The Digital NBA

STUDIES IN SPORTS MEDIA

Edited by Victoria E. Johnson and Travis Vogan

A list of books in the series appears at the end of this book.

The Digital NBA

How the World's Savviest League Brings the Court to Our Couch

STEVEN SECULAR

© 2023 by the Board of Trustees
of the University of Illinois
All rights reserved
1 2 3 4 5 C P 5 4 3 2 1
♾ This book is printed on acid-free paper.

Library of Congress Cataloging-in-Publication Data
Names: Secular, Steven, 1990– author.
Title: The digital NBA : how the world's savviest league
 brings the court to our couch / Steven Secular.
Description: Urbana : University of Illinois Press, [2023] |
 Series: Studies in sports media | Includes bibliographical
 references and index.
Identifiers: LCCN 2022051963 (print) | LCCN 2022051964
 (ebook) | ISBN 9780252045202 (cloth) | ISBN 9780252087349
 (paperback) | ISBN 9780252054587 (ebook)
Subjects: LCSH: National Basketball Association. |
 Basketball—Marketing. | Mass media and sports. |
 Streaming video.
Classification: LCC GV885.515.N37 s44 2023 (print) | LCC
 GV885.515.N37 (ebook) | DDC 796.323/6406—dc23/
 eng/20221122
LC record available at https://lccn.loc.gov/2022051963
LC ebook record available at https://lccn.loc.gov/2022051964

For my mother, Marcia—she's earned an honorary doctorate in my book.

For my wife, Anna—on to the next chapter.

Contents

Acknowledgments ix

Introduction: The International House of Hoops 1

1 The Court: Event Production, Streaming Television, and the "Glocalization" of Live Sport 29

2 The Venue: Silicon Valley, Public Finance, and the Arena as Media Platform 55

3 The Wires: Dark Fiber, Satellites, and the Global Infrastructures of Streaming Sport 83

4 The Office: The NBA's Executive Operation as a Global Media Empire 111

5 The Couch: At-Home Sport Spectatorship and the Multiplatform Viewing Environment 137

Conclusion: The House That Hoops Built 165

Notes 177

Index 217

Acknowledgments

This project began with an interest in the NBA. Not the basketball—that came later—but the organization and the person running it for most of my life: David Stern, the NBA's commissioner from 1984 to 2014. His extreme level of control and his global aspirations rendered the league a fascinating political machine. The NBA was so much more than a sports league—and still is. The NBA is an American institution, a media company, and a global political organization. The NBA's ascent during the 1980s and 1990s highlights the emergence of a modern sports media industry. Over time, the aspirations of the NFL and MLB, too, have traveled farther and farther around the world while leveraging newer and more innovative media technologies. Although the NBA offers an illustrative model, it is no longer alone in its global and digital aspirations.

It was a dream come true for me to be able to speak to David Stern before his passing in January 2020. He remained insightful, patient, and generous. Whether or not his words appear here directly, his reflections on the league's history and his own career inform almost everything that follows. It was an honor to converse with him and receive his feedback on various arguments that appear here. He did not need to lend his time to a PhD student like me—that he did speaks volumes about David Stern as a forever engaged and curious mind.

This project would have been impossible without the immense kindness of all the people who allowed themselves to be interviewed, put me in touch with peers, or generously opened their doors. I would like to especially thank Steve Hellmuth and Mike Wade of the NBA, who offered more assistance than I could ever have imagined. I would also like to thank NeuLion, since renamed Endeavor Streaming, for welcoming me and instructing a novice in the quite technical world of video streaming. The book is so much better for their believing in the merits of the scholarship.

I am a huge admirer of the work of Harvey Araton, Ira Berkow, Kim Bohuny, Ed Desser, Robert Edelman, Russ Granik, Craig Lazarus, Mark Lazarus, Terry Lyons, John Kosner, Danny Meiseles, Mike Slade, and Ailene Voisin. It was an honor to speak with each of them and pick their brains on the subject of the NBA. It was also an incredible pleasure to learn of the vast behind-the-scenes efforts that make the NBA possible, from Ruben Carbajal, Mike Chant, Mojie Crigler, Chris Halton, Troy Justice, and Andrew Nicholson. Whether or not their words appear here directly, their voices have all immeasurably improved this book.

The origins of the project may emerge from a lifelong fascination with the NBA, but the scholarship stems from my time at the University of California–Santa Barbara. I was fortunate to have had such a supportive community of people as I did in the Department of Film and Media Studies. Without the aid of the faculty, the staff, and my peers, this project would not have been possible. I want to thank Jennifer Holt, Michael Curtin, Greg Siegel, and Victoria Johnson, especially, for pushing forward my ideas and research as it evolved. They have been as generous and thoughtful as I could ever want or expect of a committee. Jen, as a mentor and adviser, played such an incredible role in my overall growth as a scholar. She empowered me to pursue any number of possible roads. I am grateful for her patience, her many hours and pages of feedback, and her always knowing precisely when to trust me and when to push the work even further. I can't imagine a version of this project without her input.

Along the way, earlier sections of chapter 3 appeared in the *International Journal of the History of Sport* and *Media Industries*, and an earlier version of chapter 4 appeared in *The Velvet Light Trap*. Thank you to Taylor and Francis, Michigan Publishing, and the University of Texas Press for the rights to reuse the ideas and writing published in these earlier pieces.

Most important, I must thank my family and friends for their support during the years of my graduate studies. Andrew Doscas and Ian Goldstein were instrumental in the process, through hours of conversation and friendship. I must thank Andrew, in particular, whose own love of basketball and of the many colorful stories about the NBA eventually rubbed off on me. My wife, Anna, has been so supportive and sturdy from the beginning of my doctoral studies, equally through the victories and the setbacks. My mother, Marcia, has spent incalculable hours reading my work, offering advice and words of support and listening to many thoughts in progress. I also would like to thank my father, Mark, and my sister, Nicole, for their encouragement and their pride in me. They all share in this achievement; this book could not have happened without them.

In closing, I would like to thank the University of Illinois Press for their belief and confidence in the book. Danny Nasset has been a steady source of support from the very beginning. Vicky Johnson and Travis Vogan, as editors on the Studies in Sports Media series, have been so encouraging and kind. Their feedback and those of the various reviewers, at the proposal stage and as a complete manuscript, were vital for improving the book and making it the best possible version. I know the book has found its rightful home.

The Digital NBA

INTRODUCTION

The International House of Hoops

In Shanghai, a basketball fan streams a game on Tencent between the Houston Rockets and Golden State Warriors, watching favorite players run across the court in Chinese-language jerseys. In Mexico City, a team of US producers meet with their local counterparts to discuss the rundown for an upcoming sporting event in the country. The producers are told that the event *must* have a "kiss cam," as fans have experienced the fun of such an activity only through telecasts. In Rio de Janeiro, a US sports league sends an envoy of executives to consult with the Brazilian league, who are subsequently advised to renovate their court, change their camera positions, and modify their rules to make the game feel more like its US peer. In Sacramento, a full data center sits in the bowels of a sports arena, in order to speed up the shuttling of 4K video back and forth between a massive video board upstairs, the team's dedicated smartphone app, and an archive of highlights housed nearly three thousand miles away.

The production of the National Basketball Association (NBA), across media platforms and across national borders, requires the coordination of thousands of employees within a number of departments, subdepartments, and development groups. Some work in New Jersey, some work in the Manhattan office, some travel between them, and some are stationed as far away as England, Mexico, China, and South Africa. I visited the NBA's Secaucus office and spoke with current and former staff members after the 2017 Finals, when the Golden State Warriors handily defeated the Cleveland Cavaliers four games to one. Despite featuring fewer games than in the previous year, ratings were up by 15 percent. In fact, the series was the most viewed Finals since 1998, the ratings peak of Michael Jordan's run with the Chicago Bulls.[1] The playoffs were then followed by what some called "the wildest offseason in NBA history," which saw stars Chris Paul, Jimmy Butler, Paul George, Carmelo Anthony, Kyrie Irving, and Gordon Hayward all changing teams.[2] The drama helped buoy coverage on ESPN, Bleacher Report (owned and operated by NBA partner WarnerMedia under the Turner banner), and the league's own NBA TV channel (also operated by Turner). As the NBA launches new programming initiatives, such as the *NBA Awards* on TNT, as social media help to transform the drama of the off-season into its own must-see television, and as the Summer League in Las Vegas becomes exciting play in its own right, the media responsibilities of the league and its employees only stand to intensify.

Today, a sports league such as the NBA makes its revenue from selling its media rights, in which distributors such as ESPN, TNT, NBC, and now Amazon and Twitter as well, pay for the rights to distribute games on broadcast, cable, or streaming platforms, profiting from the advertising that airs alongside breaks in the action. Since the 1990s, though, the NBA has entered into agreements in which it splits that advertising revenue with its media partners, and, since 2008, the league operates its own streaming platform jointly with Turner Sports through the NBA Digital subsidiary.[3] As a result, there is evidently a great deal of overlap between conceptions of sports media production and distribution, as the NBA functions as both producer and distributor in its own right. Since 2014, for instance, all twenty-nine arenas within the NBA are connected via a nationwide network of fiber-optic cables to a nondescript office building in Secaucus, New Jersey. With the rollout, the league amassed greater control over its own media operations, overseeing its own pipelines and creating a more efficient flow of data for use in everything from replay review and advanced statistics to regional cable distribution and international streaming video. Other sources of revenue also reflect this overlap of responsibilities, as merchandising is split with partners in Nike, Adidas, or Mitchell and Ness, who pay for licensing agreements with league partners. The same is true of ticket sales, or "gate revenue," which is divided between the home team and the league office, the split depending on the market size of the home team in a revenue-sharing model.[4]

A task of the league office as executor of the teams' interest is to oversee the NBA's media contracts through the collective bargaining agreement (CBA) between the franchise owners and the players' association, which splits basketball-related income (BRI) between the two sides. Russ Granik, who served as NBA general counsel and negotiated the first CBA in 1983, explains that "the league office is funded by the teams." This means that

Inside the NBA's Replay Center in Secaucus, New Jersey, from which the NBA monitors foul calls and even violations of production standards.

although the league office "*makes* money, by licensing, sponsorships, and stuff like that," ultimately "that all goes into the pot" that is divided between the players and owners.[5] Any operating costs the league office incurs are then funded by the owners.[6] Conflicts during labor negotiations, as in the strike-shortened NBA seasons in 1998–99 and 2011–12, centered on what percentages of BRI would be given to the owners and what percentage to the players. In the original 1983 CBA, players received 53 percent, a number that rose to between 55 and 57 percent in the 1999 CBA, before falling to 51.15 in the 2012 CBA.[7] These decisions greatly affected the economics of the league, which chapter 3 discusses in more detail.

While sports leagues still serve an important administrative role, then, they have come to function more as global media conglomerates in practice, as the media interests of sport have increasingly driven leagues' profitability. As of 1992, for instance, about half of the NBA's revenue were still coming from ticket sales.[8] By the 2019–20 season, this relationship has changed considerably, with tickets accounting for less than 20 percent of the league's total revenue, while the NBA's national media contracts with Disney and WarnerMedia alone accounted for about 30 percent, in addition to other revenue generated from advertising and sponsorships.[9] The NBA also profits substantially from overseas agreements with local and regional partners, such as its streaming partnership with Tencent in China for $1.5 billion over five years.[10] More than its peers in the National Football League (NFL), Major League Baseball (MLB), and the National Hockey League (NHL), one could argue that the NBA is the most globally successful team sport organization, in that it brings in far more international revenue, despite the greater domestic success of the NFL and MLB. In 2019, for instance, the NFL brought in around $16 billion, a result of massive broadcast television agreements, while MLB brought in $10.7 billion that same year, largely because of a 162-game season that offers local and national television providers the most content of any sport.[11] The NBA remains in third place, at $8.76 billion for the 2018–19 season, but its international media revenue of $500 million paces the NFL at $120 million and MLB at only $50 million.[12] On the international front, meanwhile, English Premier League (soccer) made $6.59 billion for the 2018–19 season, behind the three highest-grossing US-based leagues.[13] As sport continues to globalize, especially through emerging international streaming options, the global success of the NBA offers a great deal of insight into the cultural flows of sport around the world, as well as the status of sports league as transnational media conglomerates with multiple subsidiaries and diverse sources of income.

The case of the NBA, therefore, most effectively highlights the wider marketization and mediatization of sport since the 1980s. These interrelated processes, exemplified and driven by the NBA since the 1980s, lead to the current global state of the sports media industry, wherein leagues function as media conglomerates and sport itself functions as media content first and foremost. The case of the NBA, in particular, highlights how and why such a shift has occurred. I follow from David Hesmondalgh's definition of *marketization*, which he prefers to terms like *deregulation* or *liberalization*, as *marketization* reflects "the process by which market exchange increasingly came to permeate the cultural industries and related sectors."[14] *Marketization* best describes the transition of sports leagues from public and primarily administrative bodies into multinational, multidepartment integrated media institutions, while addressing both the regulatory and cultural dimensions of the process. *Mediatization* has been used in various capacities but emerges from political communication scholarship. The "mediatization of politics" thesis, as succinctly defined by Terry Flew, proposes that "the changing structural relations between media and politics has developed to a point where political institutions, leaders and practices are increasingly dependent upon media and conform to the logics of media production, distribution and reception."[15] The term most appropriately describes the NBA's similar efforts to manipulate basketball as media programming and its tendency to cater primarily to media interests in its directives. With the advent of internet distribution, the process of mediatization has only intensified and accelerated, as sports leagues have increasingly conceived of their sport as media content to accommodate emerging media platforms.

The mediatization argument is reminiscent of a great deal of sports media scholarship from the mid- to late 1980s, which came to see media's influence as corrupting of sport, or, at its most neutral, as a mutually beneficial commercial partnership. John Goldlust argues that, in sport's relationship with media, "television must produce a form of entertainment that ensures a maximization of the sale of commercial time and therefore the staging of the sports event is increasingly susceptible to changes in structure and form that television professionals assess will be most favorable to this end."[16] The interests of sports and media executives are thus aligned in their pursuit of profit. In this capacity, Robert McChesney is perhaps most fundamental in outlining what he terms the "symbiosis" of sport and the mass media, in which "media attention fans the flames of interest in sport and increased interest in sport warrants further media attention."[17] Sut Jhally terms this process the "sport/media complex," though he is skeptical of the idea that "before the influence of the media there was something that was pure sports."[18] More recently, Lawrence Wenner has used the concept of "MediaSport" to capture the more recent tendency of mediated sports texts to take on the corporate qualities and marketing strategies of "the Time-Warner–Cable News Network–*Sports Illustrated* combine, the Disney-ABC-ESPN brands, and the Rupert Murdoch-News Corp leveraging of the Fox television imprimatur."[19] Sports and media have moved beyond symbiosis, then, as sports leagues have become media companies in their own right and sports have transitioned from pastime into multiplatform programming. The commercial ambitions of sports and media, which were formerly separate but aligned, have become more integrated and synonymous than ever before.

These qualities are profoundly reflected in the concept of mediatization, which captures sport's wide and ongoing prioritization of media interests. Kirsten Frandsen aptly uses mediatization as a framework for describing the sports-media relationship, wherein sporting events encouraged media organizations "to bring the sports sphere and actions as close to the audience as possible" by "making use of the newest technologies—be it the telephone, at the beginning of the 20th century, or small portable cameras on athletes 100 years later."[20] Previous scholars, in fact, have highlighted the NBA as exemplary for its own investments in mediation and technology. Douglas Kellner has described the NBA as the "ideal TV sport," perfectly suited to "the era of MTV and ESPN" because of its pace, action, and attention to spectacle. "Professional basketball," Kellner argues, "has emerged during the [Michael] Jordan era as the game that best symbolizes the contemporary sports/entertainment colossus."[21] David L. Andrews has similarly proposed the NBA as an exemplary global colossus that has "seamlessly blurred the boundaries between sport, media, and entertainment sectors" as a result of "the league's ability to create multi-platform popular media spectacles."[22] As early as the 1980s, the NBA was well on its way to functioning as a media entity first and foremost, with basketball as but a secondary concern.

Since then, the NBA has been a crucial driver of the global multiplatform possibilities of sport. While the NFL first exploited the possibilities of broadcast television in the 1960s and 1970s, the fledgling NBA was better positioned to capitalize on new opportunities in cable and satellite in the 1980s, given the league's lower overhead costs and revenue. "It's not that hard to get 100 percent increases every year when you start with a number like zero or one," notes Ed Desser, who served as the NBA's vice president of international broadcasting and later became president of the television and new media ventures division.[23] The NBA had little to lose by experimenting with emergent media. During the 1980s, the creation of NBA Entertainment and NBA International thus accelerated the transformation of sport into multiplatform media content. Concurrent with a period of global deregulation, the 1990s saw the NBA consolidating control over its various properties, launching new divisions, and opening overseas offices. This centralization allowed the league to take fuller advantage of new direct-to-consumer distribution opportunities and become a more global institution. In 1994, the NBA launched League Pass, a subscription-based satellite service via DirecTV; in 1999, the league became the first to own and operate its own cable channel, NBA TV; and, in 2007, it was the first to see the opportunity in packaging together their broadcast and digital streaming rights as part of its contract extension with Turner and ESPN. Mark Lazarus, who worked with the NBA in his capacity as president of the Turner Entertainment Group, notes that, more than any other sports league, the NBA has understood its product as media content.[24] Not only is this significant in understanding the large influence of the NBA on the sports media industry, it allows us to consider NBA programming alongside scholarship of television programming and digital distribution.

In this capacity, the NBA offers a case example much like Ramon Lobato's recent comprehensive study of Netflix in the global media landscape,

Netflix Nations. In the book, Lobato described his goal as examining "how Netflix morphed from a national media company to an international one" and, subsequently, "what this case means for existing debates about global television on the one hand and digital distribution on the other."[25] My own undertaking is similar, examining instead the NBA, the sports media component of the same industrial transformation, and the inherent tensions between US-originated content and the global marketplace. In articulating the NBA as a successful media producer-distributor in its own right, I hope to contribute to our further understanding of US sports leagues as comparable to such global producer-distributors as Netflix. The NBA, like Netflix, provides a globally available media property. Ultimately, Lobato has highlighted how Netflix's international rollout and catalog system allows its content to remain simultaneously local and global. Netflix shifts our conception of cross-border media flows, Lobato explains, in "the fact that it can effortlessly combine the local and the global *within the one platform* and constitute itself as many different products simultaneously."[26] The NBA, in the simultaneity of its own international platform and the purposeful transformation of the sport to accommodate new global audiences, offers further evidence of this phenomenon beyond the case of Netflix. Framed by the mutual processes of marketization and mediatization, this book examines the motives and mechanics that encourage and enable the contemporary media ecosystem.

Rather than take a purely historical view, however, *The Digital NBA* offers a snapshot of these industrial forces in practice by selecting key constellations in the worldwide production and distribution of the NBA and sports media. These sites include the event, the venue, the wires, the office, and the couch. Each space was selected for its multiple dimensions of sport, media, technology, and culture in order to highlight and interrogate the global machinations that bear on the NBA's operations. Tracing sports media through these nodes, rather than offering a straight chronology, best positions the arc of the book to demonstrate the variables that have enabled, constrained, and influenced the circulation and consumption of basketball over time, across the multiple iterations and alternate possibilities of each site. Through the case of the NBA, then, the book seeks to illuminate the historical evolution and contemporary state of the sports media industry, as the NBA and its peers have transformed from primarily administrative organizations into multibillion-dollar media enterprises. The NBA, as the most globally pervasive of US sports leagues, most profoundly reflects the ongoing commercialization of culture, as multidirectional cultural flows are increasingly leveraged in service of greater media profits.

A (Pre) History of the NBA

Formed in 1946, when the Basketball Association of America (BAA) merged with the National Basketball League (NBL), the NBA arguably came of age in the mid- to late 1980s, transforming from a professional sports organization into a media industrial entity under the direction of David Stern, who served as the league's commissioner from 1984 to 2014. By the 1980s, the NFL's own historical trajectory served as an important model for the NBA's growing media ambitions. During the 1960s, with the help of CBS and NBC, the NFL had become a "major spectacle" on television and began to overtake the popularity of baseball.[27] Because both networks were reluctant to disrupt their Monday night sitcom and variety programming, ABC was able to win *Monday Night Football* in 1970, at $8 million for thirteen games. ABC eventually parlayed their NFL rights and *Wide World of Sports* into total network success by the mid-1970s, finally supplanting CBS and NBC and sparking a major sports-rights bidding war, primarily over the baseball, professional football, and college football rights. In 1977, the NFL negotiated a four-year, $656 million deal (between the three networks), six times the value of their 1964 deal with NBC and CBS. For the first time in the NFL's history, television revenue surpassed ticket sales as a source of team income. This gap only intensified in 1982, when the NFL netted a five-year, $2 billion deal.[28] The NBA had its sights set on the same outcome, parlaying the game's media value into overall success.

To this point, the NBA's path had been quite different. After the 1946 merger between the Basketball Association of America and the National Basketball League, forming the NBA as it is known today, the league received its first major television deal in 1965, when a still-desperate ABC sports department took a flier on the league.[29] By 1969, after steady increases in attendance and television viewership, Tom Tolnay of *Back Stage* speculated that the NBA could be on the verge of "big-time money" because of the mutual benefit to the league and ABC. Sunday afternoon games during the 1967–68 season averaged an 8.2 Nielsen rating and 27 percent share.[30] In 1969, *Broadcasting* ran a feature on the "sport TV pie," with a great deal dedicated to the rise of basketball under their contract with ABC—ratings growth, attendance growth, and sold-out advertising.[31] An unnamed network official speculated their contract could rise by millions the following year, and it did: in 1970, the NBA signed a three-year, $16 million contract with the network.[32]

In 1973, however, the NBA left ABC for CBS, infuriating ABC Sports president Roone Arledge, with whom the league had made a handshake agreement to stay. In March 1973, ABC took legal action against the league, alleging that it had acted in bad faith.[33] By August, the network lost, allowing the NBA to stay with CBS and affirming the three-year, $27 million agreement with the new network. In his decision, New York County Supreme Court justice Hyman Korn framed the issue as one of control: "the provisions for greater NBA control . . . though unfavorable from a network's standpoint are certainly beneficial to the teams. Surely, a party may not be faulted for obtaining for itself every contractual advantage it can."[34] The NBA's desire to maximize control over its own media production and distribution would dictate its actions for decades to come, including the creation of NBA Entertainment, an internal production division (as discussed in chapter 1) and the league's eventual departure for NBC (as discussed in chapter 4).

In 1976, the NBA merged with a rival professional basketball league, the American Basketball Association (ABA), taking four new teams into its ranks: the San Antonio Spurs, the Denver Nuggets, the Indiana Pacers, and the New York Nets.[35] From its launch in 1967, the ABA had sought to force the NBA into a merger, first by poaching top basketball talent, such as Connie Hawkins and Rick Barry, and then by filing an antitrust lawsuit in 1969.[36] "There is going to be a merger. Under no circumstances can a merger not come true. It's just a question of when," said Carolina Cougars owner Jim Gardner at the time.[37] The plan succeeded, in part, as the NBA agreed to negotiate the terms of a merger in 1970, but these efforts were put on pause by an additional antitrust suit filed by Oscar Robertson over the "reserve" clause, which was allowing NBA teams to hold players to contracts for as long as the team wanted.[38] The Robertson suit was settled out of court in 1976, eliminating the clause and opening the door to free agency and, in turn, to a final settlement with the ABA.[39] By that point, the ABA was hemorrhaging money because it lacked a national television contract and because it had used exorbitant salaries to entice players away from the NBA.[40] The NBA's broadcast partner CBS pushed strongly for the merger with the rival ABA, hoping that the influx of teams and stars would boost NBA interest, which had also been on the decline. "We would like to see certain ABA teams in the NBA," said CBS president Robert Wussler at the time. "I think it would be better TV production if the Denver Nuggets, with David Thompson, and New York Nets, with Julius Erving, were in the NBA structure."[41] With pressure mounting, the two sides agreed to a set of terms in August 1976, in which each of the four incoming ABA teams would pay an entrance fee of $3.2 million and receive none of the NBA's television revenue until 1980.[42]

By the start of the 1980s, however, the demand for televised professional basketball had grown only incrementally, and the NBA remained in dire financial straits. Ratings on CBS were sagging, and most of the league's franchises were losing money and on the brink of bankruptcy.[43] The 1982–83 season saw only seven of the league's twenty-three teams turn a profit, as the Utah Jazz, Indiana Pacers, Cleveland Cavaliers, and San Diego Clippers were likely to either fold or merge in some way.[44] One of the contributing factors was a rise in player salaries, which on average was equal to 60 percent of a team's basketball revenues, the highest proportion of any sport. The reason was partly the years of competition with the ABA, which had pushed the league into larger and larger contracts.[45] The NBA league office, represented by David Stern, proposed a salary "cap" to attempt to limit what teams could spend.[46] The NBA Players Association, led by general counsel Larry Fleisher, was extremely displeased with the proposal. As one insider on the side of the NBAPA explained, "What the owners are doing is, they're asking the players, 'Save us from ourselves.' The owners are asking the employees to stop the owners from spending."[47]

The salary issue was nonetheless very real, and teams were on the brink of foreclosure at a pivotal moment for the future of the league. The task became one of convincing the union to accept the cap, or one of making concessions to them that would allow them to accept the cap. Stern's idea to sweeten the deal, inspired by an unimplemented 1979 proposal to the NFL by Ed Garvey, executive director of their players association, was to offer a guaranteed percentage of gross revenues.[48] In late March 1983, the two sides met in New York, hoping to come to an agreement and avoid a labor strike come April 3.[49] Stern's new offer overcame the skepticism about the cap, and the collective bargaining agreement was signed. The salary cap would be instituted, as well as a salary floor, but players would now receive a guaranteed 53 percent of gross revenues from basketball-related income.[50] As revenues rose, therefore, so too would player salaries. "It seems nearly everybody is happy about the NBA's new collective bargaining agreement," reported David Dupree of the *Washington Post*, "which both sides agree is a landmark settlement."[51] After advertising the first successful CBA, the NBA steadily began to turn its fortunes around. The league re-signed with CBS for a four-year, $173 million contract in 1985, and then left CBS for NBC's offer of $600 million over four years in 1989.[52] Throughout this time, the NBA would also make greater investments in cable distribution, through multiple deals with TBS, ESPN, and USA Network, and as well as agreements with emerging satellite operators for overseas distribution, as discussed in chapters that follow.

Ultimately, the evolution of the NBA into a multifaceted global media empire thus illuminates the wider transformation of sport into multiplatform media content and sports leagues into modern media conglomerates. Ahead of the 2014–15 season, the NBA signed a nine-year extension with its television and streaming partners, Turner and ABC/ESPN, for a combined $24 billion.[53] The following year, US sports fans collectively watched 31 billion hours of live sports, leading to higher prices for sports channels on cable and satellite services. In 2016, pay television customers paid $18.37 per month for sports programming, 40 percent of the total bill, up from only $2.85 in 2001.[54] The US sports industry, moreover, generated more than $19 billion from its media rights in 2017 alone, overtaking revenue from ticket sales for the very first time. That same year, in a report prepared by PricewaterhouseCoopers (PwC), on the "Global Entertainment and Media" outlook for 2018 to 2022, PwC cited the NBA alongside Netflix and Amazon as comparable "giants" that are "converging on global markets." In addition to Netflix and Amazon, the report included the NBA's League Pass over-the-top (OTT) service in the same conversation as Hulu, HBO Now, and CBS All Access.[55] As new streaming competitors emerge, such as Amazon and DAZN, media rights revenues are expected to rise even higher.[56]

Global Sports Television: Frameworks, Formats, Flows

Over the past several decades, the NBA's executive office has come to operate as that of a genuine global media conglomerate, with divisions such as "NBA China" and "NBA India" functioning as distinct subsidiaries within the league's corporate structure. More recently, the NBA took the extraordinary step of investing equity in a Brazilian professional basketball league, Liga Nacional de Basquete, even sending personnel to help them comply with the NBA's standards, a clear example of the NBA's vast capital and expanding corporate power. To understand the NBA, therefore, is to understand an increasingly integrated sports and media industry, the digitization of sports spectatorship, and the capitalization of cultural flows within a multiplatform media ecosystem. The flexibility of cable and streaming television, respectively, have afforded the NBA greater scheduling control on linear television and a more global address through digital platforms. As a result, the NBA has continued to excel internationally. As of 2005, 15 percent of the league's broadcast revenues came from overseas.[57] By 2013, 10 percent of the NBA's *overall* revenue came from its international operations, a seemingly small number, but one that topped the performance of both the NFL and MLB.[58] As international players have steadily come to define the league, including the 2019 NBA Rookie of the Year win by Luka Dončić of Slovenia and the 2021 NBA Finals and Finals MVP win by Giannis Antetokounmpo of Greece, the NBA's gambit for global success has worked, and foreign-born players have brought with them an altogether more global audience. The transnational expansion and vertical integration of the NBA thus reflects historical shifts within the media industries, as the league deploys the media strategies of more established global companies such as Disney, WarnerMedia, and Netflix.

In Timothy Havens's periodization of the globalization of television, he differentiates between the widespread international exchange of programming from 1957 to 1972, "as nation after nation introduced television broadcasting," and a second wave from 1985 to the present (as of 2006), which grew from the worldwide explosion of commercial broadcasters and "the spread of cable and satellite channels around the world."[59] As the demand for television programming increased in the 1980s, the major Hollywood distributors were ideally positioned to succeed, sitting on their vast programming libraries. Havens describes how the dream of US producers in the 1960s had been "a world in which domestically tailored programming would find general entertainment audiences both at home and abroad," a fully efficient global ecosystem that could overcome national differences.[60] The case of the NBA and sports television demonstrates how this global vision was fulfilled with the aid of a privatized media environment and increasingly advanced distribution technologies, from satellite and cable to streaming.

Various scholars have examined the deregulatory atmosphere that gave rise to a transnational commercial television industry. David Hesmondalgh's choice of the term *marketization*, as discussed earlier in this introduction, highlights "the process by which market exchange increasingly came to permeate the cultural industries and related sectors." In contrast to Havens's two distinct periods, Hesmondalgh describes various overlapping waves, including the marketization of television in "advanced industrial states" from 1985 through 1995, which saw "the pulling apart of public service television," and another wave from 1992, which saw the "convergence of the cultural industries with telecommunications and information technology."[61] Jennifer Holt, who further explores these trends in her examination of the construction of transnational entertainment empires in the 1980s through the 1990s, argues that a combination of neoliberal policy and new communications technology resulted in "a great acceleration of global commerce."[62] These trends overlap with the rise of the NBA, which was able to take advantage of opportunities for self-distribution during the 1980s

The Big Ticket
Networks Pay Scalper Prices For Sports Rights

	Rights Fees (in millions)	Contract Year (year/total years)	Final Season of Contract
National Football League			
Fox	$4,400	2/8	2005-2006
CBS	$4,000	2/8	2005-2006
ABC	$4,400	2/8	2005-2006
ESPN	$4,800	2/8	2005-2006
Total	**$17,600**		
National Basketball Association			
NBC	$1,750	2/4	2001-2002
Turner	$890	2/4	2001-2002
Total	**$2,640**		
Major League Baseball			
Fox	$575	4/5	2000
NBC	$475	4/5	2000
ESPN	$455	4/5	2000
FSN**	$185	3/4	2000
Total	**$1,690**		
National Hockey League			
Fox	$350	1/5*	2003-2004
ABC	$250	1/5*	2003-2004
Total	**$600**		
NCAA College Football Championship			
ABC	$700	2/7	2004
NCAA College Basketball Tournament			
CBS	$1,725	5/8	2002
Olympics			
NBC	$715		Summer 2000
NBC	$555		Winter 2002
NBC	$793		Summer 2004
NBC	$613		Winter 2006
NBC	$894		Summer 2008

* The first year of the NHL contract begins with the 1999-2000 season. **FoxSportsNet

In 1999, with a lucrative contract with NBC, the NBA's total television revenue had finally overtaken that of Major League Baseball.

and 1990s to become a genuine media conglomerate with global aspirations. By the 2000s, moreover, the ascent of video streaming platforms provided even "lower barriers of access and cost," as Brett Hutchins and David Rowe explain, which has only "multiplied the number of media companies, leagues, clubs, and even individual athletes that can produce and distribute content for online consumption."[63]

The International House of Hoops 13

For these reasons, Victoria E. Johnson has gone as far as to describe sports leagues and conferences themselves as "fully-fledged media institutions of the post-network era," a period defined by its fragmented audiences across multiple platforms and devices.[64] In Johnson's work on the state of sports media during this period, moreover, she argues that sport "epitomizes a paradox" in that it remains "the most quintessential network-era programming" in its mass appeal and resonance, yet it is also "particularly well suited to new business practices, media outlets, and modes of viewer involvement that are enabled by the distribution flexibility and technologies characteristic of the post-network era." Johnson also argues that, historically, the NFL has been "foundational" in "shaping the business of televised sport."[65] Travis Vogan notes the same in his study of NFL Films, arguing that the division helped the league to "manufacture an image that sets the gridiron game apart from other sports and . . . [distinguishes it] from other sports organizations."[66] The NFL's impact on sports television is indisputable, as a result of both NFL Films and its work with ABC on *Monday Night Football* beginning in 1970, and the NFL continues to most profoundly exemplify the practices of the network era of television. The NBA, which ascended during the period of cable television, direct-broadcast satellite, and internet distribution, more powerfully exhibits the paradox at the heart of the global multiplatform era in its ability to "engage *both* a broad(cast) audience and increasingly narrower niches within that audience."[67] The NBA has more effectively demonstrated and perpetuated the sports industry's investment in flexible distribution on a global scale, as the league grows at a far faster rate than its contemporaries. In 2017, NFL revenue sat at $17 billion, a 7 percent increase over the previous year. The NBA's revenue, while admittedly smaller at $7.4 billion, was a staggering 25 percent increase from 2016.[68] The NBA is a media conglomerate especially suited to a multiplatform, post-network era.

The onset of the COVID-19 pandemic, beginning in China in December 2019 and initiating worldwide national lockdowns by March 2020, undoubtedly slowed down the meteoric trajectory of the sports media industry. The NBA, NHL, and MLB each paused their seasons to forestall potential outbreaks, returning months later but without fans. The moves hampered gate revenue and media revenue as well, from a combination of shortened seasons, rating cannibalization, and audience fatigue.[69] The NBA and NHL sustained estimated losses topping the $1 billion mark, and MLB surpassed $3 billion in losses.[70] The NFL, which does not begin its season until August, was able to sustain a full season without interruption, though it also suffered from a ratings decline and lower ticket sales, leading to potential losses between $3 billion and $4 billion.[71] As the major US team sports have resumed in 2021, and as the steady dissemination of the COVID-19 vaccine has enabled larger fan attendance, sports are poised to return to same rate of global growth that was once anticipated. The NBA and NHL, for instance, both saw substantial ratings increases since launching their 2021 seasons. The NBA's ratings were up by 34 percent through the league's first twenty-seven games, and the NHL's were up a more modest 8 percent through the first month of its season.[72] Both the NFL and NHL, in fact, signed substantial new television rights agreements in March 2021. The NHL signed a seven-year multiplatform deal with ESPN for $420 million per year, double its previous arrangement with NBC, and the NFL's multiple deals with NBC, CBS, Fox, ESPN, and Amazon added up to a whopping $10 billion per year.[73] In the post-network, multiplatform era of television, the businesses of sport and television are more deeply integrated than ever before.

While the COVID-19 Pandemic has not diminished the ongoing success of the sports media industry, it offers a useful inflection point, serving as a reflection and extension of various preexisting media trends that seem poised to continue, such as the digitization of the arena space, the privileging of the at-home spectator over the in-person audience, and the globalization of the event and telecast as encouraged by the proliferation of streaming platforms. In combination, the trends reflect an ongoing bid for global media "efficiency," in which integrated content producer-distributors such as Netflix, HBO, and sports leagues have all increasingly privileged programming that will be the most engaging to viewers across borders. Russell Wolff, former senior vice president of programming in ESPN's Star Sports operation in China and later executive vice president and general manager of the ESPN+ streaming service, has discussed the drive for "pan-regional efficiency" versus "local appeal."[74] In the past, this remained a crucial balance for U.S.-based pan-regional channels, such as those by ESPN and MTV, which had experienced difficult launches in the late 1980s and 1990s, before they introduced tailored programming blocks to much greater success.[75] This strategy aligns with the NBA's earliest strategies, which also relied on customized local programming, such as *Dunk Street* and other overseas versions of the NBA's *Inside Stuff* magazine show, as discussed in chapter 4 of the present book. Over time, however, the advancement of streaming and internet distribution has encouraged the league to keep investing in the internationalization of the sport in ways that can offer a more inclusive media text.

The influx of international athletes into the NBA, for instance, has transformed the sport to more effectively reflect styles of play from overseas and thus better engage fans outside the United States. By the 2003–4 season, 16.6 percent of all players on opening day rosters were identified as international, a number that jumped to 19 percent by 2005–6.[76] The NBA would set its all-time record ahead of the 2016–17 season with 25.1 percent of players born outside the United States.[77] By 2010, sportswriter Jonathan Abrams chronicled some of the specific basketball techniques that had followed foreign-born athletes into the league. Among them was the "Euro step," a particular kind of stagger-step drive toward the basket in which a player takes advantage of the permitted two steps without a dribble, a move since adopted by US athletes. "Considering the well-established presence of foreign players in the NBA . . . and with the awakening sense that the best international players have become more clever and skillful than many American players, the mimicry becomes almost necessary," Abrams explains.[78] This mimicry, of course, also created a product that could more readily engage audiences across national borders. Overseas, NBA fans could better recognize in the NBA the kind of basketball being played within their home countries. At the same time, telecasts could highlight international players and their stories. The NBA began to prioritize its own multicultural globality, putting the league in an ideal position for the ongoing turn toward a global multiplatform media economy. This strategy reflects the

In 2017, the NBA released special edition short-sleeved jerseys for Chinese New Year, to be worn by the Houston Rockets, Golden State Warriors, Toronto Raptors, and Washington Wizards, in order to incorporate more fans outside the United States.

NBA's wider efforts to offer both a globally legible media product and a locally distinctive one, as circulated through the live event itself, the streaming mediation of the event, and the digital infrastructures that allow video to be shuttled across national borders.

The NBA's internationalization efforts also extended to changes at the level of the uniforms, the "costuming" of the game. For the 2013–14 season, the league began to periodically use short-sleeved jerseys. Sal LaRocca, the NBA's vice president of global merchandising, cited the global marketplace as the incentive for the move and noted that the league tries "to stay ahead of the curve."[79] The move was coupled with the decision to place corporate sponsor logos onto jerseys, which moved the look of the sport even closer to that of soccer. While this was no doubt driven by the potential for extra revenue, Adam Silver specifically referred to soccer in justifying the change. In 2014, he called the move "inevitable" and explained, "increasingly as we see Champion's (*sic*) League and English Premier League televised in the U.S., I think it's going to become more acceptable and more commonplace for our fans as well."[80] After the league officially announced the move for the 2017–18 season, Silver reiterated his point and also noted the possibility of foreign companies investing, in the hope of expanding the league's growth overseas.[81] The twofold move of short sleeves and corporate logos, therefore, was directly meant to facilitate a pan-regional legibility, one that follows the pace and demands of the global marketplace.

In recent years, similar efforts can be observed in narrative programs such as *Criminal* (Netflix), *Narcos* (Netflix), *Chernobyl* (HBO), and *Game of Thrones* (HBO), which similarly seek multinational audiences through a multinational, and sometimes even multilingual, audience address. In this way, the NBA parallels a wider industrial shift back to pan-regional programming, as demonstrated by robust internet television distributors, including HBO and Netflix, the latter of which can "effortlessly combine the local and the global *within the one platform* and constitute itself as many different products simultaneously," as Ramon Lobato argues in his comprehensive study of the streamer.[82] The widespread growth of streaming platforms and their "library" approach to programming has thus created new possibilities for international efficiencies. Chuck Tryon, for instance, describes the efforts of Netflix to acquire "local content that appeals to international audiences," which can coexist with content directed more specifically toward other cultures.[83] Over-the-top platforms are increasingly designed to be inclusive. Through the NBA's own global appeal and use of streaming distribution, this integration allows for greater legibility and equivalence across national boundaries and marketplaces.

At a Jr. NBA event in Vietnam, participants wear jerseys with NBA logos and hold signs promoting the League Pass streaming platform.

These kinds of cultural and media flows are exemplified within the television format trade, which offers scholars a viewpoint that is simultaneously historical, industrial, and theoretical. The format, as Albert Moran explains, provides "an outer shell or organizing framework that permits or facilitates the making of a program."[84] Formats, therefore, highlight various loci of control and power between the format "devisor," the program producer, and the broadcaster across national and international lines. Yet the format also remains an ongoing process of "aggregation and accumulation" in which "subsequent adaptations of a format-based program can add, cumulatively, to its system of knowledge."[85] The format offers a productive framework for approaching the NBA as a format divisor and the multidirectionality of influences as the sport globalizes over time. The reciprocal absorption of knowledge is reflected in the NBA's changing style of play, as in the growing popularity of the Euro step and in its greater incorporation of signifiers from soccer, which have helped the sport to better address international audiences.[86] By privileging international *performance* on the court, the NBA is able to more effectively globalize its media.

Especially pertinent, then, is Paul S. N. Lee's concept of "amoebic" media, a process of cultural adaptation that is reminiscent of the television format yet is both broader and more specific. Lee's work, which focuses on the case of Hong Kong, proposes four useful models for understanding the adaptation of foreign cultures: the parrot, the amoeba, the coral, and the butterfly. The amoeba, specifically, describes programs that retain the same basic content across localities but that change in their outward packaging, "like an amoeba which appears different in form but remains the same in substance."[87] Such changes are often superficial, as with a game show or talk show that becomes localized through its hosts. It is thus a concept that offers a meaningful foundation to explain the nature of sports television. When Michael Keane, Anthony Y. H. Fung, and Albert Moran specifically categorized sport as a globally distributed television format, they cited Lee's conception of the amoeba in order to describe its particular method of "repackaging" content.[88] Similarly, Tony Schirato has explored the relationship between formats and televised sport, arguing that "formats invariably mold sport" by the "logics, imperatives, narratives, and technologies of television."[89] This research demonstrates how NBA programming ultimately embodies the amoebic logic described by Lee in service of addressing international audiences more inclusively by the 2000s. The concept of the "amoeba" is a useful framework for comprehending the nuances of sports television as format, which speaks beyond television formats to deal with a broader process of cultural adaptation.

In many ways, the internationalism of amoebic formats is reflected and further explored in Marwan Kraidy's concept of hybridity. For Kraidy, hybridity refers primarily to culture, but the concept is useful in that it "retains residual meanings related to the three interconnected realms of race, language, and ethnicity."[90] Proposing an alternative framework of transculturalism, Kraidy draws attention to the difference between the "corporate transculturalism" that seeks to use hybridity as a corporate marketing tool and the "critical transculturalism" that retains a more progressive political potential. *The Digital NBA* charts the development of NBA media content as a particularly amoebic and flexible format that engages cultural hybridity for primarily commercial pursuits. Taking that point of view is not to claim a complete absence of more authentic expression, but authenticity is certainly not the central objective. Kraidy's conceptualization is useful in integrating intentionality into cultural globalization without slipping into straightforward imperialism.

An inquiry into imperialism, then, is crucial to the examination that follows. For John Tomlinson, imperialism is necessarily a "purposeful project," which is "the *intended* spread of a social system from one center of power across the global."[91] Others, like Daya Kishan Thussu, offer more flexible conceptualizations. While Thussu acknowledges the productive potential of "contra-flows" from the global South to the North, he argues that "the American hegemony of global media cultures" is ultimately strengthened by the paradigm, since the localization of media content can "effectively legitimize the ideological imperatives of a free-market capitalism."[92] Thussu's conception leaves room for both a clear-cut intentionality and the lack thereof, emphasizing instead a more systemic imperialism. For Thomas Lamarre, the television format trade, as one such system, "discovers compatibility, convertibility, or equivalency between national culture" and seeks to transform the local into the regional.[93] I will demonstrate, through the case of the NBA and its relationship with overseas basketball leagues and talent, that the local has been made increasingly global.

The tension between local cultural expression and transnational corporate cultures has been further explored in the work of Silvio Waisbord and Michele Hilmes. Waisbord recognizes a multiplicity of local voices in the television format trade, but he warns that such instances may not be diverse in any meaningful sense and are moreover shaped by profit-driven motivations. While formats "cannot be seen simply as transmission belts for Western values," as they remain "essentially open," Waisbord notes that "formats are not entirely malleable," since "copyright holders ultimately determine what changes can be incorporated."[94] Like others, he characterizes the

The Kings debut a new court with a redesigned lion emblem and small Hindi logos c. 2017.

television format as being at the center of a relationship between national belonging and international corporate interests and characterizes cultural flows as more multidirectional and complex than straightforward cultural domination. Similarly, Michele Hilmes emphasizes the productive aspects of these global flows, arguing that "sweeping invocations of 'Americanization' or globalization tend to obscure the ways that cultural influence works, and always has worked, across lines of many different kinds."[95] The case of the NBA demonstrates, however, that, while flows may be more reciprocal, they may continue to serve the interests of the more dominant party.

Scholars have frequently approached the globalization of sport in the context of cultural flows, which often reflect the integrated forces of marketization and mediatization, in essence if not in name. Toby Miller, Geoffrey Lawrence, Jim McKay, and David Rowe are interested in the effects of corporatized sport and what the process of commercialization means for culture as it grows transnationally. "The move towards a global sports complex is as much about commodification and alienation as it is to do with a utopian internationalism," they argue.[96] Their argument is also reflected in the work of Raymond Boyle and Richard Haynes, who discuss the influence of corporate sponsorships and note how "the lexicon of sports language has been transformed by the discourse of advertising and marketing." In combination with sport's "visibility and focus on symbols, winning, competition, partisan fans," they argue, few other cultural forms are as "representative of a national identity."[97] I would propose that such universal themes are precisely what make sports programming so flexible and easily adaptable across national boundaries. Michael Serazio, similarly, highlights the similarity between religious universals and sport in sport's "ability to serve as a vehicle for existential elevation in a fashion that faith formerly fulfilled" and its simplified "quandaries of right and wrong amidst the pluralistic ambiguity of a complex, messy world," as are manifest in collective social practices.[98] Sport can offer faith, community, and clear sides across geographic borders.

Sohail Daulatzai has argued as much in his work on the NBA and Islam, which highlights how these forces are also ripe for commercialization. Most broadly, Daulatzai examines how sport's position in the global cultural landscape emerges from the synergistic relationships between multinational corporations and international marketing conglomerates, which seek to reach diasporic publics. This relates especially to the NBA's global success as "a cultural expression of the marginalized in American society—namely, African Americans"—that has moreover been commodified through "systems of production and distribution firmly rooted in Western capitalism."[99] While the global status of sport can indeed demonstrate a kind of utopian internationalism, as Miller and coauthors note, sport still remains bound up in capitalism and commodification. "Like literature, film, or any other cultural form, the NBA must be viewed as a mediated expression that can, and often does, reproduce dominant Western discourses," Daulatzai argues.[100] Like Marwan Kraidy's differentiation between corporate and critical transculturalism, basketball's Western values are increasingly downplayed in favor of a multicultural and utopian discourse that can be more easily sold on an international scale.

An understanding of global television formats can thus help us to better explain the internationalization of sport, which is often packaged and distributed according to the tenets of the format trade. A greater understanding of sport, moreover, can help us to explain the globalization of television proper, as sport remains one of the most significant and widely consumed forms of entertainment around the world. The case of the NBA offers vital information for a more dynamic understanding of the relationship between sport, media, and globalization on both cultural and industrial levels.

An Industry's View of Itself

As a media industrial entity, the NBA employs its own producers, writers, and editors that operate in much the same way as the media workers explored by industry sociologists and ethnographers. Sports media scholars such as Sut Jhally have made such a comparison, highlighting how the "directors, producers, camera operators, editors, and commentators are inserted between the live event and the home audience."[101] The NBA, with the help of its television partners, has been particularly adept at developing its star players as television stars proper. The league's many producers, directors, writers, marketers, and players (as actors) all work to contribute to the form of basketball's mediation. As a result, Victoria E. Johnson argues that "sports television is a *practice* that is cultural and experiential as well as economic and textual" and as "something people do in particular historical contexts."[102] For these reasons, Johnson continues, "sports and television can only be interpreted discursively, at the intersection or conjuncture of industry, text, social context, and audience engagement in key historical moments."[103] With this premise in mind, the field of media industry studies is most crucial to the work that follows by providing a methodological framework for the integration of industry, culture, history, and text.

Though the field is expansive and features multiple approaches, I follow Jennifer Holt and Alisa Perren's conception in *Media Industry Studies: History, Theory, and Method* (2009). While acknowledging the flexibility of the field, they understand it as an integration of "political economy's interest in ownership, regulation, and production with cultural studies' interest in texts, discourses, audiences, and consumption." The "challenge," moreover, is to provide a sophisticated-enough interdisciplinary model that can "acknowledge the complexities and contradictions of media texts" and the consumption of those texts.[104] It is not enough to combine political economy and cultural studies frameworks; one must remain attentive to the nuances and complexities of the medium. In their call for a "critical media industry studies," Timothy Havens, Amanda Lotz, and Serra Tinic address the same concern as Holt and Perren by arguing for an examination of "the micropolitics of institutional operation and production practices." The crucial "missing link" between political economy and cultural studies, they argue, is "the way in which institutional discourses are internalized and acted upon by cultural workers." In other words, they seek to parse the tensions between creative workers and corporate institutions and to unpack how artistic, social, and financial forces work through the text and through labor "within actual practice."[105] This approach to media industry studies thus incorporates the larger forces of ownership and regulation while remaining attentive to the complexities, contradictions, and discourses of specific media, per Holt and Perren's provocation.

In *Inside Prime Time*, Todd Gitlin explains his method thus: "I tried to make sense of . . . discrepancies, evasions, and blind-spots," as "many special pleadings add up to an industry's view of itself."[106] I intend to offer the same for the sports media industry, as exemplified by the NBA, using interviews and site research to better grasp and more effectively interrogate industrial practices, power hierarchies, and day-to-day operations. My sources, therefore, encompassed both interviews and site visits. Interviews included people from various backgrounds and occupations, at various levels of management, with the intention of offering a wide range of perspectives on the history and operations of the NBA, its partners, and its peers. The interviews can be grouped as follows: current and former NBA executives, NBA event and production personnel, team executives and personnel, executives from NBA partners (including Turner, ESPN, and Starwave), and the sportswriters that covered the NBA's ascent.

Site visits included the NBA's production and distribution headquarters in Secaucus, New Jersey. Here the league houses its digitized archival material, dated as far back as 1982, with films and physical media dated considerably earlier. It serves as one of two colocation centers (or "colos") through which all the NBA's video passes, along a nationwide fiber-optic cable system that the NBA purchased from Zayo Group.[107] Site visits also included the facilities of two of the NBA's partners in distribution and technology—Endeavor Streaming, which oversees the NBA's international streaming platform from their Technical Operations Center in Plainview, New York, and longtime cable partner ESPN, which oversees many of the league's most significant games, including the NBA Finals, from their Bristol, Connecticut, headquarters. In addition, I visited Golden 1 Center, home of the Sacramento Kings franchise, to better understand the league's integration of national and international media distribution from the perspective of a team exemplary in that area.

Following John T. Caldwell's call for "cross-checking" industry "disclosures," I situated such ethnographic information alongside historical trade publications and news sources.[108] These materials helped build a chronology of events that could be further interrogated by alternative ethnographic sources. Among the historical materials useful to my own project were articles and features from *Variety*, *Broadcasting*, *Broadcasting and Cable*, *Back Stage*, the *New York Times*, the *Washington Post*, the *Wall Street Journal*, *USA Today*, and *Sports Illustrated*, in addition to more contemporary news sources from ESPN, *Vice*, *Wired*, and *Forbes*. I also tracked the historical transformation of the sport's media strategies, where possible, through NBA archival footage and promotional materials. Game telecasts are available officially through their League Pass streaming package as "Hardwood Classics" and more unofficially through user uploads on YouTube, where I was also able to gather various NBA promotional spots. The sports media text itself offers primary insight into the representational strategies of the league, which includes their invocation of international cultures in order to more effectively market the league globally. In his book *Ball Don't Lie!*, Yago Colás describes his own methodology as first employing "literary analysis to identify the key elements of the myth in question" and then drawing on "existing historical and sociological research to situate this myth in and against the overlapping contexts, in basketball and society, in which it emerged."[109] This project is, essentially, the inverse—I undertake new industrial, sociological, and historical research, in combination with preexisting critical approaches to sport and media texts, such as those employed by Colás, in order to stage a full account of the NBA as a global (and globalizing) media institution.

The interrogation of media industrial practices, and the examination of how "institutional discourses are internalized and acted upon by cultural workers," following Havens, Lotz, and Tinic, offers a particularly appropriate framework for examining both the NBA and sports media more widely. Michael Serazio's *The Power of Sports: Media and Spectacle in American Culture* (2019) takes this exact approach, applying it especially to worlds of sports journalism and sports production. On the subject of the NBA, specifically, Pete Croatto's trade press book, *From Hang Time to Prime Time* (2021) also uses interviews in order to craft a clear chronology of the NBA's rise. There are also examples of academic works on the NBA's history, which have used testimony to provide a critical inquiry into the NBA's evolution as a sports league, including David Surdan's *The Rise of the National Basketball Association* (2012) and Adam Criblez's *Tall Tales and Short Shorts: Dr. J, Pistol Pete, and the Birth of the Modern NBA* (2017). Other works have focused on the league as a media institution, including John A. Fortunato's *The Ultimate Assist: The Relationship and Broadcast Strategies of the NBA* (2001) and Frank P. Josza Jr.'s *The National Basketball Association: Business, Organization, and Strategy* (2011), which offer comprehensive accounts of the NBA's function as both a media and cultural business. Ultimately, *The Digital NBA* updates and expands on these accounts by integrating industrial perspectives with historiographical context in order to reframe and enrich scholarship on media conglomeration, cultural globalization, and sports media industrialization. Using the case of the NBA, this book intends to offer a comprehensive survey of the global aspirations and machinations of the sports media industry.

From Court to Couch

In tracking and interrogating the process of production, circulation, and consumption within sports media, the first chapter is "The Court," which examines the production of the NBA event itself and how it has evolved over time to incorporate a more global address. In the mid-1980s, as cable and satellite distribution opened up possibilities of a more global programming ecosystem, the NBA reacquired their international media rights in order to grow the league abroad. To do this, the NBA embarked on a series of overseas exhibition contests and tours in order to build a more tangible local presence. This strategy is most pronounced in the Atlanta Hawks' tour of the Soviet Union in July 1988, which was spearheaded by Hawks and TBS owner Ted Turner and NBA commissioner David Stern, who both sought to parlay the tour into an agreement for NBA games on Soviet television. Today, as the media ecosystem has evolved considerably, teams in the United States regularly use their games to market themselves to multinational audiences. This is reflected in the Houston Rockets' efforts in China, the Sacramento Kings in India, and the Milwaukee Bucks in Greece. Sports programming is distinct, therefore, in its hybridity as spontaneous performance and produced media content. This chapter examines this relationship, the role of the commercial sponsor, and the extent to which live sport is both determined by media interests and impervious to their influence. Increasingly, event production is influenced by the fans watching at home, within the United States and around the world, as the league's writers and producers integrate international iconography into NBA games through player uniforms, court designs, and branded game break activities. While the influence of media interests on the live event is necessarily limited, given sport's improvisational nature, corporate sponsors play a fundamental role in determining the structure and execution of the proceedings.

The second chapter examines how the venue itself plays a fundamental role in the possibilities of sport's production, distribution, and circulation. In the 1990s, as many major cities underwent an "arena boom," taking advantage of vast new opportunities in public financing, the NBA also saw an opportunity to take greater control of the sport's production. From 1990 through 2005, as twenty-four of the NBA's thirty teams moved into new "state-of-the-art" arenas, the league imposed strict construction guidelines in consultation with then-broadcast partner NBC on particular camera placements, for example, that were intended to enhance the look of the game on television. Today, as teams such as the Sacramento Kings and Golden State Warriors move into the latest "state-of-the-art" homes, virtual reality, augmented reality, and other offerings from Silicon Valley tech firms have guided the path of live spectatorship further into mediated spectatorship. The arena space has come to be regarded as a media platform in and of itself by the individuals and institutions programming the content circulating through its walls. Ultimately, an examination of the sports media industry at the arena level highlights the roles of predatory capital, global media interests, and Silicon Valley tech firms in steering the media infrastructures of sport; the tension between sport as both civic good and commercial entity; the global geopolitical relationships that manifest in the arena space; and the mediatization of the venue itself.

The third chapter highlights the evolution of the wires, the cable and satellite infrastructures that influence the possibilities of the global circulation of sport. In the mid-1980s, when the NBA sought to consolidate control over its own media production and distribution, the league office began to require that each team mail VHS tapes of their nightly games to the NBA Entertainment headquarters in Secaucus, New Jersey. Today, this media infrastructure has become significantly more advanced. By the start of 2015, for example, each of the league's twenty-nine arenas is connected by fiber-optic cable to the league's production and distribution headquarters, which remains in Secaucus. The wires, purchased from a company called Zayo Group that specialized in disused or "dark" fiber, have created a more seamless flow of data between the NBA and its distribution partners around the world. By tracing the path of the physical cables that have enabled this ecosystem, chapter 3 illuminates the vast network of forces that enable and constrain sports media content and demonstrates leagues such as the NBA as the ultimate corporate authority. From the NBA's distribution hub in Secaucus, the wires also travel to Endeavor Streaming in Plainview, New York, and Turner's Techwood Campus in Atlanta, Georgia, two external entities that work to facilitate the NBA's streaming distribution. While Turner manages the NBA's domestic streaming distribution, through a jointly owned subsidiary called NBA Digital, Endeavor oversees the NBA's international streaming operations for all countries but a handful, including China. The programming and maintenance of a single international streaming platform by Endeavor, especially, highlights a global media ecosystem that encourages media content that will be most engaging for a multinational audience, one that is similar to Netflix's streaming efforts around the world.

The fourth chapter, "The Office," examines the space in which the NBA's executives make decisions that will trickle down and affect the performance of the sport itself. In the 1980s, their decisions reflected the league's "less is more" media strategy, in which the number of games on television were purposely reduced in order to make each one feel more like a can't-miss event and boost the NBA's ratings averages. By the early 1990s, amid the NBA's rapid international media expansion and the upcoming 1992 Olympics in Barcelona, which would propel the league into even greater levels of worldwide exposure, the NBA made plans to open a series of regional "satellite" offices—in Hong Kong, Barcelona, and Melbourne—to help with marketing and cultural penetration in the regions surrounding them. The establishment of regional offices indicates the next step in the NBA's operation as a legitimate media producer and distributor is enabling the more effective localization of its television programming like *Dunk Street* in Canada, *Fastbreak* in Japan, and *Rafaga* in Mexico. As the league office becomes increasingly diffuse, executives delegate to a wider and wider net of allied agencies, much as other genuine conglomerates in WarnerMedia or NBCUniversal do. Eventually, the NBA begins to adapt its own league operations, launching the Women's National Basketball Association (WNBA) in 1996 and making plans for a professional football league in collaboration with NBC and Turner. By mapping the NBA and its operations at the executive level, the relationship between sport, the media industries, and global capital are made increasingly clear, as the sport of basketball becomes a distant priority to the NBA's commercial media interests.

The fifth and final chapter, "The Couch," examines the vast multiplatform media ecosystem of televisions and smart devices, as the industrial forces of sports media move from the court, into the arena, through the wires, across the floors of the NBA's corporate offices, and into the home viewing space. Ultimately, sports leagues are in a dialectical relationship with their audiences. The NBA wants its media content to be accessible wherever there are the most viewers, but, at the same time, viewers can watch only where the NBA is made available. As viewers cut their cable subscriptions en masse, for instance, the NBA has expanded the reach of its streaming service, League Pass, and made available specialized feeds tailored to specific interests. At the same time, many major cable providers have since launched or are set to launch streaming services of their own, including ESPN+ and NBC Peacock, rearranging revenues as cable subscriptions continue to decline. With the increased adoption of smartphones, moreover, social media platforms and sports news apps have partnered with sports leagues to build a multiscreen ecosystem that can direct attention toward telecasts or other lucrative media outlets. The recent widespread legalization of sports betting in the United States, moreover, has taken this a step further, enhancing viewership by allowing audiences to wager on the outcomes of games.

The book concludes with an in-depth examination of the NBA's COVID-19 "bubble" games that took place at Walt Disney World from July to October 2020. As a made-for-television event in a highly mediatized environment, the bubble offers a culmination of the interrelated forces of the court, the venue, the wires, the office, and the couch in practice. By tracing the global flow of sports media, from its live performance through its mediation and consumption, *The Digital NBA* is able to illustrate the causes and consequences of sport as secondary to the interests of media content and capital in the multiplatform media era.

CHAPTER 1

The Court

Event Production, Streaming Television,
and the "Glocalization" of Live Sport

"Can anyone find a color printer?"

In Houston, people are rushing through the bowels of a sports arena. Another last-minute change, in a series of seemingly endless last-minute changes. Now the league's logo needs to be *clearly* visible on the back of the cards held by the presenters. A mock-up of the graphic is made, but where is the color printer? No one seems to know.

An executive in charge of the league's live production approaches, asking to change the order of introducing the team mascots. The event script is rewritten, as quickly as possible, in order to be distributed in both paper and electronic copies to all the relevant parties.

Suddenly, the laptop crashes.

• • •

As the raw material that will be edited and broadcast to many millions of attentive viewers around the world, the live sports event is fundamental to the larger sports media ecosystem. The NBA, for example, features 1,230 games per regular season, with nearly one hundred more in the postseason and at least a dozen "Global Games" played overseas across the NBA's preseason and regular season. The National Hockey League (NHL) consists of a similar number of games at 1,271, and Major League Baseball (MLB) features an extensive 2,430 games in addition to its own lengthy postseason. The National Football League (NFL) plays the smallest number of games, at 256, but the small number of games has had the effect of increasing the significance of each game—television ratings for the NFL games are regularly higher than those of any other sport in the United States.[1] A typical basketball season, therefore, features more than four thousand hours of media content between its regular season and postseason and a baseball season features double that number. Understanding the relationship between the live event and the media event is thus essential for making sense of the sports media industry as a whole.

Live event producers, who operate independently from the television side of the production, must walk a delicate line between entertaining the in-person audience and entertaining the viewers at home, whose interests sometimes overlap and at other times conflict. The NBA offers an especially illuminating example of the modern sporting event and its relationship with television, in the league's increasingly multinational address and its incorporation of digital media technologies as live engagement tools. As this chapter will highlight, NBA events often integrate local cultural touchstones with US ones in service of the league's commercial interests and those of its media partners and sponsors. In doing so, the league draws on the logic of television formats to adapt both mediated and unmediated elements, undergoing processes of localization when it suits international needs and globalization in order to become more accessible to fans across regions. The case of the NBA thus demonstrates the complicated relationship between mediation and liveness, the various layers of globalization, and the extent and limitations of television as an influential force. Ultimately, the NBA's global strategy reflects the direction of the broader sports media industry and, at the same time, serves as a culmination of the NBA's distinct approach to live events since the 1980s.

In late 1985, the league reacquired control of their international television rights from CBS, its broadcast partner at the time. The decision was a crucial and history-altering one, as the NBA thereafter pursued a global audience more fervently than it ever had before. For many years, basketball had been a pastime enjoyed around the world, especially in countries around the Mediterranean, such as Greece, Italy, and Israel. Once the NBA stood to benefit more substantially from that popularity, the league sought new ways to grow the global visibility of NBA-brand basketball in particular. By the end of the 1980s, the NBA embarked on a number of exhibition tours and training camps to better integrate its athletes into cultural landscapes outside the United States, while also using the tours as cover to negotiate new television deals with national governments and broadcasters. The Atlanta Hawks tour of the Soviet Union in July 1988 offers an ideal example of the NBA's early approach to the global sporting event, as discussed later.

By the 2010s, the NBA's strategy evolved to accommodate a much more extensive schedule of overseas events, relying on a vast network of league personnel stationed around the world and tasked with researching local audiences and their viewing habits. International fans, the NBA found, desired a US sporting experience, complete with kiss cams and T-shirt tosses.[2]

The blending of US cultural touchstones with ones from the local community where the particular NBA event is staged, moreover, finds a parallel in the United States, where domestic event producers emphasize both hyperlocal signifiers and ones from cultures overseas. Teams such as the San Antonio Spurs run special events like their "lotería" night, which appeals to fans watching around the world for its authenticity. Similarly, the Sacramento Kings' incorporation of Hindi and Chinese characters into their uniforms and court signage works to enhance appeal to overseas audiences. The processes of internationalization and localization thus function in tandem to craft a sports event that will reach the widest possible audience, and the event's producers seek to entertain both the in-arena crowd and the at-home viewers. The multiple interests—local, global, live, media—work simultaneously in unison and in conflict during the live sports event.

Sports and the Media Event

Writing about new media in the late 1980s, cultural scholar Bernard Miège has argued that "some sporting events are now not only produced *for* television but *in function of* television re-transmission," citing major tennis tournaments, the 1984 Olympics in Los Angeles, and the FIFA World Cup as examples that "are as much audiovisual entertainment as they are live sporting events."[3] Miège offers an expansion of Robert McChesney's fundamental theory of sports-media "symbiosis," in which "media attention fans the flames of interest in sport and increased interest in sport warrants further media attention."[4] Miège's claim goes further than McChesney's, then, in asserting that the interests of the media event have come to exceed those of the sporting event alone. The subsequent years have produced a number of more striking examples, such as Ted Turner's creation of the Goodwill Games in 1986 as a Summer Olympics competitor, driven by the many hours of programming that the venture could offer TBS and its global television partners.[5] More recently, the launch of the Big3 summer three-on-three summer basketball league and relaunch of the XFL highlight expanding opportunities for upstart sports leagues through multiplatform media rights.[6] While it is true that the commercial interests of television increasingly influence the business of sport, a through-line in this book, the sports-media dynamic is considerably more complicated on the hardwood of the court itself, as sneakers squeak at random and fans cheer or boo of their own free will.

This complexity is at the heart of Daniel Dayan and Elihu Katz's description of the "media event," which they define as the "high holidays of mass communication" that "demand and receive focused attention."[7] Crucially, Dayan and Katz describe the production of the media event as involving three particular partners across the live performance and its mediation, and whose interests may or may *not* coincide: "the organizers of the event who bring its elements together and propose its historicity; the broadcasters who re-produce the events by recombining its elements; and the audience, on the spot and at home, who take the event to heart." Dayan and Katz describe these collaborations as a "contract" in which "each side undertakes to give something to the others in order to get something in return."[8] The audience, which is included in the "frame" of the television event and observed by the at-home viewer, thus retains a large degree of leverage in this relationship. For this reason, sports organizations like the NBA must be sure to cultivate fan engagement in the arena space in order to maximize excitement in fans at home. As Mike Chant, the NBA's senior director of team programming, explained, "if you can create an environment in-arena that is exciting, that translates well on TV."[9] While the financial value of the television product

Through the example of a Milwaukee Bucks fan cam that features photo filters, the excitement of in-arena fans is mediated and translated to fans at home.

exceeds that of the event and its attendance, the broadcast remains dependent on the entertainment derived from the live performance and the in-arena production.

In another foundational examination of the relationship between live and televised sport, Margaret Morse argues that the performance of sport becomes significantly modified by its mediation. She describes how "the constant use of extremely long lenses both narrows the angle of view and flattens space," and "the convention of instant replay shows the same play two or three times from different angles and points of view."[10] The television mediation of sport, then, exists in a realm unto itself, with a distinct spatiality and temporality that is no longer purely representational. Instead, television emphasizes "only points of action and body contact, to the detriment of the 'overall geometry of the game.'"[11] Television encourages a greater disparity between what the in-person audience and the home audience experience, and the home viewer gains something in the trade-off. The camera bestows them with a closer eye to the action and the nuances of the performance, even though they lose a sense of the total picture.

This tension between the live and mediated versions of sport provides the bedrock for a great deal of sports media scholarship, including that of Miege, McChesney, and Morse, as well as that of John Goldlust, who highlights how live sport increasingly obeys the logics of "good television."[12] Sports leagues do enjoy a degree of independence, since the conclusion of events remains open-ended, but power ultimately lies with the interests of television. Goldlust compares the production of sports to an independently produced television series: "For as long as particular shows maintain their rating power, they establish a sound bargaining position for contractual renewal and increased remuneration for all concerned with the production."[13] Though a push-pull of power exists between the sports and television industries, Goldlust acknowledges, the situation encourages both parties to accommodate the interests of "good television," who are inclined to extract as much profit as possible from the performers and from the audience. What Goldlust does not directly identify, however, is the crucial role of the commercial sponsor in the equation, which is the party that is most profoundly shaping the development of sport and television, as both separate and conjoined entities.

Sport scholars Raymond Boyle and Richard Haynes conceptualize such a sporting triangle between sport, television, and sponsors in which "sport is strategically managed and marketed to produce maximum commercial yields for sports federations, media corporations, sponsors and advertising concerns."[14] The identification of the sponsor as an entity distinct from sport and television is crucial for understanding the influences at work on the live sporting event, which features spontaneous actions that remain just beyond the reach of television's influence. The live event is not beyond the reach of sponsors, however, who continue to occupy a fundamental role in shaping the production. If one integrates Dayan and Katz's concept of the contract, then two triangles of interested parties overlap: between the event's organizers, broadcasters, and audience and between sport, sponsor, and television more broadly. On the industrywide scale, the interests of television often influence the development of the sport, and indeed sponsors play a fundamental role in shaping the production of television. During the live event, however, only the sponsors can influence both sport and television by working through the autonomy of event organizers and audience members over the broadcasters.

T. Bettina Cornwell, Clinton S. Weeks, and Donald P. Roy highlight the various approaches that might be available to sponsors, "such as simple brand logos, which are minimal by nature and cannot carry the wealth or quality of information that more complex communications can," and more involved "activations," which entail the "collateral communication" of a sponsorship.[15] Cornwell, Weeks, and Roy cite the example of beverage company SoBe, which "leveraged its title sponsorship of the Summer and Winter Gravity Games" by using a strategic combination of "media advertising, regional and national sweepstakes, local radio promotions, venue signage, and on-site sampling."[16] Though passive signage is indeed useful for established brands, as a reminder and reactivation of a memory, more complex activations are useful in creating "a web of connectivity among a firm's various sponsorship activities," thus cultivating a more "unique position in consumers' minds."[17] This often leverages specific live events, which "are chosen because of significant overlap between the target audience for the event and the target market of the brand," drawing on the positive associations of a particular sporting event and "establishing a link between the two."[18] At the same time, the actions of a sponsor cannot appear to be overtly commercial, Cornwell, Weeks, and Roy argue, or else a "change-of-meaning may be triggered" and any associations with that brand might become more negative than positive.[19]

Such tensions are evident in the production of the NBA's live event, especially, which relies on writers and producers working to carry out the sponsors' vision. Event organizers must determine the most effective activation that can build positive associations between the event and the sponsor, attend to any unique requests, and deploy them at the optimal time during the game so as not to undermine the audiences' trust in the sporting qualities of the performance and so as to maximize fan entertainment. Although the improvisational nature of the sporting event exceeds the interests and control of sponsors, sponsors' needs inevitably play a strong role in shaping the contours of the sporting experience by influencing game breaks and calls to action by the audience that effect the overall impact of the event, both in person and at home.

Media and the Sports Event: The McDonald's Open and the Atlanta Hawks Tour

The relationship between sports and sponsors, and the influence of the latter on the events of the former, was especially evident in the NBA's business strategies during the 1980s. In 1982, the league created a new division called NBA Entertainment (NBAE) to serve as an in-house production outfit and video archive, capitalizing on the expanding programming possibilities offered by cable television. Inspired by the earlier success of NFL Films, the production division of the National Football League, NBAE was conceived by NBA executive vice president and later commissioner David Stern as being "something bigger and broader" in its responsibilities. "Entertainment sounded right, if a little too pretentious," he added, "but when you don't have much, you might as well flaunt what you want to have."[20] Beginning in 1982, therefore, NBA Entertainment became a production arm for television and promotional materials as well as a storehouse for all the league's telecasts. As the league's archive began to grow, these tapes would become crucial in the NBA's media production, distribution, and promotional ambitions.

By December 1985, NBAE's capabilities had evolved considerably and the division was regularly producing home video releases, commercials, and events for the NBA All-Star Game. With a reinvigorated relationship with incumbent broadcast partner CBS, and greater leverage at the negotiating table, the NBA landed a four-year, $173 million contract, a significant improvement on its previous four-year, $88 million deal.[21] Less reported on, however, was arguably the most significant feature of the new arrangement. CBS, previously, had overseen the international distribution of most major NBA events, paying the league around $250,000 for the right to do so. In Italy, however, where the league retained its own television rights, distribution rights generated close to $200,000 in that single territory alone. "So we figured if we can't make more than $250,000, if we have all of the games and the territory of the entire world to do it, then there's something wrong with us," explained Ed Desser, who served as both general manager of NBAE and director of broadcasting at the time. "So we let the deal expire and spent the next several years developing an international business from scratch."[22] In order to boost the worldwide demand for NBA's television programming, the league next embarked on a mission to expand the league's physical presence through a number of exhibition tours and tournaments.

In October 1987, the NBA cosponsored its first international basketball tournament, initially called the World Basketball Open, with the International Basketball Federation (FIBA). The Milwaukee Bucks, as the league's representatives, would face off in Milwaukee against the Soviet national team and the European champions, Tracer Milan of Italy.[23] From very early on in the process, the NBA went about looking for commercial sponsors. McDonald's, which was planning a more aggressive marketing push into the Soviet Union, quickly signed on as the title sponsor, making the tournament the keystone of its efforts.[24] Thus the World Basketball Open became the McDonald's Basketball Open, a title that the tournament would hold through its final meeting in 1999. The NBA was also able to secure significant international broadcast arrangements, capitalizing on the attention of Italy and the Soviet Union. Globally, the tournament was aired live in Italy and in tape-delayed broadcasts in twenty-five other countries.[25] After CBS, the league's incumbent broadcast partner passed on the rights to the open, the NBA came to an agreement with ABC to air the title game between the Bucks and the Soviet team and with TBS for the two preliminary games.[26]

The McDonald's Open was important to the league, not only for establishing a stronger presence in the international basketball landscape but also for evolving the NBA's approach to marketing and sponsorship. In order to ensure that NBA sponsors received the most substantial benefits, the league purchased all the commercial time from ABC and TBS for an undisclosed amount, offering their regular sponsors a minimum of three thirty-second spots that would air internationally. In doing so, wrote Michael Hiestand of *Adweek*, "the NBA will have moved beyond being a mere supplier to become a full-service marketer."[27] ABC was more than happy to oblige. As Bob Iger, then vice president of programming for ABC Sports and later CEO of Disney, explained, "They opted to bear the risk. Since we had no programming scheduled for the time slot, it's found money."[28] In turning around and selling the time to sponsors like McDonald's, the NBA could reduce those costs for the league and allowed the US brands to expand their international presence, capitalizing on the worldwide footprint of the event's broadcasts. A triangular relationship was thus established between sports, media, and sponsors, in which the sponsors' interests were the most thoroughly valued. At the event level, moreover, the influence of the sponsor was privileged by both the event organizers and broadcast partners, in order to reach the widest possible audience. In a telecast that aired on Italian television, for example, as players from Tracer Milan and the Milwaukee Bucks raced up and down the floor, large McDonald's logos surrounded every side of the court, clearly visible to both the in-arena and at-home audiences, providing the company with a valuable opportunity for transnational exposure.[29]

Upon the success of the McDonald's Open, the league formed a new division called NBA International (NBAI) in late 1987.[30] Tasked with providing and selling telecasts to the NBA's overseas broadcast partners, the league hoped to advance its global distribution and capitalize on the growing interest in its product. The division worked in close cooperation with NBAE, which continued to archive game footage and sometimes oversaw the advertising packages and foreign-language dubs in the feeds that were being sold by NBAI.[31] The relationship was so close between the NBAE and NBAI, and the league office still such a small outfit, that Ed Desser came aboard and worked in the divisions simultaneously, as vice president and general manager of both. "At one period of time, I had three different business cards I was walking around with," he remembered, "As there were new things to do, they just sort of got thrown on my plate."[32] The foundation of NBAI, then, reflected the league's increasing perception of the sport as lucrative media content and itself as a media company.

In January 1988, the upstart NBAI sold fifty-two games to the Pan-European satellite service Super Channel, putting the league in around nine million homes across Finland, France, West Germany, East Germany, and the Netherlands. Through the Dallas-based International Broadcast Systems, which helped to engineer the agreement, the NBA also formed the NBA South American Network for its own satellite distribution, which broadcast to Argentina, Brazil, Chile, Ecuador, Paraguay, Peru, Uruguay, and Venezuela. IBS also helped to secure a twenty-five-game deal with Imevision, the Mexican government-run television station.[33] The international distribution of the NBA had doubled over the prior three years, once the league took back control from CBS. In addition to those already mentioned, the NBA had agreements for one or two weekly taped games with Bandeirantes in Brazil, Icelandic TV, Spain's TVE, Great Britain's BBC, and Berlusconi in Italy.[34] It would be at least another year before MLB, comparably international in its player makeup and marketing, formed its own international division. By 1991, MLB reached only sixty-one countries on television, while the NBA had grown to reach seventy-five.[35]

The NBA's global media expansion was aided, moreover, by the ongoing relaxation of regulations in countries that had previously prevented US programming from gaining dominance on government-run airwaves. After "the rise of market-based political ideologies ushered in during the Reagan and Thatcher era," explains media historian Michele Hilmes, "public broadcasting systems were privatized and restructured to compete in the marketplace."[36] This put US media producers in the best possible position, as the "vast programming libraries" of major Hollywood studios "made them uniquely capable of fulfilling the rapidly growing demand for programming worldwide," per global media scholar Timothy Havens.[37] By 1988, the United States would account for an estimated 75 percent of the world's television export revenues, aided by the global proliferation of commercial operators. By that time in Western Europe, for instance, there were seventeen satellite-to-cable channels, of which eight were supported by advertising and required highly profitable programming.[38] "We were opportunistic," recalled the NBA's Ed Desser. "We took advantage of the technologies that developed. At the same time, internationally, there were more and more channels being launched. . . . NBA programming had a brand name, and so we took advantage of that."[39] As the global television marketplace became increasingly lucrative for US television producers, the NBA would be among them, followed by other professional sports leagues in subsequent years.

The league's pursuit of global success strategically encompassed both media distribution and exhibition events, in which the latter provided a stronger local presence that could be parlayed into a larger television audience. After the success of the inaugural McDonald's Open, for example, the Atlanta Hawks embarked on a nearly two-week exhibition tour of the Soviet Union in July 1988, which saw the Ted Turner–owned Hawks compete against the Soviet national team in Tbilisi, Vilnius, and Moscow.[40] Though depicted as a diplomatic endeavor, the tour enabled David Stern and the NBA to meet with Soviet officials on the league's television presence there. The Turner Broadcasting System, which arranged the tour, also sent its executive vice president Robert Wussler with the mission of lobbying the Soviet government to allow their athletes to play in the NBA. TBS had already established a relationship with Gostelradio, the Soviet television and radio bureau, after the two cosponsored the production of the inaugural Goodwill Games in July 1986, an international Olympic-style competition that was broadcast from the Soviet Union using TBS equipment and personnel.[41]

No Soviet athlete had been granted permission by the Soviet government to play professional basketball in the United States, due to the FIBA rules that would thereby prevent those players from competing for their country in international competition.[42] Turner's primary incentive was to lobby the Soviet government to allow its players to sign with the Hawks. If the Hawks could acquire Soviet players, and TBS could promote those Soviet players, then the channel might cultivate a more lasting presence in the Soviet Union, a potentially massive and emerging market for television. The NBA itself also stood to benefit from the exposure. Commissioner David Stern and TBS personnel would thus use the tour to negotiate television rights and the movement of players to the NBA.[43] Ultimately, Stern would offer Gostelradio a package of NBA games free of charge, banking on long-term market penetration over immediate profits.[44] Ultimately, the trip became "a watershed moment for the league," after which the league began to accelerate its global plans, noted Kim Bohuny, a TBS employee during the tour and later senior vice president of International Basketball Operations at the NBA.[45] The stated goal of the endeavor, to "bring down the wall between Eastern and Western Europe and allow the Eastern European players to come and play in the NBA," would finally come to pass the following year, when FIBA at last voted to admit professionals into the Olympics and other international tournaments, paving the way for Soviet players to join the NBA without relinquishing the ability to compete for their home country.[46]

A few months after the Hawks' Soviet tour, in October 1988, the Boston Celtics were set to travel to Madrid for the second McDonald's Open. Like the first open, TBS would televise the preliminary matchups while ABC covered the championship round. Globally, the tournament was expected to be televised in nearly sixty countries.[47] The NBA, in conjunction with these exhibition events, continued to explode across international television screens. Spain and Italy, in particular, had grown into "basketball hotbeds," with regular television highlights and newspaper coverage.[48] Greece, too, had continued to evolve as a major basketball market, especially after introducing commercial television. In fall 1988, the Greek government launched an experimental state-run satellite service, which retransmitted from Sky Channel, Superchannel, CNN, MTV, RAI-1, RAI-2, TV5, and Spain's TVE.[49] Sports were now being broadcast during prime-time hours, with basketball and soccer becoming especially successful.[50] Basketball counted as three of the top five programs for the month of January 1989, consistently netting an audience share between 24 and 27.[51]

By February, after the Atlanta Hawks' tour through the Soviet Union the previous summer, the same was becoming true there. The Soviet Union was set to begin bimonthly taped broadcasts of NBA games, using the condensed versions produced by NBA Entertainment. There would be fourteen games for the remainder of the season, filled in with six minutes of commercials from Coca-Cola and Mastercard.[52] Like the McDonald's sponsorship of the World Basketball Championships, other US companies eagerly sought to penetrate the Soviet market. As an additional gesture, the NBA invited Rimas Kurtinaitis, after winning the Lithuanian three-point contest, to participate in the NBA's competition at All-Star weekend. This would be the first and only time the NBA would make such a gesture, likely because other players had a negative response to inviting a non-NBA athlete to compete in a league event. The decision reflected the NBA's evolving effort to address an altogether more global audience by featuring foreign-born stars, a strategy that would become more prominent in the years to come.[53]

The NBA's actions as a global media institution during this period thus illuminate the mechanics between sport, media, and sponsors at the level of the event. While media interests may inform the league's decision-making and investments in particular international events, the presence of sponsors such as McDonald's and Mastercard are able to more directly affect the experience of both the live sporting event and its mediation, through signage and branded game-break activities, as the next section will discuss. Ultimately, the greater the internationalism of a sport and its events, the more substantial the benefit will be to the global commercial interests of both the league and its sponsors.

Producing the Global Sports Event

By the close of the 1990s, NBA Entertainment gave rise to a new subdivision, Live Programming and Entertainment (LP&E), which was tasked with overseeing the live production of All-Star Weekend and the league's various global events. Since 2006, the NBA has played at least three and as many as six preseason games per year overseas, plus a small number of regular-season games. In 2017, the NBA held a record five regular-season games in Mexico and the United Kingdom.[54] In addition to a director and producer, a typical NBA event relies extensively on the script department housed within LP&E, which employs a script supervisor, a script writer, and a script coordinator, though the roles of the latter two positions are sometimes combined.[55] The script department serves as a crucial "hub of information," explained writer and coordinator Mojie Crigler. "We get all the information about a show from the producers and directors and we put that information into various documents."[56]

Among these documents is the *script*, which helps to coordinate lighting cues, commercial breaks, activities such as dance teams and giveaways, and center court interviews. More central than the script, however, is the *rundown*, which itself has two versions—a long rundown and a shorter "quickie" rundown. The rundown takes the form of a spreadsheet that includes time codes and lighting, sound, and any pyrotechnics for those activities—who is entering the court, when and from where, and if anyone must accompany them. "There is not anything that is left to chance," Crigler adds. "It's all planned out."[57] The script coordinator and writer, moreover, must coordinate with sponsors and supervisors on any changes, such as new graphics or activities moving up or back within the program. With every change, the script and the rundown must both be updated and properly aligned and redistributed to the entire crew. For the All-Star Game, for example, the distribution ("distro") list is massive. It includes both twenty to thirty printed copies in large binders and an electronic mailing list of at least one hundred people. Changes are constant in the six to eight weeks leading up to an event and even while the game is in progress. The writer may have to craft a new introduction or line of copy and run it out to the event MC or PA announcer with seconds to spare.[58]

While the script department is following dictates from supervisors, including the NBA's executive in charge of live programming or the head of overall content, the event producer is the individual that is balancing the sometime contradictory interests of the NBA, its sponsors, and the interests of the live audience. As Anne Wright, a former NBA producer, explained, "I'm given sponsorship assets that we either have to create activation—like build the creative for it, whether it's a contest, or a video-board element, fan cam, or whatever—but sometimes we're told what it is and sometimes we have to pitch ideas, based on what we think will work for that audience, or what assets we have for entertainment, like mascots or dancers, anything."[59] Ultimately, there are templates for time-outs, halftime, pregame intros and warmups, and so on. "So I just built a show based around those blocks of time that I had.... We plug in a show. First quarter, first time out, usually the dance team would come out. You can tag it at the end with a fan cam until the ball is inbounded, that kind of thing. Those are things I would be doing to produce. I basically collect all the things we *have* to do and then within that make it entertaining."[60]

The interests of the sponsors, therefore, are valued most highly within the structure of the event. The need for branded activities, such as fan cams and T-shirt tosses, are dictated downward from the uppermost executive levels, and those individuals in charge of programming the event must follow those requirements. A tension is evident, therefore, between the larger corporate institution, in this case the NBA, and the personnel who are tasked

At NBA Fan Day, part of the 2017 Global Games in Shanghai, Klay Thompson of the Golden State Warriors participates in a three-point contest alongside Chinese celebrities. The logo for Vivo, a Chinese tech company, is emblazoned on the side of the ball rack, reflecting the confluence of US and local brands and cultural touchstones.

with executing those interests while keeping the audience entertained. In this way, the creative labor of the live sports event is reflective of the writers, directors, and producers of narrative television, who also must attract and maintain particular audiences, but whose true autonomy is suspect, as creative personnel are often beholden to sponsor relationships first and foremost. As Dallas W. Smythe has argued in his foundational work on the "audience commodity," the nonadvertising content of television functions as a kind of "free lunch," in that the ultimate "purpose of the mass media is to produce audiences to sell to the advertisers."[61] By highlighting the mechanics of live event production, the relationship between the live event and the media event becomes increasingly apparent. Rather than through commercials, the sporting event provides sponsors with access to both an in-person and an at-home audience through active branded festivities like shot contests and fan cams, as well as passive in-arena signage, both of which have proven effective in reinforcing positive associations between an event and a company.[62]

These dynamics are evident in the actual text of the event script and rundown, which is the product of the script department's labor. In the script for the 2015 NBA Global Games event in Shenzhen, China, between the Charlotte Hornets and the Los Angeles Clippers, spaces are left for sponsors to be added later. During the team entrances and warmups, the in-arena announcer is given space to thank all the NBA's event partners, including Adidas, American Airlines, Gatorade, and Marriot, as well as more local companies, such as Master Kong, Harbin Beer, and Mengniu. For particular breaks in the action, such as the first time-out of the first quarter, fan interactions are branded by those sponsors. During Global Games Shenzhen, for example, NBA writers scripted a "Mengniu Puzzle Challenge" wherein two contestants "race to solve a giant Mengniu puzzle. With that completed, they'll grab a basketball, dribble to the basket, and make a layup. The first to complete the challenge will take home a special prize from Mengniu!" Every interaction with fans by the master of ceremonies, Edcon, is scripted. "They're getting close," the script reads, "the puzzle is starting to come together . . . it looks like—yes, it's the new NBA Mengniu Milk Carton!" During the first time-out of the second quarter, there is another branded activity, the ZTE Hot and Cold Challenge, but this one has not yet been as fully conceptualized. Instead, the script reads simply that contestants will make their way to the "ZTE Prop/Prize." "You did it!" Edcon will tell them, "You've won a (TBD PRIZE) from ZTE!" Even though the game is not yet clear, the sponsor and its role are definitive.

The rundown works together with the script by including details such as time codes, graphics that will accompany the activities, and notes on how many participants are involved in each one. The rundown for the NBA Global Game event in Shanghai, for another example, features the same Mengniu Puzzle Challenge and notes that the main video board will accompany the game with Mengniu graphics. The rundown thus offers the widest perspective of the event, for the widest range of personnel, while the script provides the necessary information for the relevant performers. Ultimately, the NBA's writers work diligently to craft the most entertaining show possible, writing jokes for the MC and creating minigames that will be the most fun to fans inside the arena. Their creativity is restricted, however, by the limits of the sports event, in which they can write only within the allotted timeframes of the game breaks, as well as the needs of the sponsors, who may propose or approve of any activities that will be associated with their brands. Keeping the sponsors happy is paramount, perhaps more so than keeping fans entertained, insofar as those interests conflict. In the triangular relationship between sport, sponsor, and media, the sponsor remains most important to personnel in the live programming and event department.

Localizing the Global Sports Event

The NBA's 2015 events in Shenzhen and Shanghai also call attention to the ways in which global and local interests have been merged in meaningful ways. While fans want a recognizably American sporting experience, the NBA's writers and producers work to translate those features into distinctly local terms. In this capacity, the NBA's process of localization is aligned with that of the global television format trade, which similarly draws on a flexible program template that can be efficiently adapted to various local markets. Albert Moran defines the television format as containing "a core or a structuring center" or "that set of invariable elements in a program out of which the variable elements of an individual episode are produced."[63] The format, moreover, is an ongoing and never-complete process in which knowledge from subsequent iterations are absorbed into the format package to the benefit of the copyright holder.[64] The NBA live event, as a recognizable form that is also flexible enough to incorporate local cultural touchstones, is driven by a similar commercial motive and invokes the same intercultural dynamics that are at work in the television format trade. The same is true of overseas NFL and MLB events, both of which have either planned or played games in Mexico City and London, though neither league has been as globally aggressive or comprehensive as the NBA to this point.[65]

Just as television formats rely on local broadcasters to adapt programs from their original form, the NBA's overseas event production is conducted with the aid of the NBA's relevant local offices, which are most thoroughly versed in the interests of local fans. In this particular case, NBA China aided in the process of translation and localization, but NBA Latin America would help for any events in Mexico and NBA India for the league's recent events in India. Anne Wright recalled that "we would try to think of things that were super local because that's the exciting thing for us," but often the local offices would ask for "the real authentic NBA experience."[66] This balance is clear in the inclusion of activities such as the kiss cam and dance cam, which the NBA used in both Shenzhen and Shanghai, but crucially chose to attach them to the non-US sponsors Harbin Beer and Clear Shampoo, respectively, in an effort to enhance the legibility of those activities for the fans.[67]

Making such decisions can often prove difficult. The producers are placed in a position where they must follow the wishes of local partners and sponsors, but the execution of those requests is sometimes at odds with the NBA's expected version of the event. "There [were] always things that didn't make sense to us because of the culture, but those are what the sponsor needed,"

Wright explained, including props with unexpectedly large dimensions or materials that were very obviously unsafe. For a game activity that needed to use branded placemats from which participants would shoot baskets, for example, the mats arrived as a plastic material that was far too dangerous for people to use on a slippery hardwood floor. Mojie Crigler, script coordinator, similarly noted difficulties in translation, which can often choose the wrong equivalent of a word with multiple meanings. She recalled giving the first draft of a script to a translator to look over, only to discover that *court* had been translated with the Chinese word for a tribunal court and *shot* with the word for a gunshot.[68] Such difficulties are a by-product of adapting an American cultural product to a local context, which do not always fit together neatly.

The process of localizing the NBA event thus reflects the mechanics of localizing global television formats, in which a similar tension remains between the original program and its many local adaptions. Daya Kishan Thussu has argued that the localization of US media content continues to "legitimize the ideological imperatives of a free-market capitalism."[69] The dynamic is evident not only in television programming but in the adaptation of the live sports event, prior to its mediation, as the script and rundown are filled with the language of capitalism. "Ladies and gentlemen, please log onto NBA flagship store by tapping 'NBAStore.cn' on your mobile phone for going shopping NBA Global Games Official Merchandises," the arena announcer tells fans during halftime, in language that has clearly been translated back into English from the local dialect. "Meanwhile, we have set up several NBA Stores to provide our fans Adidas jersey, T-shirt, caps, Spalding basketball and the other authentic accessories." The NBA event, therefore, fuses the local language and cultural touchstones with US sponsors and consumption patterns in order to promote the commercial interests of the NBA and its sponsors.

In his analysis of the global format trade, Silvio Waisbord draws on Roland Robertson's concept of "glocalization" to describe the process in which cultural diversity serves as a business strategy rather than a political project, "not informed by respect for or interest in preserving 'multiculturalism' but rather to maximize opportunities for commercial gain."[70] Marwan Kraidy has described similar machinations as "corporate transculturalism," which "emphasizes cultural fluidity as a tool to make corporations more profitable."[71] Since the very first McDonald's Open in 1987, the NBA in particular has drawn on the transculturalism of multinational events in order to market NBA basketball and its partners to a multinational audience. More recently, events such as the Global Games have catered to more localized interests, by focusing on particular cities or regions such as Shenzhen and Shanghai, Rio de Janeiro and Brazil, and Mumbai and India. This approach is "glocal" in its integration of local cultural interests with US commercial imperatives through the global popularity of a sport such as basketball. The approach is similar, moreover, to McDonald's own approach to glocalization, which utilizes the flexibility of its brand to offer more local products, including the McHuevo in Uruguay and the McBurrito in Mexico, that can still be recognized globally as a McDonald's product.[72] Taking the concept into the realm of media, Waisbord goes on to describe the concept of "McTelevision," in which television formats demonstrate the "selling of programming ideas with a track record that are sufficiently flexible to accommodate local cultures to maximize profitability."[73] The practice is evident, also, in the NBA's live events. NBA productions in China, India, or Brazil, for instance, are adapted to local fans and cultures, balanced against the league's established brand identity, in order to maximize profits.

In this way, the NBA's strategy is reflective of MTV, among the most globally successful of US television channels, which discovered the glocal approach after initial failures. Their initial strategy assumed that US popular music could serve as an international language, but the "one-channel-fits-all approach" ultimately could not gain any local traction. Instead, they launched MTV Taiwan, India, Japan, Korea, etc., and introduced more customized local programming blocks to much greater success.[74] "Despite MTV being a global brand, we are local in approach," explained David Flack, senior vice president of MTV Asia's Creative and Content Division in 2003. "We reflect the taste and demands of our viewers and this differs in each market. Thus the need to create specific channels (in each country) that meet the needs of our target audience."[75] Ultimately, MTV glocalizes its content "by establishing joint business ventures with local corporations."[76] Other major global media producer-distributors have used similar alliances, including Netflix, which signed agreements with Mexico's TV Azteca and Grupo Televisa and Brazil's Globo for more local media content as the Netflix platform expanded into Latin America.[77]

This is deeply reminiscent of the NBA, which uses its own league satellite offices, drawing on their expert knowledge of the local landscape to create the most effectively glocalized event. Danny Meiseles, the NBA's president of content, noted that "the regional offices are very much involved" in the league's strategic use of local talent to craft localized content.[78] The live sports event, at the initial script stages and prior to any mediation, thus reflects the commercial interests of its media partners and sponsors. In this way, the producers and writers of the NBA's live programming department, like the creative personnel of a television program, remain restricted by the commercialism of the endeavor. Creative autonomy is limited by formal elements such as time-outs or commercial breaks, as well as the prioritization of sponsorship within the content itself, such as the branded activities and prize giveaways that function as live product placement. The affinities between the NBA and international television producers thus highlight the league's ongoing and evolving status as a legitimate global media conglomerate.

Globalizing the Local Sports Event

With the NBA's expanding number of global exhibition events, the NBA's integrated media and event strategy established in the 1980s has only intensified, encouraged by emerging media technologies such as streaming that have allowed for an even wider and more simultaneous audience. As with the NBA's invitation of Rimas Kurtinaitis to All-Star Weekend in 1989, the NBA has continued to draw on foreign-born athletes to more effectively reach audiences overseas. "When there is a local affinity for a player because he's from that market, then obviously there's more affinity for watching our games and buying our products," explained Danny Meiseles, NBA president of content. "We saw it with Yao Ming, we see it with players from Europe, Brazil, Australia. You see it all the time."[79] As streaming platforms such as NBA League Pass can reach more fans more simultaneously than ever before, the NBA has increasingly sought to incorporate international performances and iconography into the live event so that these elements can be broadcast to the widest possible audience.

This incorporation is evident at the level of the NBA franchise, many of which have pursued a more global audience through their team events, capitalizing on the new opportunities from streaming and social media platforms. The Milwaukee Bucks, for example, have strategically pursued Greek fans and audiences as a result of their Greek star player, Giannis Antetokounmpo. During a live event, the team aired a video package produced by their Greek television partner that congratulated Antetokounmpo for making his first All-Star team in 2017.[80] By using the live arena space, the video could be viewed across Greek linear television, the US and international versions of the League Pass streaming platform, and the Bucks' Facebook and Twitter pages as well.[81] Ramon Lobato has highlighted that Netflix is significant for its ability to "effortlessly combine the local and the global *within the one platform* and constitute itself as many different products simultaneously."[82] For sports, this is possible within the same *program*.

By the Bucks' airing the package in the arena, it was broadcast worldwide through the NBA's streaming platform.

The Sacramento Kings are another team that uses the multiplatform ecosystem to their advantage, using the live event and its subsequent mediation to more substantially address an overseas fan base. Ahead of the 2017–18 season, the team revealed two new alternative court designs, one in Hindi and one in Chinese characters, that would be used during select games aired in those nations.[83] The "global court" also features a redesigned Kings logo, which uses a more traditional lion logo than the standard Kings basketball design in order to be more recognizable in India and other overseas nations.[84] For the 2017–18 season, Nike released "city edition" jerseys for every NBA franchise, and the Kings' version featured a version of their lion logo as well as a white "soccer-style" chest stripe.[85] While some Sacramento

Greek basketball fans congratulate Giannis Antetokounmpo on making his first All-Star team, in a video that circulated across Greek linear television, the Bucks' in-arena video board, NBA League Pass, and the Bucks' Facebook page.

48   CHAPTER 1

fans were critical of the look, the effort to better engage international Kings fans was evident.[86] The courts and jersey have also been combined with various "international theme nights," including a "Lunar New Year Celebration" and "Bollywood Night." Throughout these events, the Kings rely on multiple social media platforms to more effectively address local fans, including the Chinese platform Weibo.[87] In 2014, when the Kings launched the first Hindi-language website in the NBA, the team's president at the time, Chris Granger, stated that the organization's goal was "to become India's home team."[88] The Kings have pursued this mission by cultivating a live event that can take advantage of the global media ecosystem.

Although the Kings serve as exemplars of the global NBA franchise, others have pursued their own international audiences. In addition to the example of Greek star Giannis Antetokounmpo and the Milwaukee Bucks, the city edition jerseys of the Houston Rockets and Golden State Warriors both feature Chinese characters.[89] Like the Kings, many teams also feature various international "heritage" nights that are broadcast overseas in the country of note. The New York Knicks held their first "French Heritage Night" against the Charlotte Hornets in order to feature their own French player in Frank Ntilikina and the Hornets' Nicolas Batum and Tony Parker.[90] Mike Chant described the live event as "an extension of a team's marketing effort," which is especially clear in the specialized theme nights and local-themed jerseys. "The people who are at your games are your biggest fans," Chant continued, "so how you present your games is in essence how you present your brand to those fans."[91] In a global media ecosystem, moreover, these efforts are broadcast simultaneously to fans around the world, thus encouraging teams to incorporate those viewers into its team brand, as the Kings have done to remake themselves as India's team. Semiotics scholar Marcel Danesi has argued that global brands, "by co-opting local signification systems and blending them with more global ones," encourage individuals "to see themselves as members of local and global communities at once."[92] The NBA and its franchises, beginning at the level of the live event, have similarly worked to blend US and non-US interests in such a way as to craft a more marketable global identity.[93]

At the same time that various franchises have taken on an altogether more global identity, other teams have gone in the opposite direction, marketing themselves as more distinctly local. The San Antonio Spurs, for example, released their 2019–20 season schedule online in the style of "lotería cards," translating team names into Spanish and designing new logos for every team franchise, in a bid to draw on the city's Mexican heritage and thus market the localism to fans in San Antonio and throughout

Latin America. "Lotería is such an authentic aspect of Hispanic culture, and staying true to the team, the city and the culture here is an important aspect of the work we do," explained team creative designers Justin Winget and Owen Lindsay.[94] On October 26, 2019, the team subsequently held a Hispanic Heritage Night, wherein they handed out sets of lotería cards to fans in attendance.[95] Similarly, the Brooklyn Nets have pursued localization by incorporating the area's relationship to street basketball and hip-hop history. For the 2019–20 season, for instance, the team launched a new concrete-gray court, which was surrounded by a white subway tile pattern. Their city edition uniforms, moreover, paid tribute to local rapper Notorious B.I.G. by featuring his particular neighborhood, Bedford Stuyvesant, or Bed-Stuy, in place of the team's usual "Brooklyn" text.[96]

This process of relocalization is aimed at the same sort of global success that teams like the Kings and Bucks had. Local fans can feel great affinity with their local team, and fans overseas can feel great kinship with their adopted teams. The Spurs can use local Hispanic roots to fashion themselves as the team for Latin America, for example, and the Nets can reimagine themselves as the team that represents New York hip-hop. Just as

The San Antonio Spurs' lotería cards, which were used as a promotional tool to reach a more international sample of fans.

NBA uses kiss cams and dance cams in its overseas events to blend local experiences with an American one, identifiably local elements like the Nets' subway court design and Bed-Stuy jerseys work to engage fans around the world through their distinctly American qualities.

Teams can either market themselves directly to fan bases outside the United States, as the Sacramento Kings have to India, or be more indirect by using recognizably local elements to appeal to multiple groups of international fans, irrespective of national borders. Both strategies have the effect of globalizing the address of the live sporting event and the ultimate goal of global commercial success. The NBA's Mike Chant, who travels around the country to view and improve each team's live production, understands the increasing importance of the global audience. "I'm trying to get the people who focus on in-arena to try think a little bit more globally because their content is being distributed globally," he explained, most often through the NBA's own international streaming platform.[97] The examples of the Bucks, Kings, Spurs, and Nets, moreover, demonstrate this strategy in action, as their events have taken on an increasingly global hue in order to solicit the widest possible audience.

At the same time, glocalization of the event does not necessarily equate with genuine cultural diversity or social progress. In the realm of television formats, Silvio Waisbord notes that "copyright holders ultimately determine what changes can be incorporated; they remain 'the author' of the text despite a variety of national adaptations and audiences' interpretations," much as the NBA controls the adaptation of its own live events into various local contexts.[98] In keeping with Marcel Danesi's argument, moreover, that global brands encourage individuals "to see themselves as members of local and global communities at once," the NBA and its franchises blend local and global elements in pursuit of greater overall profit, as reflected in Marwan Kraidy's suggestion that "cultural fluidity" is often used "as a tool to make corporations more profitable."[99] In the case of the NBA, individual writers and producers may try to make the live event as entertaining as possible for fans inside the arena, but the profit motive remains at the root of the endeavor, limiting the paths that personal creativity can take.

Conclusion: Global Games

The NBA's contemporary approach to live events is the culmination of the league's strategy since the 1980s, when the McDonald's Open and Hawks Tour presented new opportunities for the NBA to pursue an altogether more global audience, in combination with the league's reacquisition of its own international television rights from CBS. Since then, the league has drawn from the logic of television formats to translate and adapt its events into local contexts around the world, growing its own cultural footprint as well as the visibility of its corporate sponsors. Simultaneously, the NBA has undergone a localization of events abroad and a globalization of domestic events. While global events rely on the league's satellite offices to adapt NBA events to local contexts, the NBA's domestic events have become increasingly global in order to better address overseas fans, building greater cohesion across its adaptations and multinational audiences.

The writers and producers doing the legwork of these translations are seeking to primarily entertain the audience in front of them, but they are afforded only so much creative autonomy, much like their counterparts working in narrative television, who are similarly trying to make captivating works that will hold an audience's attention in service of the network and its sponsors. As a result, the live sports event offers insights that exceed the subject of sport alone, providing a window into the mechanics of creative labor within a predominantly commercial enterprise. By examining the live sports event, then, as the starting foundation for the NBA's media event, the triangular tension between sport, media, and sponsor can be better understood. Although the interests of the live event can sometimes supersede the NBA's media interests, as writers, producers, and performers alike all seek to appeal to the in-person audience first and foremost, the commercial interests of the NBA's sponsors still rule over the enterprise through the many branded contests and giveaways that pervade events around the world. The live event stokes as much excitement as possible in its audience, and the methods for doing so often function as marketing tools for local and national brands, such as the dance cam and kiss cam tied to Harbin Beer and Clear hair products in the case of the Global Games Shenzhen event.

The institutions of sports and media are heavily integrated, but the event-specific relationship between the event organizers, the broadcasters, and the audience illustrates the extent to which sport remains distinct from the media industry. Broadcasters are beholden to the excitement of the live event; if it is boring, or seats are empty, or no one seems excited, audiences at home are less likely to stay tuned to that channel. The in-person audience, then, holds some leverage as the party that is being addressed directly, which allows them to participate in the proceedings or disrupt them, in conflict with the organizers' wishes. The audience has the power, in other words, to act out their excitement or not.

The event organizers, meanwhile, have the job of unifying the expanding number of interested parties, both creative and corporate. The producers and writers must abide the desires of the audience, the sponsors, and their league supervisors while integrating the league's local and global cultural interests into the event. Ultimately, event writers and event producers prioritize the entertainment of the live audience. The impact of their creativity may be curtailed by the extensive sponsorship and the ultimate mediation of the event, yet their effort still demonstrates a powerful and underlying tension between the individual and the institution. The sports event thus provides a crucial starting point for understanding the integrated sports media industry on a global scale. By illuminating the creative and commercial conflict at the heart of the endeavor's rawest material, the event establishes a looming tension that threatens to undermine the increasingly lucrative sport and media partnership, as the two institutions become more deeply aligned from the court to the arena, through the system of cameras and cables, and into viewers' homes.

CHAPTER 2

The Venue
Silicon Valley, Public Finance, and the Arena as Media Platform

The Arena as Media Platform

A towering glass-and-metal structure sits at the end of a city street. Climbing the steps and walking inside, through automated smart turnstiles, one is immediately greeted by the gigantic video display hovering above the arena floor. The board is at eye level from the entrance and illuminates the thousands of seats that descend into a bowl shape around the court. At more than six thousand square feet, the board is both the largest in the NBA and the first one with 4K Ultra HD picture quality.[1] Golden 1 Center, the home of the Sacramento Kings, was constructed between 2014 and 2016 and intended to be the highest-tech arena in the NBA. Ultimately, Golden 1 Center highlights the issues most central to the arena as a fundamental component of the sports media ecosystem: the involvement of Silicon Valley technology firms, the use of public funds, and the conception of the arena itself as an immersive real-world video platform.

Such trends began to intensify in July 2020, when the NBA resumed with a bubble format after the rapid expansion of COVID-19 and the stoppage of play in multiple professional sports. Based in Walt Disney World in Orlando, Florida, the twenty-two participating teams performed for an at-home television audience in order to fulfill the league's media contracts. Without fans, cameras were moved closer to the action, and the league used archival audio of prior games to create artificial crowd noise inside the venues in an attempt to make each event feel normal for both players and viewers. Though the format would prove temporary, as the NBA and other leagues have since welcomed back in-person fans, many of the new digital elements remain an ongoing part of the arena space and epitomize the extent of the modern sports arena as a programmable platform. This chapter examines the origins of such a phenomenon prior to COVID-19, beginning from the NBA's deepening investment in arena mediatization during the 1990s, through the cases of Golden 1 Center and other recent arena projects such as the Golden State Warriors' Chase Center and the Los Angeles Clippers' Intuit Dome, which are heavily tied to Silicon Valley capital. These investments are mirrored overseas in countries such as Brazil, where the NBA and major media companies have been extensively involved in the development of arenas and other physical structures.

Before and since COVID-19, then, sports league executives and team personnel, as well as their digital technology partners, have come to perceive venues as "massive media platforms," explained Chintan Patel, chief technical officer of Cisco UK and Ireland, which includes "the whole end-to-end experience," extending from "the moment that person leaves home" until that person returns.[2] As a result, venues have become increasingly mediatized spaces, utilizing digital tools to maximize fan engagement and augment the physical experience of sporting spectatorship. Andrew Shannon, director of emerging technology with the NFL's Atlanta Falcons, explained that much of his franchise's focus is on "removing all the barriers" to the in-person experience by decreasing telephone usage, long lines, decision-making, and invasive security. "How do we get rid of the 'gunk'?" Shannon asked.[3] By transforming the venue into an immersive media platform, sports leagues and their franchises are able to reduce the "gunk," programming the arena space in ways that effectively refocus and monetize spectators' attention.

Ian Bogost and Nick Montfort have succinctly defined the media platform as "a computing system of any sort upon which further computing development can be done," which "can be implemented entirely in hardware, entirely in software (which runs on any of several hardware platforms), or in some combination of the two."[4] In the case of the arena, the combination of hardware and software is evident in the screens, mobile applications, and Wi-Fi access points that surround the space, all of which are controlled by the team as the central mediating entity. In this way, the relationship between host arena and the user-spectator is reflective of Tarleton Gillespie's analysis of platforms, in which "YouTube must present its service not only to its users, but to advertisers, to major media producers it hopes to have as partners and to policymakers."[5] Gillespie also identifies the tensions that platform operators such as YouTube must navigate "between user-generated and commercially-produced content, between cultivating community and serving up advertising, between intervening in the delivery of content and remaining neutral."[6] One can begin to see the affinities between a platform such as YouTube and the "lived" experiential media platform of the arena, as league and team personnel similarly negotiate between community and commercialism, producing and distributing content that will benefit their own organization and their sponsors while trying to leave the performance itself as untouched as possible. The excitement of the event, moreover, is largely derived from the crowd's participation, which is simultaneously broadcasted or streamed for the benefit of the team, just as other kinds of platforms profit from user-generated content.

Much of the outreach and engagement with audience members, as users, is oriented around the variety of screens that adorn the walls of the arena. Greg Siegel has discussed how the large-screen video displays that occupy center court or outfield walls, in particular, are often used to direct audience members to participate in specific ways, such as clapping, dancing, or even kissing.[7] Screens also provide advertising throughout the arena and can simulcast the game action while attendees wait in line or visit the restroom. The contemporary arena thus functions as a "complete entertainment environment," Siegel explains, in a response to a supposed "crisis" that "the sporting event in itself is thought to be insufficiently entertaining in an era of richly diversified, highly mediatized leisure consumption."[8] Göran Bolin has examined the use of video displays in shopping malls in similar terms, which also serve as "structuring devices" that direct customers' attention within an increasingly mediatized space.[9] More recently, one's personal mobile device has become a further source of engagement through dedicated team applications (or apps) that allow attendees to view highlights, order food, and ascertain wait times for various queues.

As the arena increasingly draws on digital communication to augment live spectatorship, the in-person audience can be described as participating in "networked spectatorship," as Holly Kruse proposes in her analysis of horse racing and off-track betting, in which fan publics are connected across "the racetracks, homes, off-track betting facilities, farms, and auction sites that constitute its nodes" through the multiple communication technologies that circulate within those spaces.[10] Rather than the mass address of large-screen video displays, connected personal devices allow spectators to experience a greater illusion of control and customization. But the format can also amplify estrangement, a tension that is made clear in Fiona Allon's discussion of the screened environment of the "smart house," wherein "communication technologies are invested with the responsibility for social connection, bonding and civic participation at exactly the same

A view of the Kings' dedicated mobile app while seated at a live game.

The Kings' "mission control," which monitors the data generated within the app.

time as they increase the possibilities for communities to become fragmented and dispersed."[11] Whereas new outlets of communication provide a greater potential for interpersonal bonding, a more individualized address often results in a more fragmented experience, especially between fans with smart devices and those without them.

In the case of the arena, as in the smart home, such divisions can occur both within the walls and outside them, extending into the wider community. Allon, for example, describes what amounts to technological haves and have-nots, as the "high-tech enclaves and premium network spaces" that "exist in stark contrast to the abandoned landscapes of the excluded."[12] Nick Couldry and Anna McCarthy, similarly, have noted how "the spatial orders that media systems construct and enforce," including the mall, the arena, the smart house, and any kind of highly mediatized space, "are highly complicated, unevenly developed and multi-scaled. . . . The development of electronic media is a spatial process intertwined with the development of regimes of accumulation in capitalism."[13] The unevenness is apparent in the stratified area of Silicon Valley and its unofficial annex, San Francisco, explains Andrew Ross, where new media companies that were attracted to the city's "bare-plaster, low-rent ambience" as a "grassroots alternatives to corporate America" have since discovered a "perfect engine for pumping value into depreciated land assets," thus extinguishing the very same qualities that initially brought companies into the Bay Area.[14]

The institution of Silicon Valley is also of central importance to the development of the modern arena through the close relationship between the NBA and various tech executives and financiers. By "Silicon Valley," I include the high-level Bay Area executives, venture capital firms, and hedge fund managers, as well as their shared interests. Included is the web of relations and decision-making that favors a particular economic and cultural status quo. Thus, I would also include the investors, perhaps not located specifically in the San Francisco Bay Area, who have an interest (financial or otherwise) in what happens to Silicon Valley businesses. During the 2010s, especially, such individuals perceived the NBA to be the same kind of depreciated asset once seen in the commercial zones of San Francisco and transformed the NBA's physical spaces and constructed new high-tech arenas, often with the aid of public subsidies and incentives that have maximized profits and left local governments in debt. This chapter thus interrogates the mutual evolution of the tech and sports industries on a global scale and the impact of the relationship on the arena as a distinct media platform. To do so, the chapter first chronicles the NBA's participation in the explosion of new arena construction during the 1990s, the events that led to the marriage between Silicon Valley and the NBA, the emergence of the wired arena, the expansion of the NBA's construction projects overseas, and ultimately the COVID-19 pandemic as both a culmination and extension of the arena as an increasingly digital space.

NBC and the Facilities Requirements

Ahead of the 1990–91 basketball season, the NBA left its longtime broadcast partner CBS for NBC. Not only did NBC offer the NBA an astonishing $600 million over four years, an almost 250 percent increase over the previous CBS deal, the league's new home also proposed a larger degree of creative autonomy.[15] The NBA was able to participate more fully in production and marketing, expanding its capabilities and influence as a multiplatform media company, a subject discussed in greater detail in chapter 4 on the office. As much as the NBA was involved in NBC's depiction of the sport on screen, Dick Ebersol, president of NBC Sports, and the network were also deeply involved in how to improve the production and distribution of NBA basketball, including the construction of its arenas. On the network's recommendation, for example, the NBA decided to install "low slash" cameras, which were best able to "capture low-angle replays and live shots of the benches, coaches, and players between plays."[16] To do so, the NBA had to remove premium seating to the chagrin of its arena and team owners. Steve Hellmuth, who worked in NBA Entertainment at the time and later became president of media operations and technology, recalled the meeting where the decision was announced. "The chief marketing officers [of the teams] were there and they were literally going to storm the stage and just do me in right there, because they were losing large swathes of seats in the corners."[17]

For David Stern and the league office, the tradeoff between attendance revenue and a better media product was no real contest. "We were listening to our network partners with respect to what would make the game a better production," recalled Stern in a 2015 joint interview with Dick Ebersol. The low-angled slash cameras, for instance, were able to improve and distinguish the NBA's presentation by privileging its intimate elements. "You see their facial expressions, you're seeing them sweat, it's a much more kind of in your face intimate program," explained Ed Desser at the time.[18] Changes within the arena, then, were driven by the demands of the telecast and the at-home audience. "We have sacrificed seats in arenas to put cameras because we realize that 99 percent of the people who are watching the game are watching it through television," noted the NBA's senior vice president of communications at the time, Bryan McIntyre.[19]

The new camera placements would be concretized within the league's "facilities requirements," a document that stipulated the organization of each camera within each venue.[20] During the NBC era, this meant eighteen cameras—one providing the standard broadcast view from midcourt, which "maintains a wide enough angle to allow all 10 players to be seen," while the others are "utilized for cut-away shots during breaks in the action or replays," thus providing "isolations on key players" to "visually enhance storylines."[21] Among them were the low slash cameras requested by Dick Ebersol, as was an overhead camera, two "super-slow motion cameras," and "two mini-action baseline cameras [that] are designed to cover action on the low post," according to NBC producer Tommy Roy.[22] Meanwhile, camera technologies have improved and the NBA now uses more than thirty cameras, though the division of responsibilities across the feeds remains essentially the same, a balance of intimacy and overall legibility.[23]

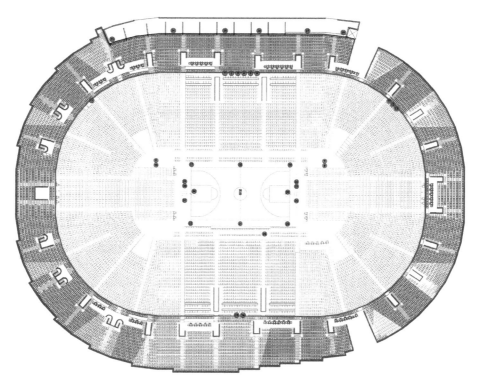

A diagram of the NBA's camera requirements as of 2017, as outlined by Rossetti Architects for an arena project proposal in Seattle.

The Venue   61

The NBA's camera placements, as encouraged by NBC, "forever changed the architecture of the buildings," noted Steve Hellmuth.[24] The changes were enforced through the NBA's strict facilities requirements. Hellmuth recalled an issue with the Pepsi Center, home of the Denver Nuggets, sometime after it opened in 1999. "I was writing memos to David [Stern] saying, 'this building is out of compliance, the cameras are too high.'" Stern, angry, called the Nuggets ownership and demanded they fix the issue or else "find another place to play these games, because you're not playing them in this building." To this day, adds Hellmuth, there is a "three foot drop where the cameras are," because they used jackhammers to drill down and lower the floor.[25] Aside from the example of the Nuggets arena, the placement of cameras was generally less contentious when a new arena was being constructed, which enabled the league and the network to guide the architecture from the ground up. "The new arenas were easy," offered Stern, "and so we began sending entire teams out to build the new buildings, and interestingly enough, every building in the NBA has now either been brand new or remodeled three times."[26] Between 1990 and 2005, the NBA opened a staggering twenty-one new arenas across its thirty teams, not including various renovation projects.[27] Arena construction became an opportunity to retool, bringing all its venues up to the NBC-era broadcast standards, a synergistic integration of the telecast and the media capabilities of the event space.

The Stadium Boom and Public Funds

The NBA's explosion of new arenas was part of a larger stadium boom that began during the 1990s. This growth was made easier by the more widespread availability of taxpayer funding for new constructions. Though publicly financed stadiums began much earlier—the Boston Braves baseball franchise became the first in 1953 when they moved to Milwaukee, enticed by a new $5 million stadium paid for entirely by public funds.[28] Cities soon began to bid against one another, and franchises from all major sports jumped to new locations, lured by growing subsidies. Between 1960 and 1969, twenty-one new sports venues were built for $513 million, 63.2 percent of which was paid for by public funds. Between 1970 and 1979, twenty-five new venues were constructed for $1.76 billion, of which 94.6 percent was publicly financed.[29] The trend continued into the 1980s and 1990s. Between 1990 and 2013, notes sports-law expert Roger L. Abrams, more than ninety-five sports venues were newly built across the major team sports, using $27 billion in funds from public treasuries.[30] Neil deMause and Joanna Cagan, in their book *Field of Schemes* (2008), situate stadium subsidies within a larger trend of subsidy abuse in the 1980s and 1990s, wherein local governments paid off companies to stay local.[31] Direct subsidies, in the form of taxes and tax-exempt bonds, are often further supplemented by indirect subsidies, such as stadium naming rights, personal seat licenses, and tax loopholes, that generate further revenue for the venue and its construction.[32] Even less direct, hidden subsidies have also developed—in the form of public land clearing, parking lots, and new roads and highways—that can positively affect the profitability of a stadium.[33]

Stadium owners and their supporters promise an ultimately rejuvenated local economy that makes such costs worthwhile. Most evidence, though, is to the contrary. When there is an increase in local economic activity, it can often be attributed to an "expenditure substitution," in which money is simply shifted "from one entertainment source to another."[34] Another form of expenditure substitution also takes place when money for the stadium is taken away from important public or infrastructural needs: transportation, parks, housing, waste, and so on.[35] George Lipsitz highlights the relationship in his analysis of St. Louis and its relationship to the then-local Rams football franchise. "No one publicly recognized the contributions made by 45,473 children enrolled in the St. Louis city school system" when the St. Louis Rams won the 2000 Super Bowl over the Tennessee Titans, yet "eighty-five percent of these students were so poor that they qualified for federally subsidized lunches." Therefore, Lipsitz argues, "revenue diverted from the St. Louis school system through tax abatements and other subsidies to the Rams made a crucial difference in giving the football team the resources to win the Super Bowl," even though the students "did not score touchdowns, make tackles, kick field goals, or intercept passes for the team."[36]

Reports conducted by stadium boosters fail to take into account that sort of diverted costs or spending leakage—the money that is taken out by owners and not reinvested locally, as the owner of a more typical local business might.[37] In fact, most of the money introduced to the local economy by sports venues leaves the community in the pockets of the franchise or stadium owners. As Lipsitz notes in the case of St. Louis, "subsidies for professional sports teams and other corporations do not 'trickle down' to the majority of the population, but instead function largely as a means for transferring wealth and resources from the poor and the middle class to the rich."[38] A new publicly supported stadium, therefore, is a significant boon to franchise owners—which is why more and more have sought to build them during the last thirty years.

In turn, the alleged obsolescence of venues has only continued to accelerate across all sports. In a 1998 piece in *Public Administration Quarterly*,

Howard Frank, Sandra Lopez, and Sonia Santana note the already shrinking life cycles of sports complexes. Citing the example of Miami Arena, which the Miami Heat abandoned after only ten years of service, they put the mean life span of arenas at 17.7 years.[39] Often it is "technological obsolescence," they note, that has been used to justify the public subsidization of arenas, despite little evidence that they will stand long enough to pay back the profit.[40] DeMause and Cagan take up this planned arena obsolescence as a tactic for public financing, with owners "alleging that [the] old stadium is obsolete, insufficient to cater to the demands of modern fans, or even on the verge of physical collapse."[41] In their 2008 update to the book, they point out that the stadium boom, despite predictions, never really dried up, and obsolescence remains a key strategy for justifying new stadium construction: "The breakneck pace of new sports facilities, each with more revenue-generating luxury suites and ever-vaster concessions concourses, has left owners scrambling faster and faster to keep up with the Joneses."[42] In the choice between "renovation" and the "wrecking ball," as Frank, Lopez, and Santana put it, demolition is often more cost-effective than renovation.[43] The most recent renovation of Madison Square Garden, which took place from 2011 to 2013, cost nearly $1 billion, far more money than an entirely new arena would have cost.[44] Demolition, moreover, comes with the possibility of public subsidy, which renovation and retrofitting do not. The NFL, for example, saw the construction of sixteen brand-new stadiums between 2000 and 2020 with the help of $5 billion in public funds, not including any hidden and indirect subsidies.[45] Obsolescence is thus a strategy by owners—a crucial tactic in selling the necessity of newness.

High Upside: Silicon Valley and the NBA

After the initial "stadium boom" and the NBA's interest in retooling its arenas to improve the quality of its telecasts, the financial and technological interests of the league changed substantially. After a labor dispute and work stoppage during the 1998–99 season, and Michael Jordan's retirement shortly thereafter, the domestic television audience steadily dwindled, dropping from an average Nielsen rating of 4.3 in 1998–99 to a 3.3 average for the 1999–2000 season.[46] As the NBA headed into a new round of negotiations with NBC for a possible rights extension in 2001, ratings on the network had fallen by 38 percent over the course of their $1.75 billion investment.[47] As the league inched closer to the start of the 2001–2 season, Michael Jordan officially announced that he was returning to the NBA as a member of the Washington Wizards. NBC and TNT quickly set about reorganizing their schedules to accommodate more Wizards games, which had been entirely left off of the national slate.[48] Despite the attempt to recapture the old magic, however, an older Michael Jordan was not enough to turn around the slumping NBC ratings, which would ultimately hold a 2.9 average for the season, the same as the disappointing previous year. Having lost $100 million on the NBA during the previous season and being projected to lose another $200 million during the 2001–2 season, NBC decided to walk away from their longtime partner.[49]

In January 2002, the NBA officially announced a new deal with ABC/ESPN and Turner, totaling $4.6 billion over six years, the details and implications of which will be discussed more fully in chapter 4.[50] Ratings on ABC, however, continued the precipitous decline that began at NBC, falling every single year from a 2.6 average during the initial 2002–3 season to a 2.0 average for the 2006–7 season.[51] The team owners' assertion of sustained declines in revenue, moreover, grew into contentious negotiations for a labor agreement between ownership and the players by the summer of 2011. David Stern declared that twenty-two of the league's thirty teams were losing money, and the NBA itself was expected to lose another $300 million, already having lost $300 million the year before. The owners asked that the current revenue split, wherein players made 57 percent of the gross team revenue, be dropped to as low as 40 percent.[52] Owners' claims rather conveniently ignored the NBA's looming television extension with ABC/ESPN and TNT, which was to total $24 billion over nine years, an increase of $17 billion over the previous deal signed in 2007.[53] In the end, after a labor lockout, with nearly two months of the season lost, the owners won—the revenue split was lowered to 51–49 in their favor.[54]

The turmoil of these events provided an opportunity for a greater influx of financing from the technology and venture-capital firms of Silicon Valley. After the new labor agreement allowed team owners to receive a more substantial percentage of a franchise's revenue, in addition to growing opportunities for publicly financed arenas, the NBA became a "high upside" investment. In 2011, before the lockout, Michael Jordan purchased a controlling stake in the Charlotte Bobcats for less than $200 million, and the Philadelphia 76ers sold for only $280 million. After the new revenue split, the Memphis Grizzlies, in a much smaller market than Philadelphia, sold to Robert Pera for $377 million. Soon after, in May 2013, Vivek Ranadive purchased the Sacramento Kings for a record $534 million, before being trumped by the sale of the Milwaukee Bucks for $550 million to hedge-fund managers Wesley Edens and Marc Lasry.[55]

Valuations continued to skyrocket: in January 2014, *Forbes* valued the New York Knicks as the top team at $1.4 billion, followed closely by the Los Angeles Lakers at $1.35 billion, with the average NBA franchise valued at $635 million.[56] In August 2014, former Microsoft CEO Steve Ballmer purchased the Los Angeles Clippers, for an NBA record $2 billion, far above the *Forbes* valuation at $575 million the previous January. He told ESPN's Ramona Shelbourne, "It's not a cheap price, but when you're used to looking at tech companies with huge risk, no earnings and huge multiples, this doesn't look like the craziest thing I've ever acquired. . . . There are great companies out there like Amazon with absolutely no earnings and a huge market cap and lots of risk. There's much less risk. There's real earnings in this business. There's real upside opportunity."[57] Indeed, by January 2016, as the fruits of the new television contract set in, *Forbes*'s valuation of the New York Knicks more than doubled to $3 billion, followed once again by the Los Angeles Lakers at $2.7 billion. The average NBA franchise was estimated to be worth $1.25 billion.[58] By 2019, this number had increased to $1.9 billion, overtaking the average value of a MLB franchise, at $1.7 billion, for the first time.[59] As the NBA became a low-risk and high-upside investment, nearly half of all NBA teams now have majority owners with backgrounds in tech or investment management.[60]

At the close of the 2014–15 season, the Golden State Warriors won their first championship since 1975 over the Cleveland Cavaliers, in what many considered to be a victory for Silicon Valley business principles. One year later, the *New York Times* ran an in-depth feature, "What Happened When Venture Capitalists Took Over the Golden State Warriors."[61] Only a few weeks afterward, the *Wall Street Journal* similarly declared, "The Golden State Warriors Have Revolutionized Basketball," as the team remained on pace to win seventy-three games, breaking the seemingly unbeatable record of seventy-two wins set by the Michael Jordan–led Chicago Bulls in 1996.[62] Majority owner Joe Lacob "was not the first venture capitalist to buy a franchise," Bruce Schoenfeld wrote in the *New York Times* article, "but he is the first to operate one according to what might be called Silicon Valley precepts: nimble management, open communication, integrating the wisdom of outside advisers and continuous re-evaluation of what companies do and how they do it."[63] In a similar vein, the more in-depth *Betaball: How Silicon Valley and Science Built One of the Greatest Basketball Teams in History* explains how the Warriors' new ownership group placed "a greater emphasis . . . on finding technological solutions to lingering problems and using proprietary analytics to unearth latent advantages their employees already possessed."[64] Ultimately, the Warriors' success symbolizes the deepening marriage between the NBA and Silicon Valley as two institutions with aligned media ambitions.

In joining up with the NBA, Silicon Valley found the ideal platform for the global dissemination of its various technologies. As an increasing number of venture capitalists from Silicon Valley have bought their way into the NBA, the league has imported (and invested in) an even greater number of cutting-edge technologies within the arena space, including virtual reality and video streaming platforms. Aside from the corporate sponsorships— Nike, Adidas, Under Armour—that get passed along in the visual information of the broadcast, we have also witnessed the display and deployment of specifically Silicon Valley products in new ways. In addition to the Sacramento Kings' investment in, and use of, the virtual reality platform Voke, the Kings conducted a start-up pitch competition with a $10,000 grand prize and a $5,000 investment in all four finalists from team owner Vivek Ranadive.[65] In another instance, Steve Ballmer's purchase of the Clippers became an outlet to deploy his Microsoft products. In an interview with *Reuters* after taking over the team, Ballmer expressed his displeasure that the personnel had been using Apple iPads at practice and made plans to switch them all over to Microsoft Surfaces.[66] Yet another example was when the Golden State Warriors came to a three-year agreement with Zoom in 2016 that gave the team access to Zoom's video conferencing services in exchange for in-arena branding opportunities.[67] The interests of Silicon Valley executives and financiers are thus able to piggyback on the NBA's global broadcasts, benefiting from both direct investment in the NBA and from an expanded consumer base.

Silicon Valley thus offers capital and technological know-how and the NBA offers paying customers and a global distribution system. The NBA benefits from this influx of capital and the potential to expand its distribution range, and Silicon Valley benefits from greater access to a global sports-watching public. The relationship has only deepened. In July 2016, the NBPA, the players' labor union, announced a yearly technology summit in San Francisco to be led by Warriors forward Andre Iguodala. The summit was intended to offer "networking opportunities with senior executives and influencers" and "workshops designed to identify opportunities for players to pursue both during and after their NBA careers."[68] Moreover, after longtime NBA commissioner David Stern retired in 2014, he did not stay in the world of sport, nor did he stay very retired. In an October 2016 interview with Sam Amick of *USA Today*, Stern noted that he had been serving

Zoom signed a three-year deal with the Golden State Warriors in 2016, giving the team access to its video conferencing services in exchange for in-arena branding opportunities.

as an adviser to a venture-capital firm and three startup businesses.[69] The NBA and Silicon Valley have transformed each other, perhaps irrevocably, becoming a combined titan of tech, media, and business.

Code and Concrete: The Case of Golden 1 Center

Nowhere is the relationship between Silicon Valley and sport clearer than in the arena space, and perhaps no arena provides a more illustrative example than the NBA's Golden 1 Center, the home of the Sacramento Kings. Golden 1 Center, which officially opened for the 2016–17 season, features its own data center, 900 miles of cabling, virtual reality capabilities, a 6,100-square-foot 4k video display, and chatbots "to improve fan engagement" by using artificial intelligence to "understand what people need and want."[70] Levi's Stadium in Santa Clara, home of the NFL's San Francisco 49ers, had arguably held the title of "highest-tech sports stadium" before

Golden 1 Center. Opened in September 2014, Levi's Stadium features 400 miles of cabling, 1,200 distributed antenna systems, 2,000 Sony televisions, and a Wi-Fi router for every hundred seats.[71] Golden 1 Center, in comparison, features a router for every *seventeen* seats.[72] The case of the Kings, though exceptional in its extremity, demonstrates the further mediatization of sport, the possibilities for sports teams as global media brands, and the future of sports spectatorship, especially as Steve Ballmer's Los Angeles Clippers are set to open the Intuit Dome in 2024, a similarly "state-of-the-art" arena in the Inglewood area of Los Angeles.[73]

In focusing on the case of the Sacramento Kings, as a pace setter for the wider sports-media world, we can better understand the modern spectatorial experience of sport and its implications for global sports fandom. The Kings, through their massive video display, mobile app, and use of virtual reality, offer a newfound level of mediation within the stadium space itself, combining two formerly distinct forms of spectatorship in live viewing and home viewing. The display was part of a larger plan by Kings majority owner Vivek Ranadive, dubbed "NBA 3.0," which seeks to "use technology and data to reboot the Kings" and "remake the league."[74] Ranadive expands on NBA 3.0 in his own words, adding, "with technology you can expand social networks, you can give people an opportunity to participate and identify with [sport] in ways that haven't been done before."[75] With its NBA 3.0 directive, perhaps no franchise is more reflective of the Silicon Valley–fication of the NBA than the Sacramento Kings.

In a video walkthrough of the Kings' Golden 1 Center, offered by CBS Sacramento, the arena's massive 4K video display, the largest in North America, hovers above the arena floor, visible from the moment one enters the arena and from nearly every corner and corridor.[76] A similar feature, by KCRA, describes the nearly one thousand miles of cable, operated on "enough electricity to power an entire city," through a data center comparable to those owned by Amazon and Google.[77] Perhaps most striking is "mission control," in which staff monitor user data from the Kings' dedicated mobile app, which can point out the shortest concession and restroom lines. Through the app, fans can check this information, check player and game statistics, order food to be delivered, and even request an adjustment to the temperature near their seats.[78] Mission control also mines fans' social media presence, taking stock of their thoughts and preferences. Owner Vivek Ranadive gives examples using food: "if you have a fan tweeting that their pizza is cold, we know that. If we know that the fan is there with his kids, he likes hot dogs . . . we'll come and give him hot dogs. Even before you have a chance to become unhappy, we make you happy."[79] Golden 1

The Kings' Golden 1 Center features its own Tier 4 data center, the only one housed inside a professional sports arena.

Center privileges its own highly mediatized environment above and beyond the live performance of basketball.

Since the opening of Golden 1 Center, Ranadive and the Kings have also begun to experiment with virtual reality. For the start of the 2015–16 season, after an investment in virtual-reality (VR) company Voke, which placed their "stereoscopic panoramic camera system" throughout the arena, the Kings began to offer virtual-reality livestreams of select games.[80] The venture was part of a larger NBA trend, as the league itself partnered with NextVR in 2015 and began to broadcast one game per week in virtual reality by the 2016–17 season.[81] The Kings' plans for VR have gone beyond broadcasting, however, to the actual in-person audience. Team minority owner Paul Jacobs, former CEO of mobile chipmaker Qualcomm, described tentative plans to offer virtual replays for fans who are present but far from the court: "Whether they're way up in the high seats or they're in a box but not sitting courtside, you still want to give them that courtside experience."[82] Jacobs also noted the possibility of offering specially priced tickets for a "movie-theater-like space inside the stadium with high-end VR headsets" so that fans would "still be there to feel the roar of the crowd and be part of it but be watching in a slightly different way."[83] After Kings partner Voke was acquired by Intel in 2016, the Kings and Intel expanded their partnership beyond VR alone.[84] Ahead of the 2020–21 season, Golden 1 Center was designated as an Intel research and development site, testing the company's

70   CHAPTER 2

True View platform for "volumetric video," which would allow for VR from a 360-degree perspective.[85] While Golden 1 Center might offer an exceptional level of mediation of the spectatorial experience, it highlights increasingly viable paths for the deepening mediatization of sport and the arena's status as an experiential media platform.

Despite the promise of cutting-edge features of the Kings' new home, Golden 1 Center relied on the same kinds of troubling financial tactics that have come to define modern arena construction. Besides receiving a public subsidy of $255 million from the city of Sacramento, the Kings were asked to pay only $20 million to terminate their ongoing lease at Sleep Train Arena, leaving the city struggling to pay off the remaining $30 million of debt. When the San Francisco 49ers left Candlestick Park for their own new "state-of-the-art" stadium in Santa Clara, the city of San Francisco opted for demolition rather than seeking a new tenant, favoring a development project that they believed would better recoup their own outstanding debt.[86] Sacramento has hoped to find a long-term money-generating solution to the empty Sleep Train Arena problem, which has left them grappling with the strong possibility that demolition is the only viable option.[87] Yet destruction also comes with environmental costs. The original demolition plan for Candlestick Park, for instance, called for an implosion, which was quickest but would have significantly increased the risk of spreading silica dust and asbestos. Instead, after much debate, the city opted for a wrecking ball applied in sections, so that water could be hosed over the wreckage to try to minimize the spread of dust into the nearby neighborhood of Bayview-Hunter's Point.[88] By leaving Sleep Train Arena for Golden 1 Center, the Kings saddled the city with debt from which it is unlikely to recover.

Architectural or structural obsolescence, as in the cases of Sleep Train Arena and Candlestick Park, are no longer the only discourses that may encourage new arena construction. In the age of the fully wired stadium, with data centers and miles and miles of fiber-optic cabling, there are also discourses of new media obsolescence. Greg Siegel noted the early instance of wired stadiums in the late 1990s into the early 2000s, as stadiums became Disneyfied "complete entertainment environments," highly mediatized and technologized, giving a "technocultural form" to the "convergence of sports, media, and entertainment."[89] The mediatized stadium, he rightly argues, is part of "the corporate class's celebration and fetishization of its own technologization."[90] But these stadiums, as monuments to newness and the next, are also monuments to ephemerality. Wendy Chun, for instance, asserts that "new media exist at the bleeding edge of obsolescence" and thus live and die by the update: "the end of the update, the end of the object." To be unupdatable is to be obsolete.[91] The modern arena, as a highly networked environment, exhibits a similar drive for the latest state-of-the-art media technologies. Likewise, these arenas come to rely more and more heavily on the update. Ranadive, in fact, compares the arena to a giant Tesla: "Every single night, your Tesla updates. So we need to have that same philosophy when it comes to our arena: every single night, the arena updates and improves itself."[92] But it is one thing to update software; it is another to update a massive half-billion-dollar structure. To be unupdatable, for an arena, is most often to be demolished.

Ultimately, Kings management has addressed the possibility of obsolescence under the guise that they have left themselves room to combat it, that the arena is "future proof." In an interview with NBC's Sacramento affiliate, KCRA, Vivek Ranadive explained that "One of the goals I had is that I wanted to future-proof [Golden 1 Center], so that there wasn't something new that happened ten years out and you say, 'I wish we could have done that.'"[93] In *Wired*, the team's vice president of technology, Matt Eclavea, expanded on their plans: "A lot of thought goes into what it'll look like in five years. . . . I want to put it in now. It's a lot easier than dealing with sheet rock."[94] He continues, as paraphrased by David Pierce, that "Golden 1 Center's setup has enough headroom for 10, even 20 years of innovation before anything could possibly overwhelm their network."[95] As I observed during my visit to the arena in 2018, however, the reality is much less striking in person, consisting of extra wire racks that provide the capability to increase bandwidth for technological improvements, should that become necessary.

"Future-proofing," of course, is a rhetorical manipulation, as the industrywide trend of shrinking arena life-spans, obsolescence, and public subsidy has only grown more pronounced. Ultimately, only so much technology is future-proof. Ranadive and NBA teams like his—the Warriors, the Bucks, the Cavaliers—sell the innovative nature of their arenas and broadcast capabilities. The Kings, for example, promote their use of bitcoin, Google Glass, Voke VR, and—as of June 2016—chatbots "to improve fan engagement" by using "artificial intelligence and natural language processing to understand what people need and want."[96] But when such media inevitably become obsolete, it will fall to local fans and taxpayers to fund the cleanup. In 2016, MLB's Texas Rangers successfully petitioned the city of Arlington to construct a new $1 billion stadium, $500 million of which will come from taxpayers.[97] In the NBA, the Milwaukee Bucks received approval in 2015 from the Wisconsin state government for $250 million in government funds toward their new arena, despite the combined $6 billion net worth of their owners, hedge-fund investors Wes Edens, Marc Lasry, and

Jamie Dinan.[98] In a wired stadium made of both concrete and code, the burden of media obsolescence falls on the public. The discourses out of Silicon Valley, naturally, obscure this outcome, preferring to sell cutting-edge newness. But as such individuals enter NBA circles in greater numbers, pledging a technological revolution as Ranadive has, these accelerating "advancements" bring with them an accelerated obsolescence. No amount of future-proofing can stop habitual technological change, nor can it overcome the appeal of a newly built and publicly funded new stadium.

International Investments: The Case of Brazil

In December 2014, a partnership was announced between the NBA and Brazil's Liga Nacional de Basquete (LNB). The NBA had long made deals in foreign markets, but the deal with LNB was something new; it was not simply the NBA spreading its product to as large a consumer base as possible. Instead, the two leagues would work together, collaborating on "innovative marketing" and "enhanced game presentation" to increase fan engagement and improve business and player development.[99] The NBA would receive an equity stake in LNB and lend its money, personnel, and business acumen to facilitate the league's growth, while LNB would provide the NBA with stronger ties to the International Basketball Federation (FIBA) and the still-expanding global basketball market. The deal, noted sportswriter Zach Lowe at the time, continued "the NBA's quest for global sporting dominance and potential interest in eventually unifying the sport at the highest level under one set of rules."[100]

As the NBA has looked overseas to expand its product and its profits, the league's strategies reflect the Silicon Valley partnership that has defined its team ownership. Brazil, in particular, has been presented as a major frontier for integrated producer-distributors like Netflix and the NBA.[101] Netflix installed web servers and technological infrastructure to prepare the nation for its own media initiatives, and the NBA similarly purchased a stake in the country's national basketball league and renovated its sports venues in order to more effectively cultivate both an NBA audience and a pipeline for future athletes. Jeunesse Arena, in the Barra da Tijuca region of Rio de Janeiro, "passed NBA's most stringent tests and met all technical criteria," which allowed them to host all NBA trips to the country for exhibition games from 2013 to 2015, the last time the league visited as part of its Global Games initiative.[102] More recently, in place of live games in Brazil, the NBA launched the NBA House event, which took place in Rio de Janeiro in 2016 and São Paulo in 2019. Staged during game nights and weekends, the festival-like event includes NBA Finals viewing parties, photo opportunities, virtual-reality experiences, and basketball skill challenges, all intended to build local excitement for the NBA in Brazil.[103] The strategy, which enabled the NBA to establish a stronger overall presence in the country, has been an unqualified success. In October 2019, the Brazilian media conglomerate Bandeirantes acquired the rights to both regular season and playoff NBA basketball for its broadcast network, "Band," the first time in fifteen years that the NBA's regular season will be shown on free-to-air Brazilian television.[104] While the league will continue to air on pay-TV through SporTV and the local ESPN channel, the deal with Bandeirantes allows the NBA to reach a wider audience in Brazil than ever before, capitalizing on the interest that had accumulated through their various initiatives in the country.[105]

Success in Brazil is especially significant because of its history as a major market for soccer. More recently, though, soccer's market power has been declining. In the 2018 World Cup, Brazil was eliminated in the quarterfinals, for the third time in the last four tournaments.[106] As Ewan MacKenna of the *New York Times* explained, "Brazil's national team is in many ways a shadow of its famous past," which has not sat well with a fan base that favors winning. The dearth of talent, he went on to argue, is caused by infrastructural troubles. The last three presidents of the Brazilian Football Confederation having been brought up on corruption charges, and no strong managerial voice remains to direct the future of the sport. Talent has suffered, star players look to leagues overseas, and, in the end, the whole sport has lost its luster.[107] At the same time that soccer faces infrastructural weakness, the NBA has stepped in to bolster Brazil's basketball infrastructure, growing the sport's cultural distinction and reshaping the game in its own image. Working with the local government's sports secretary, Marco Antonio Cabral, the NBA built a multisport complex in the Rocinha area of Rio de Janeiro, the country's largest favela, and designated Brazil as the South American home for the league's Junior NBA program. The complex, moreover, offered youth programs to teach "the fundamentals of the sport while instilling core values" such as "teamwork, respect and sportsmanship."[108] In September 2018, the Rocinha even appeared as a playable level called "Rio Favela" in the *NBA LIVE 19* video game, which helped to highlight the NBA's initiatives in the area. The official website of EA Sports, the game's publisher, describes how the area is "surrounded with violence and natural effects of poverty and over-population," but the "the Jr. NBA program, a grassroots youth league, carries heavy influence among the city's youth."[109] By including Rocinha alongside the NBA's US counterparts, EA Sports elevates the cultures of Brazilian basketball and offers a purely positive depiction of the NBA's intervention in the country.

The NBA's construction and outreach in Brazil, combined with soccer's decline and the NBA's input into Brazil's own national league, LNB, have thus created a massive future there for the NBA. But it also leads to uncomfortable questions, much like those about the financing of arena construction in the United States, which can draw from public resources for private gain. On the one hand, the Brazilian endeavor provides "social benefits" for "a community as complicated and delicate as Rocinha."[110] On the other, the NBA cannot be considered a solely altruistic organization for the public good, as it also remains a for-profit media conglomerate. The relationship with Brazil's government allows the NBA direct access to the school system to instruct children and inculcate them as consumers of an NBA-specific brand of basketball. The same was true in China, where the NBA agreed to a deal with the Ministry of Education to build a "fitness and basketball development curriculum in elementary, middle and high schools," which aimed to "provide enhanced basketball training to at least 3 million students by 2017."[111] One cannot discredit the genuine social good that the NBA has provided in these places, both currently and historically. Terry Lyons, former vice president of international communications, recalled a visit to China in the late 1990s, during which the league worked with the US Department of State to provide computers to a makeshift school for the children of migrant workers.[112] The NBA has used its reach and power for true charity. At the same time, the NBA benefits from these agreements by more effectively cultivating future fans and future athletes, in order to maintain the league's global footprint and profitability. The commercial incentives cannot be disregarded.

Such questions are not unique to the NBA, whose efforts are part of a broader investment in the Brazilian market by foreign media interests. When Netflix, for instance, found that Brazil's poor internet coverage was making its widespread adoption impossible, it began to install internet servers around the country free of charge and provided even more to local telecommunications firms, in order to create a high-speed broadband infrastructure that would allow the platform to succeed in the future.[113] Like Netflix, the NBA improved Brazil's basketball infrastructure, ostensibly for free, in order to benefit later. In this regard, Brazil is only the latest in a long line of examples in which Western media interests, including the NBA, have sought to cultivate what were perceived to be lucrative and unsaturated markets. In the 1980s, as discussed in chapter 1, the NBA offered China and the Soviet Union free telecasts in order to grow its own brand.[114] Ted Turner assisted in the Soviet Union, in particular, as he had already established a presence there for TBS.

Turner continued to expand the presence of his properties in Russia into the 1990s, where he proceeded to wire the country for high-speed internet. Ailene Voisin, sent by the *Atlanta Journal-Constitution* to cover the 1994 Goodwill Games in St. Petersburg, recalled the juxtaposition of a struggling country, in which people were forced to sell toilet paper on the street, having among the most developed internet infrastructures in the world. "Laptops were always sketchy around different cities and countries," she remembered, but because "we connected from St. Petersburg, it was a piece of cake. And that was all because Turner was broadcasting the games and needed to have state-of-the-art equipment over there."[115] More than twenty years later, Turner's strategy was still evident in both Netflix's and the NBA's investments in Brazil: short-term financial sacrifice for long-term growth. When PricewaterhouseCoopers published its 2018–22 outlook on global media, these actions illustrate why it considered the NBA to be every bit as powerful a global competitor as Netflix.[116]

The NBA's recent success in Brazil has since encouraged the league to pursue the strategy elsewhere. In February 2019, the NBA announced that it would launch its own twelve-team pan-African basketball league, the Basketball Africa League (BAL), in partnership with FIBA and former US president Barack Obama, who will have an unidentified but "hands-on" role in the new league. "Combined with our other programs on the continent," announced NBA commissioner Adam Silver in a statement, "we are committed to using basketball as an economic engine to create new opportunities in sports, media and technology across Africa."[117] The league was set to begin its inaugural season in Senegal in March 2020, but the season was postponed because of the coronavirus pandemic.[118] In December 2019, moreover, the NBA announced plans to include a Mexican professional basketball team, the Capitanes de Ciudad de México, as part of the league's developmental "minor" league, the G-League, for the 2020–21 season, a major step toward one day including a full professional team from Mexico among its ranks.[119] The NBA may remain a sports league in name, but it is also a media conglomerate with worldwide cultural and political influence. Just as integrated producer-distributors such as Netflix and Turner spent money on local internet capabilities to ensure greater potential audiences, so has the NBA built venues and entire leagues to increase its own popularity around the world. The NBA's success in Brazil, and similar actions in Mexico and across Africa, presents strong indications of similar international maneuvers to come.

Conclusion: The Bubble and Future Trends

After the postponement of the 2019–20 NBA season because of the onset of the coronavirus pandemic in March 2020, the NBA relaunched with a "bubble" format in July, in which the twenty-two participating teams remained inside a hotel at Walt Disney World in Orlando and played games across three courts without fans.[120] The mechanics of the bubble turned out to be temporary, and the NBA launched its subsequent 2020–21 season in December without the bubble format but with limited fans in certain cities. The league's time in Orlando reflected ongoing trends in the arena space. Without in-person spectators, for instance, the NBA was able to focus even more intently on the mediation of the event. The bubble began with eight production trucks and with camera placements, which had been such a significant issue since the NBC era, that could also be moved even closer to the action. The corner "slash" cameras were moved closer to the floor and a "rail-cam" moving along the sideline could be used with greater frequency.[121] "These are things that, in our traditional coverage, we have not been able to do, either because of fans or because of safety," explained Chris Brown, vice president of sports production and technical operations at Turner Sports, the NBA's longtime cable and streaming partner.[122]

The adaptations to COVID-19, then, offer a culmination of the arena as a distinct media platform by highlighting the ways in which the space increasingly functions as a digital canvas. Without the sound of fans, for example, an important component of the sporting experience as discussed in chapter 1, the NBA and its media partners drew from their collective library of material to create a tapestry of artificial crowd noise to fit the flow of the action. During each game in the bubble, a team of audio personnel would watch, adjust, and integrate the noise into the broadcast feed.[123] The NFL and MLB did the same when they returned for their own crowdless seasons.[124] "Nothing is going to replace 20,000 home fans cheering for their team," explained Sara Zuckert, the head of the NBA's Next Gen Telecast department, "but we were looking at all of the opportunities to replicate that in the best possible way digitally."[125] The efforts went beyond crowd noise to include virtual fans, appearing on seventeen-foot LED screens that wrapped around the arena. In addition, all the team insignias and sponsor logos on the courts were digitally superimposed, as the floors inside the bubble were otherwise blank hardwood.[126] While digital advertising has been a common practice in international soccer, in order to better appeal to audiences from different countries, and the NBA had experimented with its use before the pandemic for its Chinese broadcasts, the bubble was the

NBA's first large-scale use of technology for it.[127] In order to replicate the normal experience of sports spectatorship, the investments ultimately highlight the contemporary status of the arena as a unique and immersive media platform, with crowds, logos, and advertising all function as digital content circulating through the hardware and software that surrounds the space.[128] The arena-as-platform, therefore, must deliver content to spectators-as-users while navigating the interests of users, advertisers, partners, and policy makers alike, a clear reflection of Gillespie's analysis of the traditional platform host.[129]

Though the NBA's bubble for the 2020 postseason offered new heights for arena mediation, it was also in keeping with the precepts of arena construction during the preceding decade, as venues such as Golden 1 Center used dedicated apps to augment fan engagement as an end-to-end user experience from home to home.[130] With the recent and upcoming construction of more major sports venues, the trend is likely to continue. The Golden State Warriors, for example, left their Oakland, California, home for Chase Center, a new state-of-the-art arena in nearby San Francisco, for the 2019–20 season.[131] The Los Angeles Clippers are set to leave Staples Center, their home since 1999, to move into a newly constructed arena in the Inglewood area of Los Angeles by 2024.[132]

Virtual fans "attending" games via the wraparound LED screens of the bubble.

By building these new arenas from the ground up, teams like the Kings, Warriors, and Clippers are able to more comprehensively invest in the digitization of the space, from screens to VR to easier mobile ticketing. While paperless ticketing is depicted to fans as faster and more convenient, it also allows teams to maintain greater control over the resale market and offers new areas for potential monetization by providing a more substantial amount of trackable information on each person entering the building. "Everything's about the data and how you mine the data and direct marketing to the consumer," explained Steve Hall, president of Signature Sports Group.[133] Paperless ticketing is in keeping with the initiatives behind dedicated team or leaguewide mobile apps. The Kings offer the convenience of seat delivery and estimated wait times, and the app is also providing them a plethora of salable information that will be used for their own or their partners' benefit. With the onset of COVID-19, moreover, paperless ticketing has only become more widespread because it is contact-free. The small number of NBA teams that have allowed a limited number of fans to attend games in person, including the Cleveland Cavaliers, Utah Jazz, and Houston Rockets, have required all ticketing to be mobile.[134] The ostensible motive here is the health and safety of spectators, but the result is still the greater ability to track the behavior and preferences of attendees. There is little reason to believe, therefore, that the previously common use of paper ticketing will ever return, even with the resumption of full in-person attendance.

In making plans for the Clippers' new arena, owner Steve Ballmer's ambitions extend beyond ticketing to the synergistic potential of a wholesale digitization of the space, designing the arena's ability to stream games more effectively. In a conversation with the *Los Angeles Times*, Ballmer noted his potential interest in forgoing a traditional cable agreement, allowing the Clippers to control their own distribution via a streaming platform. "I want to at least try to make digital technology a vehicle for pushing the sports viewing experience forward," explained Ballmer. "If that's not part of a relationship we can have with our partner—because most of the partners want digital rights in addition to cable rights—that to me is an issue."[135] The construction of the Clippers' Intuit Dome allows the team to build that infrastructure into the arena, whether or not such an arrangement materializes in the near future. Ultimately, these initiatives are in keeping with the capitalization and digitization efforts of Silicon Valley–affiliated ownership since entering the league, as well as the NBA's own history of pushing the boundaries of mediation beyond the sport itself, such as the league's removal of seating for the betterment of camera placement. As ever, Silicon

Valley and the NBA are aligned in their pursuit of profitability and technological innovation.

Unlike the case of Golden 1 Center and other recent arena projects, however, the Clippers' Intuit Dome and the Warriors' Chase Center were both funded privately rather than through public financing, for an estimated $1.8 billion and $1.5 billion, respectively. The Warriors' Chase Center even billed itself as the "the first privately financed modern sports arena."[136] Crucially, though, the arrangement was not the Warriors' first choice—the organization lobbied but simply failed to secure subsidies from the City of San Francisco. "That's just not the philosophy in San Francisco," noted Rick Welts, the Warriors' president, while adding that cities "should" give money towards venues due to their overall contributions for residents.[137] Nonetheless, the private construction of a new venue remains a high upside investment, just as when Silicon Valley financiers bought into the league in the early 2000s.

Despite the billion-dollar costs, both the Clippers and Warriors will quickly make back their money by leasing office space in their new complexes. As landlords, rather than tenants, the teams can also profit from events aside from basketball. "We're transforming from being a basketball team that rents its building to a sport and entertainment organization that's responsible for every aspect of its business," Welts stated. "At Chase Center, we will own and operate this building. We'll book and manage all the events. We're responsible for the security. If there's a stray piece of paper on the plaza, that's our fault."[138] The Warriors, in fact, were able to turn a profit on Chase Center before the doors even opened, securing $2 billion from lease agreements, corporate sponsorships, and ticket sales.[139] The Warriors' experience only demonstrates how unnecessary public subsidies can be, when the substantial profits stand to be made by private for-profit companies like the Warriors.

The privately financed stadium, however, is unlikely to be lasting trend. If a city is trying to keep or solicit its local franchise, the team has no reason to refuse the funds. The Clippers and Warriors would have taken subsidies or tax breaks had they been offered. The Sacramento Kings and Milwaukee Bucks, both teams with similar ties to the worlds of high technology and finance, accepted the public funds that were offered to them.[140] At best, one could argue that the success of the Warriors and Clippers with privately financed construction projects may be enough to disincentivize other cities from offering in the first place, yet the new football stadium in Las Vegas is set to receive $750 million in taxpayer-generated money toward its $2 billion budget.[141]

Moreover, the Clippers' and Warriors' own model of private funding is misleading, as the cities continue to contribute substantial amounts of money when one widens the scope of the contribution to the surrounding area and infrastructure. In San Francisco, the city is paying $51 million for necessary improvements to the city's transportation infrastructure in order to accommodate the new influx of traffic, including a new train platform, track and street realignment, and new Metro cars.[142] Similarly, in Los Angeles, the city announced plans for a monorail project connecting the preexisting downtown metro system with the Intuit Dome and nearby Sofi Stadium, the new home of the LA Rams and LA Chargers football teams, for $1 billion, for which neither of those organizations are paying.[143] The Clippers also purchased the twenty-two acres of land for the Dome from the city of Los Angeles itself, angering local residents who argued that the land could have been, and should have been, used for affordable housing.[144] The construction of the arena itself may be a private endeavor, but the full cost of development often ripples out into the community. As in the case of the arenas cited, as well as those over the last twenty years, innovation obscures the cycles of obsolescence and exploitation that are used to ensure profitability for the few at the expense of the many. The next chapter further examines issues of infrastructure, as it relates to the distribution of the NBA, and sport more widely, on an international scale.

CHAPTER 3

The Wires

Dark Fiber, Satellites, and the Global Infrastructures of Streaming Sport

A global media distribution center sits in an unassuming office park in Plainview, New York. The streaming video enjoyed by a basketball fan in Brazil streaming the Houston Rockets–Oklahoma City Thunder game, a football fan catching replays on a train in France, or a RugbyPass subscriber in China, all emanate from that building on Long Island. Endeavor Streaming, formerly known as NeuLion, programs and oversees the streaming platforms for the NBA, the NFL, Univision, and China Central Television (CCTV), among other media companies around the world. Endeavor is aided, moreover, by a global network of fiber-optic cables and satellites, crisscrossing various terrains and multiple oceans. As sport continues to transform from a broadcast and cable program into multiplatform streaming content, a vast network has emerged to facilitate its production and delivery. Its infrastructure includes companies such as Endeavor and its competitors, who manage streaming platforms and encode the video, as well as companies in the "dark fiber" business, who sell unused cables to companies for private use, including the NBA.

The roots of this system, as it pertains to sports media, emerged in the 1980s from the game libraries of leagues, which served as an in-house system of video capture and circulation, capitalizing on the advancement of computer databases and indexes. This video content positioned leagues to more easily transition into the direct-to-consumer (DTC) media platforms of direct broadcast satellite (DBS) and the internet during the 1990s. With the aid of intermediary companies such as DirecTV and Starwave, services such as NBA League Pass and NBA.com became lucrative new offerings that would give way to broadband streaming options by the mid-2000s. The evolution of DTC programming, therefore, offers important context for the modern multiplatform ecosystem of streaming sport and the global media infrastructures that both enable and constrain its contemporary circulation.

As streaming distribution has become more widespread, the intermediary firms that program platforms and keep video running properly have also grown considerably. When content owners seek to put their content online, they must turn to these firms to program and manage their branded streaming platforms, which is often more cost-effective than building capabilities internally. HBO and ESPN, for example, lacking the appropriate infrastructures for their initial HBO Now and WatchESPN ventures, both turned to the same company: the MLB-owned BAMTech (originally Baseball Advanced Media). In August 2016, BAMTech made headlines when Disney had finally had enough of leasing the firm's services for its ESPN platform and purchased 33 percent of the company for $1 billion. One year later, in August 2017, Disney bought another 42 percent for $1.58 billion, which set the company's value at $3.75 billion.[1] In a streaming media economy, the streaming intermediary is immensely valuable.

Such companies are "transparent," as Joshua Braun describes them, in that they minimize their own branding in service of their client.[2] Though the HBO name is on the marquee of the HBO Now platform, for example, it is BAMtech that first designed and operated it. While streaming intermediaries service the needs of particular clients, they have as much invested in the global availability and popularity of their own platforms, for which they are compensated through some combination of platform fees, device enablement fees, per-subscriber percentages, and revenue sharing. Streaming intermediaries do not build a platform like NBA League Pass and simply step aside; they are very much invested in a platform's ongoing global success and work with the content owner to determine how to sustain such growth. One such strategy, which is reflected profoundly in the collaboration between the NBA and Endeavor, privileges a global address both within the United States and abroad. The NBA uses the international presence of Endeavor's platform to feature players and marketing that will simultaneously address the greatest number of possible fans in the greatest number of possible countries. The result is content that is international and inclusive yet culturally vague. Intermediaries, then, are far from neutral in the process.

Streaming intermediaries, including Endeavor and BAMTech, primarily offer streaming *software* and management to their clients, but their products and services sit atop the *hardware* offered by companies like Zayo Group and its competitors, including specialized firms such as CenturyLink and Crown Castle, as well as major telecoms such as AT&T and Verizon.[3] These companies are all invested in the dark fiber business, which is the sale of fiber-optic cables that have either become disused or were simply never put into use. While regional start-ups often begin with the latter, buying up cable from regional cable companies to resell to private companies for business uses, companies such as Verizon and AT&T simply earmark some of their thousands of miles of cables for the service.[4] Dark fiber is thus a business-to-business enterprise, used by companies to securely connect their office buildings and expedite the delivery of files. In September 2014, the NBA announced the purchase of a nationwide network of fiber from Zayo Group that would connect each of the league's twenty-nine arenas to its Secaucus, New Jersey, media headquarters, as well as two distribution hubs in nearby Newark and Atlanta, Georgia.[5] Through those colocation facilities, which contain a combination of cables and satellites, the NBA's system facilitates the dissemination of telecasts around the world.

Drawing on interviews with personnel from Endeavor Streaming (NeuLion at the time), the NBA, and Starwave, as well as site visits to Endeavor and the NBA, this chapter demonstrates how a greater emphasis on streaming intermediaries and the infrastructures that underlie sports media distribution can more fully answer questions that have arisen from the growth of global streaming television. While early agreements between content owners and digital firms were often experimental, serving as fact-finding operations, these arrangements have nonetheless become increasingly central as the distribution environment has evolved and required greater

From the NeuLion fact sheet for prospective customers c. 2017, which notes the company's ability to monitor real-time data.

infrastructural capabilities. As streaming video has become more widespread and its success more vital to content owners and content distributors, the intermediary firms that program the platforms and keep the video running properly wield considerable power over those who depend on their services. At the same time, the advent of the dark fiber business has created new opportunities for leagues and content owners alike to amass greater control than ever before over their own media pipelines, with less reliance on cable and internet service providers.

Infrastructures, as Brian Larkin defines them, are "are the institutionalized networks that facilitate the flow of goods in a wider cultural as well as physical sense."[6] Larkin, then, proposes a way to think through the materiality of global television flows by examining the "mediating capacities" of the networks that facilitate distribution across space.[7] Also of significance, then, is Lisa Parks's development of a critical methodology for approaching infrastructure, which she similarly defines as "the material sites and objects involved in the local, national, and/or global distribution of audiovisual signals and data." Parks further calls for site studies and personal observation "intended to foster infrastructural intelligibility by breaking infrastructures down into discrete parts."[8] Larkin and Parks are crucial for situating the technological infrastructure of the NBA itself, which relies on a nationwide fiber-optic cable system, an international satellite system, and two colocation centers for its worldwide distribution. The process of making this infrastructure intelligible is significant, not only to better understand the physical realities and difficulties of the NBA's circulation, but to illuminate how the infrastructure encourages the globality of the NBA's media texts. In doing so, the role of infrastructure in the consumption and cultures of sport around the world can be made clearer.

The infrastructure of intermediaries, dark fiber, and satellite that underlies the delivery of streaming sport, as well as the broader streaming ecosystem that it reflects, thus highlights a dialectical relationship between cultural globalization and the advancement of communication technology. New technologies, such as streaming, facilitate vast new possibilities for distribution and enable a more substantial global address, which in turn motivates further investment in those technologies. Ultimately, the proliferation of streaming encourages the production of media content that capitalizes on transnational cultural flows in order to reach the widest range of demographics and solicit an altogether more global audience. The NBA's infrastructure, which emerged from its early DTC services during the 1990s, demonstrates the productive role of distribution in determining the global course of the sports media industry as a whole.

NBA Entertainment: A Foundational Media Infrastructure

In 1982, when the NBA's executive vice president, David Stern, devised NBA Entertainment (NBAE), Stern sent a memo to commissioner Larry O'Brien requesting three-quarter-inch Panasonic VCRs for each of the teams, at a cost of $132,500, so that they could record all the games and FedEx the tapes nightly to the league office, creating a library of materials for the league's own use.[9] The NBA's enterprise was further enhanced by its acquisition of any older video materials that it could track down from earlier broadcasts on ABC and CBS.[10] As the league's archive began to grow, and new opportunities for content arose through dot-coms and direct-broadcast satellite, NBA Entertainment formed an important media infrastructure and a hub for global communication between the central league office, its franchises, and its network partners.

The success of NBAE was enabled, moreover, by broader industrial changes, such as the global deregulation of television and the ascendance of cable and satellite as viable distribution technologies. Whereas broadcast television had frequently relegated sports to the weekend, the expansion of cable channels and their demand for programming opened more favorable opportunities for NBAE and professional basketball. "Sports television was basically Saturday and Sunday afternoons on those networks," recalled Ed Desser, the NBA's director of broadcasting during the 1980s.[11] Though ABC had found success on Monday nights with its marquee NFL and MLB telecasts, "sports media wasn't the thing," Desser added, except for "start-up things," such as a nascent ESPN airing of "third-rate college football games and college basketball out of a trailer parked out in a field in Connecticut."[12] Though cable remained the minor league to broadcast television for a majority of the decade, the medium would reach 55.6 percent of US households with televisions by 1989.[13] During the same time period, broadcast television's grip began to loosen, as the three major networks saw their average Nielsen rating decline from 50 in 1981 to 33.9 in 1991.[14] "Cable is going to need programming, and sports are the obvious solution," said Rod Thorn in 1981, the general manager of the Chicago Bulls and later the NBA's president of basketball operations.[15]

In 1982, as the NBA's broadcast ratings continued to stagnate on CBS, its partner since 1973, the league signed two two-year agreements with ESPN and USA Network for forty regular-season games and ten playoff games each, with ESPN's package airing on Sunday nights and USA's on Thursday nights.[16] Less than a year after the foundation of NBAE, the 1983 All-Star

Game became the first program to feature NBA-produced promotional materials, with a commercial using the league's most explosive highlights and concluding with a new slogan, "NBA action . . . it's Fan-tastic."[17] Reflecting the newfound opportunities available for sport on cable, NBAE soon afterward signed a deal with USA Network for the production of thirty half-time features for the season to come. USA would also air the NBA draft and the NBA awards luncheon, coproduced by NBAE and ProServ, the premier sports management firm at the time.[18] NBAE had thus found an ideal match in cable television, which offered the league greater programming flexibility and promotional opportunities than did CBS and the broadcast networks. At the same time, by archiving league content for later use or licensing, NBAE and its video library provided a crucial in-house media infrastructure that would enable the league to become a more fully integrated global media company.

Encouraged by the possibilities that computers could offer these new responsibilities, the NBA also entered the digital age at this time. In 1983, the league signed an agreement with Mohawk Data Sciences (MDS) to make its Qantel product the "Official Computer of the NBA."[19] By adding a mainframe and satellite terminals to the NBA offices, the MDS Qantel system was able to create a stronger network of communication between franchises and the league, adding another layer to the ongoing system of mailing telecasts back and forth across the country. "This network will enable teams to tap instantly into our information banks for game statistics, player contract information, attendance figures and other vital data," explained commissioner Larry O'Brien.[20]

By 1988, the NBA's computer system would incorporate the operations of NBAE, which had already amassed forty thousand videotapes during its first five years. Rather than rely on handwritten descriptions of a game's significant plays, NBAE editors could now log notable plays for each game tape into a computer, indicating the player, the type of play, and a one-line summary, using the standard midcourt angle of most telecasts as well as alternate camera angles that NBAE received for more intense replay close-ups. The log process still took the same three hours per game, but more footage could be logged and locating it became much more efficient, especially for highlights that were cross-listed between players.[21] The digitization of NBAE thus enabled the league to develop a more effective internal media pipeline, which allowed them to invest more fully and more easily in emerging DTC platforms in the subsequent decade.

Today, the process of logging NBA games remains essentially the same, only instead of receiving the footage through videotapes mailed to Secaucus,

A 1982 advertisement in *Management Accounting* promotes the Qantel system and its ongoing agreement with the NFL.

the office is directly connected to each of the league's arenas by fiber-optic cable. Like the NBAE of 1988, the NBA's Game Distribution Center compiles game highlights and descriptions and edits together the alternative camera angles for a closer-to-the-action experience. NBAE's role between 1982 and 1988 was thus one of laying the groundwork, building a global media infrastructure that could be further leveraged as communications technologies continued to advance. A few years later, the league would construct a new state-of-art forty-five-thousand-square-foot studio and production facility in Secaucus. From that studio, NBAE would produce *Inside Stuff*, a new Saturday-morning highlight show for NBC, its broadcast partner as of 1990, as well as halftime features, promotions, and its usual slate of home videos.[22] NBAE and its improved capability as a legitimate producer-distributor was thus a crucial driver of the league's broader media ambitions.

Direct-Broadcast Satellite and Dot-coms: Sport in the Early Direct-to-Consumer Era

While NBAE continued to evolve, direct-broadcast satellite was steadily becoming a legitimate domestic competitor to cable, opening up new possibilities for the expanded television coverage of sport. After launching in June 1994, DirecTV, for instance, would reach one million subscribers by November 1995, expanding to seven million by 1999 and then 12.6 million by 2004. By 2005, overall DBS penetration would reach 17 percent of US households.[23] The NBA's own satellite offering had been years in the making, beginning with early research on the possibilities of digital compression for the delivery of games. "Digital signal compression was first applied to high definition TV signals to get them to fit into 6 megahertz bandwidth slots," the standard bandwidth for television stations, recalled Ed Desser, who had since transitioned from the NBA's director of broadcasting to become the president of a new Television Ventures division.[24] "But then there was this really interesting sort of side benefit, which was 'hey, if we can use this signal compression technology to take a big fat high definition channel and squeeze it into 6 megahertz, how many standard definition signals could we squeeze onto a satellite?'"[25] From that discovery, the DBS satellite business was born and the NBA wanted to be involved, as a way to more directly reach audiences that would allow greater control for the league. At the same time, as providers DirecTV and Dish Network sought a way to differentiate their competing products, exclusive sports rights provided the ideal course.

The NBA signed on with DirecTV in 1994, as did the NFL.[26] For the 1994–95 season, the NFL's Sunday Ticket service and the NBA's League Pass service both debuted. The NFL package would provide subscribers with access to dozens of out-of-market games every Sunday. The NBA's League Pass offered customers access to more than four hundred regular-season games—any games that were out-of-market and not already televised nationally. By January 1995, the NFL's package had sold two hundred thousand residential subscriptions and five thousand commercial ones. While the NBA's numbers were not yet available, the league was careful to temper expectations. "We don't foresee this as being a mass-distribution vehicle," Ed Desser explained to *Variety*. "It's a supplement to other programming. Our expectations, frankly, are modest."[27] Nonetheless, these new systems enabled the NFL and NBA to take more control of their own distribution outside the traditional broadcast or cable paradigm, thus improving both leagues' internal pipelines for the production and delivery of media content.

Only one year after the debut of the League Pass DBS service, the league debuted its own web service, NBA.com. The site was developed in partnership with Starwave, an intermediary software company that would build and manage websites on behalf of clients, much like the streaming intermediary firms to be discussed later. Paul Allen, the cofounder of Microsoft and owner of the NBA's Portland Trail Blazers franchise, had created the company in 1993 to capitalize on the potential of the internet as a vast media delivery system. From very early in the process, Mike Slade, who had spent eight years in product marketing at Microsoft and was selected to lead the venture as CEO, sought to invest in a sports platform. "I wanted to build an online sports section, the world's biggest sports section, basically," he recalled.[28] As a result, ESPN became Starwave's first and most important partner.

Launched in April 1995, all aspects of the initial ESPN online platform had to be built from scratch, including a scoreboard and the ability to post real-time statistics. Just as intermediary companies with the appropriate know-how are now hired to build streaming platforms for their clients, Starwave was required to do the same for the ESPN website from scratch, which did not come easily at the time. "We built all the tools—the technology to parse the data, and do the content management and the ad serving, and the load balancing," explained Slade, describing features that are now commonplace in web building and hosting platforms like WordPress and SquareSpace. Tools were also built for ESPNnet.SportZone.com, as it was then called, that allowed Starwave to see who was coming, how often, and to which pages. Management could see, for instance, that traffic would peak on Monday morning when people at work could take advantage of high-speed connections at the office.[29]

This accumulated knowledge was essential for pitching advertisers on the value of internet advertising dollars over television, print, or radio. Mike Slade recalled that "The whole pitch then . . . wasn't 'this is a better presentation of your brand,' it was 'you'll get all this data and someday you'll be able to sell direct to these people.'"[30] Starwave parlayed its data collection into extensive advertising sales. *Advertising Age* reported in October 1995 that Starwave had signed eight major sponsors to contracts totaling over $1 million, including a $300,000 deal with Levi Strauss and other smaller deals with AT&T, Microsoft, and Pizza Hut.[31] The strategy is similar to those used by streaming intermediary companies today, which also collect and analyze viewer data that their clients will purchase and then leverage into more lucrative advertising and merchandising plans.

Not long after launching the ESPN site, the NBA became the first major sports league to sign up with Starwave and allow them to oversee the administration of its own web venture. "There was an interest because of Paul Allen's involvement—and also a comfort level," recalled Ed Desser to *Sports Business Journal* in 2008. "If we were going to be out on the bleeding edge, it would be good to do it with people who understood sports, understood media, and understood technology."[32] The NBA website was launched in November 1995 for the start of the season. NBA commissioner David Stern compared the website to the league's early investments in cable, which had since become a more commonplace delivery system.[33] Like the ESPN site, the NBA site would feature team pages, play spotlights, video clips, and real-time statistics.[34]

Starwave's partnership with ESPN stipulated, however, that ESPN be involved in any other sports endeavors, creating a three-way partnership with prospective clients, such as the NBA or the NFL, and splitting all advertising revenue three ways. The Starwave-ESPN platform thus remained under joint ownership of Starwave and ESPN while the NBA leased its content and brand for the NBA platform. When Starwave set about programming its additional websites, the company simply cloned much of the original ESPN site and reskinned it and then worked in any unique requests made by its client. The NFL, for example, required a toolbar across the top of the page with all the teams' logos, a feature that remained on the site until 2017.[35] This three-way partnership, from the relatively early days of internet media, thus reflected the streaming paradigm to come, with transparent intermediaries building branded platforms for their clients. Though the NBA's domestic League Pass, for instance, is emblazoned with the league's logos and branding, it is operated by Turner Sports Digital, just as Starwave and ESPN owned those early online platforms.

While reliable video streaming remained a few years away, Starwave and the NBA were highly interested in offering *audio* broadcasts of games on the website, which was aided by a partnership with Progressive Networks and its RealAudio technology.[36] Geoff Reis, who oversaw the NBA project

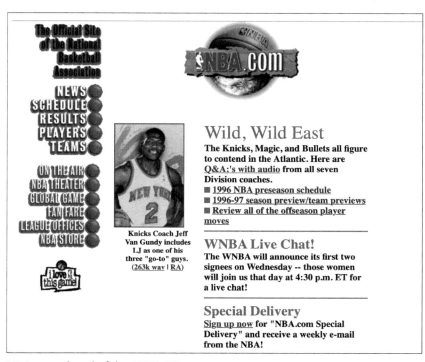

NBA.com ahead of the 1996–97 season.

at Starwave, told *Broadcasting and Cable*, "We will be putting up fresh daily multimedia content [that] NBA fans from around the world will be able to access."[37] Because bandwidth capabilities varied globally, the hope was that audio streaming would help to reach a dispersed international fan base. For the website's first Finals, in June 1996, NBA.com carried live audio from the postgame news conferences and real-time photograph stills from the games. "It's a total companion to the fans following the finals," said Jamie Rosenberg, the NBA manager of interactive programming. To that point, the operation had been successful, receiving two million hits per day early in the playoffs, rising to 2.5 million leading up to the Finals.[38]

The NBA's efforts to maintain control over these burgeoning media operations were further encouraged by larger regulatory machinations. In February 1996, the Telecommunications Act of 1996 officially went into effect, removing barriers to ownership and operation across the communications business and instigating a series of massive corporate mergers. After the bill had passed the Senate, in June 1995, Disney came to an agreement to buy Cap Cities/ABC for $19 billion, making it the largest entertainment company in the world.[39] A month later, talks began to accelerate between Turner Broadcasting System and Time Warner, already a TBS part owner.[40] In September, Time Warner bought out the remaining shares of TBS for $7.5 billion, creating the *new* largest media company in the world.[41] The following February, the Telecom Act was signed into law and the mergers were all officially approved. Jennifer Holt explains the act as "the ultimate deregulatory initiative to complete the structural convergence of the media industries that began during the 1980s" in that it allowed "broadcast, cable, and telephone companies to create convergent media empires with newly expanded boundaries."[42]

After Disney purchased Cap Cities/ABC, and with it ESPN, the purchase of Starwave became an inevitability. In February 1997, talks began to accelerate. In April, Disney announced that it was purchasing 33 percent of Starwave for approximately $100 million. Nearly a year to the day later, Disney exercised its option to buy out the remaining two-thirds of the company, folding Starwave's operations into its Buena Vista Internet Group in order to expand Disney's internet presence under a common technology platform.[43] Disney hoped to leapfrog competitors CBS, NBC, and Fox in the internet sports business by improving its own internal web infrastructure.[44] Mike Slade had seen the move coming: "it was sort of obvious they were either going to dump us, which was impossible, or buy us."[45] Starwave held too much leverage, as ESPN's expert platform manager, to exist independent of Disney's online operations and had to be brought in-house, whatever the cost, as in the purchase of BAMTech twenty years later. Renamed the ESPN Internet Ventures division, Starwave's relationship with the NBA would continue relatively unaffected. The league's audio streaming operation, which had evolved into a $19.95 audio-only League Pass, was simply moved from ESPN.com to NBA.com for the start of the 1997 season.[46]

The most extreme changes to the media landscape had occurred on the domestic front, but the NBA's primary motivation remained global. Since the launch of NBA.com, for instance, more than 35 percent of its traffic had come from outside the United States.[47] The introduction of NBA League Pass and NBA.com were intended to reach far-flung and disparate audiences, even if the technologies required more development to allow more reliable and sustained international engagement. The NBA understood the potential in NBA.com for the greater control over the administration of its brand and greater direct-to-consumer access, which could be further parlayed into an increase in viewership and revenue. "We did monetize on the website, to a certain degree, but more importantly it was a portal into the NBA, the same way social media is, to get you to video, where we really monetize," explained Steve Hellmuth, who worked on the NBA website and would later become the league's executive vice president of media operations and technology."[48] Just as NBA Entertainment was originally created to do in the 1980s through its commercials and home video releases, NBA.com was launched with the intention of creating additional value for telecasts. The strategy would be the same for an upcoming NBA-owned cable channel, which began primarily as a "barker" sales channel for the League Pass DBS service.[49]

NBA.com TV and Convergent Media Infrastructures

With NBA.com continuing to mature, the 1998 Finals between the Chicago Bulls and the Utah Jazz featured a greater integration of the NBAE's television and web efforts. Video highlights would be made available on the website during halftime, in combination with shot charts, statistics, and game commentaries from the players. Users could also use the NBA.cam service to take snapshots of the action by clicking on images from the game's eight camera angles, with the feeds updating every few seconds.[50] In addition to NBC's coverage of the event, NBAE maintained its own camera angles that could be quickly edited into a customized international feed for the league's ninety-three international television partners in 175 countries. At the same time that NBAE worked to smoothly self-distribute these telecasts, other NBAE personnel were assigned to document everything on the court and behind the scenes for home video releases and the league website as well, a reflection of how deeply the league had invested in its internet platform.[51]

Although the 1998 Finals were the highest rated in the NBA's history, worries abounded that NBC would soon lose money on the NBA arrangement.[52] To counteract the rising cost of NBA rights, NBC raised its advertising rates by as much as 50 percent over the previous year's.[53] Even more threatening to the long-term health of the agreement, rumors began to swirl that Michael Jordan would retire after the 1998 season. In February, during NBC's pregame coverage of the All-Star Game, the noted Jordan insider Ahmad Rashad offered his take on the situation: "For the first time, I believe him when he says he's going to quit."[54] As Jordan's retirement became increasingly certain, NBC noticeably began to promote Kobe Bryant, the nineteen-year-old Lakers star. "Promoting Kobe is no different than what we were doing promoting Michael in 1990," said Dick Ebersol. "Business goes on."[55]

At the same time, the looming possibility of a labor lockout and a strike-shortened season was gaining momentum. David Stern tried to downplay the growing unease, emphasizing the overall growth of the league. "We have to be able together to find a way to split this pie up, make the players even wealthier than they are, make our teams profitable, and find a way not to raise ticket prices at the rate that they've been raised," Stern told Lou Dobbs on *CNN Moneyline*.[56] By October, however, the necessary progress in labor negotiations between the owners and the players' union had not been made. Stern and deputy commissioner Russ Granik announced that the first two weeks of the season would be canceled.[57] In December 1998, the NBA canceled its schedule through the All-Star game in February. NBC tried to dismiss any talk of an entire canceled *season*, which only served to draw more attention to the possibility.[58]

NBA Entertainment, however, would use the work stoppage to expand its production capabilities and improve its video archive, in much the same way the league would later leverage the COVID-19 stoppage and restart to reimage the possibilities of its media output. With a break from logging the massive influx of nightly game footage, NBAE employees were now free to catalog older footage from the pre-NBAE era of the 1970s, which could be added to the oldies footage packages that were being distributed to international markets. An NBA History section was also added to NBA.com, which included video clips, season recaps, and player bios.[59] "We're not as busy as we'd like to be, but we're not sitting around," Adam Silver told the *New York Times*, in his new role as president and COO of NBAE.[60] While the lockout did much to hurt the credibility and profitability of the league—until then the NBA had been the only major sport without a strike-shortened season—the time off from basketball proved essential in cultivating central media operations that would distinguish the league for years to come.

In January 1999, the lockout officially ended. The schedule was expected to feature forty to forty-five games out of a possible eighty-two, a number that ultimately rose to fifty.[61] As expected, Michael Jordan announced his retirement on January 13.[62] In losing the superstar that had defined the league at its peak in the midst of "attempting to assess the damage of a labor dispute," most news coverage imagined the worst-case scenario for the NBA.[63] When basketball returned in February, the NBA also debuted a new slogan: "I *still* love this game!" The league hoped to earn back the trust of the fans by acknowledging its mistakes. Terry Cummings, a forward on the Golden State Warriors, added, "What must happen in this league, as a result of the lockout, is for everyone to become more intimate with the fans. The owners, players and fans all need each other, and we've got to show it."[64]

The push for greater intimacy extended to NBAE's evolving production approach. For the Spurs-Knicks Finals in June 1999, NBAE filmed anything and everything, including the sights and sounds of Spurs star David Robinson's ankles being taped on the sidelines, which was then stored in the NBAE archive. Under Adam Silver's NBAE, which had since grown to two hundred staffers, the driving philosophy had becoming access and intimacy. "The players and coaches understand it's our job to promote them, that we'll never use anything to harm them," Silver told *USA Today*. "There's film locked away in our vaults that will never see the light of day." The eventual plan, he explained, would be to digitize the archive and make much of it available on NBA.com.[65] All the footage that was amassed at the Finals, then, would become essential in distinguishing the NBA's online offerings.

In the interim, the video library also proved a key component of the NBA's latest media endeavor—its own cable channel. Set to launch on DirecTV and digital cable for the start of the 1999–2000 season, NBA. com TV was the first league-owned, twenty-four-hour network for any sports organization.[66] "It was another example of being opportunistic and seeing an opportunity in a growing world . . . taking advantage of the fact that sports leagues actually create more hours of programming every year than all the studios combined," explained Ed Desser. "It's a huge amount of content, so why shouldn't a sports league have a network?"[67] At launch, NBA.com TV would not feature any complete live games, acting instead as a barker channel intended to drive sales of its League Pass DBS service. During the day, the channel would feature two-hour edits of classic games (newly completed during the lockout), reruns of features from *Inside Stuff*, and other assorted NBA Entertainment-produced content. At 7 pm Eastern Time each night, the channel would go live with a news show featuring the previous day's highlights and a preview of upcoming games, leading eventually into live cut-ins and statistical updates from NBA.com. At 1 am, a fifteen-minute video package would air to sum up the night's action.[68] "We see this as an opportunity to tap into the rich array of information available on NBA.com and the vast television programming from NBAE's video and film library," said Adam Silver.[69] "This is our Web site morphed into a television channel."[70]

Operating out of the same Secaucus studio complex where the NBA produced *Inside Stuff* and its other programming, the start-up costs for the network were estimated at $10 million. DirecTV saw the addition of NBA.com TV as a further incentive to drive annual subscriptions of League Pass, which had thus far accumulated 150,000 DirecTV customers. In creating a more direct-to-consumer model, many industry analysts believed that the NBA was distancing itself from traditional television distribution deals.[71] Richard Tedesco of *Broadcasting and Cable* highlighted the promise of a channel "without network intermediaries," forecasting something like the streaming television paradigm to come.[72] The wider television industry had offered the ideal environment for NBA.com TV, which Commissioner Stern called "a convergence of the Internet, television, and basketball."[73] Over the previous few years, a web presence had come to be considered an essential asset for television programmers, a major shift since its early days as a mere curiosity. Geoff Reiss, who had overseen the launch of the NBA website and was serving as senior vice president at ESPN Internet Ventures, explained to *Broadcasting and Cable*, "ESPN is not a TV network. ESPN is sports and sports gets expressed on TV, radio, in print and on the Internet."[74]

Similarly, the 2000 Finals continued NBAE's interest in internet-television convergence, featuring sixty video cameras, thirty still-photo cameras, and approximately eighteen microphones distributed among the coaches, referees, and the court itself. After being logged in Secaucus, the footage would be stored away for future use in NBAE's multiple vaults, which had since grown to 180,000 tapes.[75] But the physical tapes had become unwieldy, given Adam Silver's ongoing plans to feature games and select footage on the NBA website. As a result, the league signed a deal with Convera, a new company from Intel and Excalibur Technologies, which would immediately begin work on digitizing the NBA's entire archive.[76] NBA Entertainment, a "once-modest operation" had "become a high-tech multimedia conglomerate," according to the *Philadelphia Inquirer*.[77]

By the start of the 2000–2001 season, the NBA's media convergence reached a new height with the launch of *The NBA Beat*, a studio show simulcast on NBA.com and NBA.com TV leading into its nightly coverage.[78] Broadcast distribution remained the primary emphasis for the NBA, but the scale of "streaming video" had made it "a very good way of serving niche products to disparate and dispersed audiences," noted Ed Desser in late 2000.[79] Because of the league's global ambition, internet distribution thus seemed a miraculous answer to the question of how to reach a global audience directly and simultaneously. Through NBAE's media and promotional efforts, star players could become more global than ever before. "With things like the Internet," explained Heidi Ueberroth, NBAE vice president for global media, "the players are known as quickly around the world as they are known here."[80] Simultaneity would become a fundamental component of the NBA's streaming strategy to come.

Baseball Advanced Media, Globalization, and the Early Infrastructures of Streaming

Given the immense promise for the worldwide delivery of media content, streaming technology continued to evolve and proliferate. Perhaps the ideal example of the "newly converged" media, noted a *Broadcasting and Cable* special report in January 2000, was "the satellite-delivered 24-hour NBA channel with 'wraparound' content from the NBA website."[81] The *Washington Post*, too, examined the ways in which internet-enhanced television was altering the sports media landscape. Many believed that sports leagues themselves would soon be broadcasting their own games and posting highlights to dedicated web "channels."[82] As a result, the streaming rights, or "internet broadcast rights," as they were often called at the time, became an increasingly valuable commodity. The NBA would continue holding onto its own rights for another several years; the National Collegiate Athletic Association (NCAA), however, set a precedent in 1999 when it sold the combined "March Madness" rights—including broadcast, cable, satellite, radio, streaming, marketing, sponsorship, and merchandising—to CBS for $6 billion over eleven years.[83]

In January 2001, the NBA announced a partnership with RealNetworks to offer audio and video streams of NBA.com TV, the first partnership between a cable channel and an internet subscription service.[84] In April, as a result of the deal, the NBA became the first professional sports league to stream a game telecast via the internet. The Sacramento Kings and Dallas Mavericks were purposely selected for the occasion, taking advantage of both teams' plethora of international stars and Mavericks owner Mark Cuban's career in the streaming audio business. "As someone who was there at the birth of the webcasting industry, to be part of the first broadcast of an NBA game is very exciting," Mark Cuban said in a statement. "The ability to watch an NBA game from almost any Internet-enabled device opens the NBA to fans worldwide."[85]

Though the NBA was the first to reach this particular benchmark, it was far from the only sport preparing for the dawn of a new distribution paradigm. In addition to the NBA and the NCAA, MLB Advanced Media (MLBAM or BAM), a division of MLB, had also been hard at work. Founded in June 2000 as a jointly owned subsidiary of all thirty MLB teams, BAM believed that a new digital economy would emerge with wider broadband adoption and better streaming video technologies. "Baseball's grand online plans rely on fundamentally different economics than the old advertising-revenue model for the Web," wrote Alan Schwarz of *Newsweek*, in an in-depth feature on BAM's work as of late 2002. "MLB is attempting to wean Web users off the idea of free, mediocre content in favor of paying for premium, exclusive and personalized services."[86] Bob Bowman, who oversaw MLB.com as CEO of BAM, explained of its overall strategy at the time, "to be successful economically, subscription services have to be the engine. . . . It's happening, and will continue to happen."[87] Indeed, Bowman's prediction would prove accurate about the oncoming era of streaming television.

By July 2005, the NBA had fallen slightly behind MLB in its streaming capabilities. The Finals earlier that summer, which saw the San Antonio Spurs defeat the Detroit Pistons over a full seven games, became the NBA's first championship series to be streamed over the internet.[88] Professional baseball, however, had been streaming games regularly since 2003, and BAM itself had grown into a key intermediary in the digital distribution business, filling the role once occupied by Starwave. BAM had been hired to oversee the launch of streaming platforms for NCAA and Major League Soccer, whose live streams would operate through MLB.com.[89] Sports programming had thus become "the killer app for streaming to your computer," according to Michael Kelley of PricewaterhouseCoopers, because of sport's volume and its global, out-of-market appeal.[90] More than half the traffic to NBA.com, for instance, now regularly came from outside the United States and, in order to better accommodate those fans, the league's website featured live audio broadcasts in fifteen languages, including Cantonese, Mandarin, Tagalog, French, German, and Spanish.[91] As the technology continued to improve and become more accessible to global viewers, an "internet TV revolution" seemed increasingly likely, according to David Lieberman's feature on the subject in USA Today.[92]

The internationalization of NBA basketball thus encouraged the further expansion of international direct-to-consumer distribution, in order to cater to fans who wanted to see their own national stars. In a major milestone, the 2006 Finals featured the German-born Dirk Nowitzki leading the Dallas Mavericks against the Miami Heat, who would go on to win the series. By that point, one-fifth of all players in the league were born outside the United States.[93] The 2007 Finals, the first to feature LeBron James, whose Cavaliers would lose to the San Antonio Spurs, also featured an NBA-record nine international players on its rosters, including Manu Ginobili of Argentina and Tony Parker of France.[94] During the series, Parker became the first European-born player to win NBA Finals MVP, in a season that saw Dirk Nowitzki become the first European to win regular-season MVP.[95]

At the same time, the NBA readied its streaming video capabilities in order to launch its new League Pass Broadband service for the 2006–7 season. For a half-season price of $109, League Pass Broadband offered up to forty regular season games a week on NBA.com, though the package remained an added feature of the satellite and digital cable service for the time being.[96] While the NBA's broadband platform went live in the United States, moreover, the league announced plans for a separate service to be sold in China, Taiwan, and Hong Kong, featuring Chinese-language broadcasts for about ninety regular-season and playoff games.[97] The moves were also tied to a revamped NBA.com, which now included ten national spotlight pages in addition to its new webcast offerings.[98] While the NBA, ultimately, became the third professional sports league to launch a streaming video service, behind the BAM-created services for MLB and Major League Soccer, the NBA remained far ahead of other US sports in its aggressive international expansion.[99]

The NBA's international and digital value influenced the subsequent rights negotiations with Disney and Turner in late 2006. In October, the league began talks with its incumbent partners about contract extensions, as the current deals were set to expire after the 2007–8 season. Digital rights were the centerpiece of the discussions, as Turner Sports looked to expand a New Media division that oversaw the websites for professional golf and NASCAR.[100] The NBA's recently launched League Pass broadband platform and the ongoing NBA TV digital cable channel were thus attractive potential properties, and the current deals did not allow either Turner or ABC/ESPN to stream any NBA content on its own platforms.[101]

Despite the value in the NBA's digital offerings, the linear television ratings measured by Nielsen had still declined every single year through the 2006–7 season, from a 2.6 average during the league's first season on ABC (2002–3) down to a 2.0 average.[102] TNT had also seen a 9 percent decline in ratings from the previous season, and ESPN had not fared much better.[103] The partners had hoped for a postseason boost, but the numbers never came. The 2007 Finals on ABC, which saw the San Antonio Spurs defeat the Cleveland Cavaliers in the shortest possible series of four games, dropped 28 percent from the previous year, itself one of the lowest-rated Finals, to a 6.2 rating.[104] John Hollinger of the *New York Sun*, and later analyst for ESPN and vice president of basketball operations for the Memphis Grizzlies, credited the decline to poor matchups, an overemphasis on cable, and promotion of stars at the expense of better teams.[105]

Hollinger's argument, however, did not take into account an increasingly fragmented multiplatform media landscape, which valued direct-to-consumer distribution more highly than ever before. MLB's BAM, for instance, which had continued to expand its streaming capabilities for itself and its various clients, had seen its annual revenue grow to $400 million.[106] Thus, in June 2007, despite the NBA's sagging domestic ratings, the league successfully negotiated a new eight-year, $7.4 billion rights deal with Disney and Time Warner, a 22 percent annual increase. Both partners gained the ability to simulcast live games on their digital platforms, while ESPN also obtained expanded global television coverage for ESPN International in Latin America, the Middle East, Africa, and Oceania. George Bodenheimer, president of ESPN and ABC Sports at the time, called the agreement a "prototype for TV sports deals going forward" in its expanded digital rights and a clause that bestowed digital rights on any future over-the-top (OTT) platforms from the rights holder. The digital discussions "kept our lawyers busy," noted David Levy, president of Turner Sports.[107] David Stern was finally ready to cash in the NBA's digital rights after he had remained patient into the twenty-first century.[108]

Turner, hoping to expand its digital content holdings to fuel its new platforms, also set its sights on NBA League Pass and NBA TV. After months of talks, a separate deal was announced in January 2008, which would see the formation of a new entity called NBA Digital. Turner would assume responsibility for operating and programming NBA TV, NBA.com, and NBA League Pass, though Turner and the NBA would sell digital advertising jointly, and NBA Entertainment would continue to produce content for the properties out of Secaucus. As part of the new deal, the NBA's digital operations would move from its New Jersey location to Turner's campus in Atlanta. Turner's David Levy called the venture "a new strategic business model and an innovative template for growth."[109] The agreement provided a path for the two organizations to become more deeply integrated and essential to one another in a tumultuous media environment. Turner obtained a more robust digital portfolio and the NBA gained the infrastructural reach and expertise that it required for its global media ambitions. The integrated operations became inextricably linked, to the degree that any future dissolution seems extremely unlikely. NBA Digital is "a real deep partnership that's going to be hard for anyone to unwind over time," noted Mark Lazarus, who negotiated the agreement as the president of Turner Entertainment Group at the time.[110]

A crucial aspect is that the NBA's transfer of digital infrastructure and operational responsibility to Turner also enabled the league to focus more fully on its global distribution. Steve Hellmuth, executive vice president of media operations and technology, noted that the majority of his duties now involve global operations. "That [agreement] has allowed us to focus one thousand percent on international up here at NBA Entertainment,"

Hellmuth explained. "Every day I spend the vast majority of my time on international, because that's where our revenues are growing very, very rapidly, and that's where our business really needs a lot of attention. So, we have Turner doing all domestic and doing a great job and then we're all focused on international."[111]

In forgoing some domestic oversight, the NBA could gain far greater international leverage, where revenues continued to expand without concern for market saturation. For the 2009–10 season, the NBA thus partnered with RayV, a digital intermediary service, to program an international-only League Pass service. For the 2010–11 season, the league revamped the platform in collaboration with NeuLion, the company that had most recently programmed the NHL's service.[112] Internationally, the NBA could more effectively self-distribute than in the domestic US market, which remained carved up by major players such as Fox Sports, ABC/ESPN, and NBC Sports. In the global shift toward streaming distribution, content owners were motivated by the greatest possible opportunity for centralization and control.

Hub and Spokes: The Hardware of the Contemporary Sports Media Infrastructure

Within a few years, the NBA opened its Replay Center in Secaucus, New Jersey, ahead of the 2014–15 basketball season. As part of the undertaking, all twenty-nine of its arenas were connected by fiber-optic cabling to that central hub. The connection helped the NBA to speed up its gameplay reviews after difficult foul calls, and the development also streamlined the league's media production, distribution, and archival process. During games, the NBA gained faster access to game footage that it could edit and post to social media platforms, and when games ended, the complete footage could be tagged and stored more quickly than ever before. The league office refers to this structure, based in its Traffic Ops Center, which monitors the video feeds as they enter the building, as the "hub and spoke" model: Secaucus acts as the hub of the wheel, the wires act as the spokes that connect it to its franchises, and arenas are the tire that makes the entire enterprise spin onward.[113]

This infrastructure was made possible by the dark fiber business, in which network providers sold unused or disused telecommunications fiber for private purposes, including the NBA's own interarena network. In this instance, the league signed an agreement with the Zayo Group, a Colorado company that maintains a global network of cables and satellites.[114] From the arena, all telecasts—whether intended to be regional, national, or international—travel to Secaucus via the high-speed arena network, or HSAN, a ten-gigabyte network of fiber-optic cables that allows the league to shuttle thirteen feeds of HD quality video at 200 megabytes per second. Each arena also provides the league with thirteen camera angles, which arrive in the basement of the NBA headquarters and are subsequently encoded for worldwide distribution.

The new speed at which video files can be stored and retrieved, moreover, also allowed the NBA to launch the NBA Content Network ahead of the 2016 season, as a global business-to-business video-on-demand service for the NBA's media partners.[115] Through the network, personnel from Turner, ESPN, MDeportes (Spain), Viasat Sport (Russia), CCTV (China), and the NBA's own franchises can sign into the system and request clips for its broadcasts or in-arena video boards. Once the order is received and approved, the file is pulled from StorageTek tape libraries, which feature robotic arms that find and grab a physical tape, place it into a reader, and send the video file onward to its destination. Each tape features 4.5 terabytes of data, or about forty full games, of which hundreds line the walls

Inside an Oracle StorageTek tape library, the same kind used by the NBA for storing its game footage.

of the silos. In all, there are about 25 petabytes of data in the NBA's library, which equates to approximately 25 million gigabytes.[116] Building on the NBA's history of video exchange, the NBA Content Network, in combination with the HSAN, thus offers a culmination of NBAE's pipeline of content delivery.

Through the opportunities presented by streaming distribution, the NBA serves as the arbiter of its own global distribution. After the H-San wires carry game feeds to Secaucus, video is sent either upstairs to the Replay Center for review or externally to one of the league's two colocation centers, or colos, in Newark, New Jersey, and Turner's Techwood campus in Atlanta, Georgia. The colos contain more cables, as well as a host of satellites, which make the redistribution of telecasts to the NBA's international

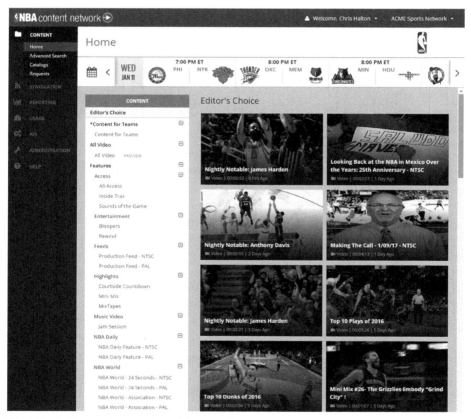

The NBA's Content Network enables media partners to download content for their broadcasts on demand.

partners easier. The infrastructure thus streamlines access for global broadcasters, while limiting the amount of data that the NBA must house on-site in Secaucus.[117] As the system of wires and satellites is made more diffuse, the NBA increasingly centralizes its control over it.

Streaming distribution thus offers content owners the greatest degree of control, direct-to-consumer access, and economic opportunity, as studio-owned platforms minimize the number of stakeholders between the content producer and the consumer. If the studio owns the wires, too, the possibilities for total control are vastly expanded. This approach is evident in the launches of conglomerate-owned platforms such as NBCUniversal's Peacock, with the assistance of parent company Comcast, the largest cable and internet service provider in the United States.[118] Similarly, AT&T's media content arm, WarnerMedia, launched HBO Max in 2020.[119] The NBA is in a similar position as a global content producer and distributor with its own streaming platform in NBA League Pass. In purchasing a network of wires from Zayo Group, moreover, the NBA took a further step toward total vertical integration.

Endeavor Streaming, Geolocation, and the Software of International Streaming Platforms

The NBA oversees much of the back-end infrastructure of game distribution itself, but it has left the front-end, consumer-facing side of its streaming platforms to intermediary firms. Turner, through its oversight of NBA Digital, has managed the NBA's domestic streaming platform since 2008. In 2010, the NBA hired NeuLion (since renamed Endeavor Streaming) to oversee its International League Pass, which includes all countries outside the United States but fourteen. In China, League Pass is overseen by Tencent, which launched its version of the service in 2016.[120] As Starwave did during the 1990s, today's firms draw on their unique expertise to design and operate branded streaming platforms for clients. The platforms require the work of specialists to design and program their interface, encode the video, track and analyze audience behavior, and oversee any problems with the finished front-end video.

Rather than rely on many different platforms around the world, US sports leagues have widely adopted inclusive international platforms, which are overseen by a single intermediary in charge of all non-US markets. Such an arrangement offers more oversight for the content owner and reduces the number of parties between the content provider and its central platform-managing intermediary. The paradigm is cost-effective, then, if not particularly easy to manage. For that reason, Endeavor Streaming is often aided by satellite offices in many of the regions it oversees for the purposes of localization. Its office in China, for example, works with local clients and will relay the proper Chinese commercials to play during advertising breaks.[121] Though international streaming platforms such as NBA League Pass and NFL Game Pass are intended to be as uniform as possible across borders, they still depend on the reinforcement of location awareness and market differentiation.

Geolocation, therefore, has grown into a central component of an intermediary's value, as firms emphasize their proprietary geolocation tools in pitches to prospective clients. Joshua Braun usefully differentiates between the operations of *geofencing*, which allows clients like Hulu and Netflix to "easily restrict access to their content to audiences in the regions they specify" and of *geotargeting*, which can "provide different versions of their content catalogues and interfaces to users in different markets."[122] For sports intermediaries, *geofencing* is a fundamental part of their job, due to the regional blackouts triggered by broadcast rights, whereby a Knicks game cannot be streaming in the New York area or games offered by a national network like TNT (or even NBA TV) will not be offered in an area where that channel is available. The in-game support team at Endeavor Streaming sets those restrictions in the game's administrative tools once the game is posted in its schedule.

Geotargeting is often a more lucrative asset, which allows intermediaries to track viewer behavior, tagged by location, and provide that data to clients to price their services more aggressively or leverage the information to advertisers. In *The Informal Media Economy*, Ramon Lobato and Julian Thomas describe the incentive for such market segmentation, which "enables media producers to price their goods according to local income levels, to control sequencing and to extract the greatest return from each market."[123] The most measurable remains, as ever, the most marketable. Companies like Endeavor make this measurement possible by programming, designing, and managing the platforms and its measurement tools; the differentiation is built into the system. Transnational flows, evidently, are not simply unidirectional. The intermediary, moreover, demonstrates that no longer do the flows derive from a simple producer-distributor agreement, but from a more complex arrangement in which these firms can significantly set the terms by which global audiences engage with media content online.

While geotargeting, at the level of platform management, allows the closing (and also opening) of borders, there is a simultaneous incentive for content that will most efficiently flow through those borders. Transnational streaming providers such as Netflix and HBO have sought to acquire "local content that appeals to international audiences."[124] The NBA, similarly, benefits from high-profile international players who can be highlighted in replays.[125] At the level of the live sports event, which provides the content that will ultimately circulate through the international streaming platforms, there have been greater efforts to address international fans, such as the foreign-language uniforms and theme nights discussed in the introduction and chapter 1 of this book. These efforts go hand in hand with the efforts of the intermediary, which has designed a platform that can address any and all international fans simultaneously. In this way, the NBA's International League Pass remains an inclusive platform, in spite of its linguistic barriers and differential pricing. The NBA uses the international presence of Endeavor Streaming's platform to feature players and marketing that will simultaneously address the most possible fans in the most possible countries.

In the realm of global streaming television, then, intermediary firms function as collaborative rights holders, though they concede far greater control to content producers than would NBC Sports or Fox Sports to its own linear television partners. With Endeavor, the NBA obtains the most effective infrastructure to reach global consumers while maintaining more leverage overseas than in its domestic operations. Through the NBA and other clients, Endeavor obtains the programming to fill its propriety platform, while receiving compensation for its services through some combination of platform fees, device enablement fees, per-subscriber percentages, and revenue sharing. The NBA's system of a hub and spokes that stretches around the world, through the cables and colocation centers, thus maximizes the league's control over its global streaming operations.

Conclusion: Toward a Post-network Paradigm

As intermediary firms become more expensive to outsource, companies with enough capital to buy a preexisting one or build their own have increasingly sought to do so. NBC, for example, launched Playmaker Media in May 2016 to service its own sports streaming operations, as well as clients from outside Comcast-NBCUniversal. TBS similarly acquired a majority stake in iStreamPlanet to bolster its streaming capabilities when its contract with MLB Advanced Media expired after the 2016 NCAA Men's Basketball Tournament.[126] Even Amazon, whose prestigious Web Services division has been hired to provide cloud services for clients as diverse as Netflix and the US

Central Intelligence Agency, found it necessary to purchase the Portland, Oregon, streaming intermediary Elemental Technologies for $500 million in September 2015 in order to better compete with BAMTech, NeuLion, and iStreamPlanet in the business of streaming video encoding and transcoding.[127] In March 2018, Endeavor, the parent company of Ultimate Fighting Championship (UFC) and Professional Bull Riders, both clients of the intermediary firm NeuLion, purchased NeuLion for $250 million. By taking control of NeuLion, renamed Endeavor Streaming, Endeavor could bring the streaming operations of UFC in-house while continuing to provide services to the NBA, NFL, and other NeuLion clients.[128]

Such activities reflect a wider post-network era of television, which Amanda D. Lotz succinctly describes as a media ecosystem "devoid of networks or channels as the distinct industrial entities they've served as thus far."[129] Emerging from the media cross-ownership made possible by the Telecommunications Act of 1996, streaming distribution has increasingly become the beachhead for further industrial consolidation and vertical integration. While the post-network era has evolved beyond the linear distribution of television programming through distinct channels, it has largely led to the reorganization of those same major corporate entities across new institutions, such as Disney's ESPN+, NBCUniversal's Peacock, and ViacomCBS's Paramount+. Some entities, including the NBA and its franchises, have used the opportunity to grow more globally and become more integrated than ever before. The intermediary firms that help make streaming distribution possible have also grown immensely by capitalizing on their unique infrastructural know-how to provide clients with essential programming services. But the most powerful entities also remain powerful, often absorbing those firms and any other companies that might be useful to in-house media infrastructures, including Disney's purchases of Starwave and BAMTech, Turner's purchase of iStreamPlanet, and Endeavor's purchase of NeuLion. With the proliferation of streaming, new possibilities for vertical integration and corporate control have emerged for companies that can afford them.

In taking on more and more distribution responsibilities, across NBA.com, NBA League Pass, and NBA.com TV, the NBA cemented its own status as a legitimate media conglomerate, building up from the media infrastructure initiated by NBA Entertainment in the early 1980s. The league's interest in global media was encouraged by cable and satellite distribution during that period, and its ambitions were vastly expanded by the simultaneity of internet distribution in the 1990s and 2000s. As the importation of international athletes became more widespread, the NBA only accelerated its investment in digital distribution in order to more directly reach a growing audience around the world. In doing so, the NBA has reinforced globalization and digitization as integrated processes. The global proliferation of streaming distribution enables integrated content providers, such as Netflix and HBO, to maintain vast libraries that can appeal to a wide demographic. Similarly, the NBA's own streaming platform features an evolving archive of games and highlights that can address any particular fan base around the world.

The drive for full global efficiency is thus accelerated by the success of streaming television and OTT platforms, in combination with the advent of "dark fiber," which provides content owners such as the NBA with even greater control over the physical delivery of internet-distributed video. Through its ownership of cables and satellites, outsourcing infrastructure only when necessary, the NBA has maximized control over its own media operations. By enabling and constraining the flow of content within and around its arenas, the NBA stands to expand its reach even further as a global media empire, as streaming distribution continues to gain momentum over linear television. In the chapter that follows, which examines the league's executive office and its evolving approach to decision-making, the NBA leaves behind almost all remnants of itself as a mere professional basketball league, as the sport is transformed into multiplatform media content.

CHAPTER 4

The Office

The NBA's Executive Operation as a Global Media Empire

Manifest Destiny

Beside Interstate 95 in New Jersey is a seemingly standard outdoor shopping center, complete with a Red Lobster, a Chili's Grill and Bar, a Starbucks, a movie theater, and various other storefronts. But, across the parking lot, tucked away from the hustle and bustle of the regular passersby, is the production and distribution center of the NBA. A bare, nondescript concrete building on the outside, the facade hides an impressive inner structure, with four circular floors wrapping around an open atrium.[1] In the center are custom NBA-brand pool tables and pop-a-shot games. The waiting area for visitors is functionally a small museum, featuring memorabilia such as Bob Cousy's 1957 MVP trophy, a life-size Wilt Chamberlain standee from Spaulding, assorted bobbleheads and All-Star Game mugs, a game ball from the ABA era, and an unopened pack of Michael Jordan fruit snacks, as well as game jerseys from Michael Jordan, Hakeem Olajuwon, and Bernard King. Even more material lines the walls between offices and conference rooms, including floor-to-ceiling posters of LeBron James and Carmelo Anthony and game-worn sneakers from Manu Ginobili in a display case. These artifacts serve as a reminder to visitors and employees alike of the global power and history of the NBA.

The NBA's production-distribution center in Secaucus, New Jersey, and its business headquarters in Manhattan, New York, operate in unison as the ultimate authority over professional basketball and its mediation by directing the actions of its teams and its overseas offices. On November 29, 2012, for instance, the San Antonio Spurs franchise gave four of the team's top stars the night off. After playing five games in eight nights, the decision was not unusual for head coach Gregg Popovich or for the league more widely. The problem was that this game, against LeBron James and the Miami Heat, was to be nationally televised on TNT. The NBA's commissioner, David Stern, fined the team $250,000, arguing that the Spurs had rested their players "in manner contrary to the best interests of the NBA. . . . Under these circumstances, I have concluded that the Spurs did a disservice to the league and our fans."[2] While the NBA is officially tasked with administering the directives of the franchise owners, the will of the league's executives can sometimes overrule owners' interests. One week later, as pundits took opposing sides across ESPN and national news networks, cultural critic Chuck Klosterman drew a broader question from the controversy: "What is the central purpose of pro sports, and how much of that purpose is solely tied to entertainment?"[3] Stern's actions highlighted the extent to which the NBA privileged its media value above and beyond its investment in competitive and meaningful play. The lesson that television came first for the NBA, if not for all US professional sports, was an uncomfortable truth for many sports fans. But the fines against the Spurs were not the first time the priority was clear, nor would it be the last.

Since at least 1984, when David Stern became the NBA's commissioner, the league office had prioritized television and its global interests above all, acting as a media company first and a basketball league second. In November 1996, Stern served as the keynote speaker at the International Council meeting of the National Academy of Television Arts and Sciences. "Our game inspires local, regional, national and even international loyalty," he told the audience. "We are truly egalitarian programming. . . . The emerging lesson for us is that the power of TV has given us global fans, and this is no longer a local thing."[4] The NBA took complete globality to be the sport's ultimate horizon, with the National Basketball Association as the world's league and David Stern as the world's commissioner. In 1996, Jeff Coplon of the *New York Times* aptly termed Stern's tenure the "Manifest Destiny Regime," adding that Stern "grasped the root law of capitalism: grow or die."[5] The NBA, formerly a professional sports organization with a global curiosity, aspired to become an international force in entertainment.

Conceptions of imperialism, then, are crucial to unpacking the NBA's strategic globalization during this period. While John Tomlinson considers imperialism to be a necessarily "purposeful project," as "the *intended* spread of a social system from one center of power across the global," others offer more flexible definitions that may be more accurate in capturing the complex consequences of the NBA's international circulation.[6] Silvio Waisbord and Michele Hilmes, for instance, have both characterized cultural flows as more multidirectional and complex than straightforward cultural domination in their discussions of international television.[7]

Daya Kishan Thussu offers a useful merger of the various viewpoints, noting that while "contraflows" are possible, the localization of media content can "effectively legitimize the ideological imperatives of a free-market capitalism" and, as a result, strengthen "the American hegemony of global media cultures."[8] For Thomas Lamarre, this effect is a systemic quality of the global television format trade, which seeks to transform the local into the regional or global through the "compatibility, convertibility, or equivalency between national cultures."[9] Ultimately, television formats are useful in explaining the internationalization of sport, which has often been packaged and distributed according to the commercial tenets of the format trade. NBA basketball, moreover, as a hybrid of live and mediated performance, available across linear and nonlinear platforms around the world, offers a valuable perspective for understanding the global multiplatform era of television at the executive level by highlighting the ways in which cultural flows can be reciprocal while still serving the commercial interests of the rights holder.

The phenomenon is evident in the examples discussed throughout this chapter, which illustrate the NBA's transformation from a cultural pastime into international media product through the purposeful decisions made within the upper echelons of its corporate offices. In the 1980s, David Stern, along with director of broadcasting Ed Desser, decided to reduce the league's television exposure in order to boost the rating averages for each game. The NBA was subsequently rewarded by a new lucrative broadcast contract from NBC that allowed the league far greater autonomy than its previous partner, CBS, had permitted. The league's media ambitions would soon extend beyond its telecasts alone to providing formatted supplementary programming to countries around the world. The programming would be produced and controlled by the NBA's own executives, aided by the opening of various regional offices, like subsidiaries within the larger NBA corporate structure. The process would eventually give way to a formatting of the NBA itself, which sought to launch new leagues in the NBA's own image, including the Women's National Basketball Association (WNBA) and a *football* league to be run by the NBA, NBC, and Turner, though that venture was ultimately aborted. The NBA, therefore, has worked diligently to extend the reach of its physical and media operations on a global scale, a fulfillment of David Stern's "Manifest Destiny Regime," even after his eventual replacement by Adam Silver as commissioner in 2014. In this capacity, the NBA reflects the actions and strategies of the companies Netflix, WarnerMedia, and NBCUniversal, as similarly integrated producer-distributors with a global reach and offices around the world.

Putting Out Fires: The NBA on CBS

By 1982, when the NBA officially launched its in-house entertainment division, the league had been looking for ways to take greater control of its promotion and production from broadcast partner CBS, a relationship that had grown somewhat tense. After an infamously tape-delayed Finals in 1980 between the Philadelphia 76ers and Los Angeles Lakers, led by popular rookie Magic Johnson, *Newsweek* called the league "the sorriest mess in sports."[10] The deciding sixth game of the series aired on a delay at 11:30 pm eastern time in every major city but Philadelphia, Los Angeles, Portland, and Seattle, as CBS affiliates opted instead to air reruns of *The Incredible Hulk*, *The Dukes of Hazzard*, and *Dallas* during May sweeps—a response to the lack of interest in the NBA at the time.[11] In a June 1981 feature in the *Washington Post* on the future of sports television, multiple network executives put the blame squarely on CBS for their mishandling of professional basketball. Taking a defensive stance, CBS Sports president Van Gordon Sauter admitted that, while professional basketball "is a very viable television sport," the "sport itself has some identity problems that need to be corrected."[12]

The NBA felt that its partner had done much to exacerbate these issues, which had worsened after an exposé in the *Los Angeles Times*. The report proposed that up to 75 percent of NBA players were using cocaine, tying the drug's popularity to the "sudden wealth" of its "young players, many from unstable families in inner-city ghettos."[13] The league at the time, sportswriters Harvey Araton and Filip Bondy noted, "just happened to be roughly 75 percent black," highlighting the obvious racism of the allegations.[14] Basketball and cultural scholar Todd Boyd, too, described how the NBA was "becoming increasingly Black" during this period, "not only in terms of population but in style of play and in its overall aesthetics." Combined with the rumors of drug abuse, this led to a perception of the league "as simply another example of Black criminality, not unlike those Black criminals represented in other aspects of society across the news media."[15] As controversy swelled and racist attitudes persisted, CBS only stoked the flames. In April 1983, for example, after a fight between Wayne "Tree" Rollins and Danny Ainge, CBS kept replaying close-ups of the fight and depicting Rollins as the unprovoked aggressor. Rollins explained later, "CBS made it look like the big black guy jumped on the little white guys. . . . [The Hawks] sent [CBS] the tape showing what happened, and they didn't use it. Nobody saw him with a clenched fist, taking a swing."[16] Even as late as November 1984, during a fight between Larry Bird and Julius Erving, CBS aired multiple slow-motion replays of Erving punching a restrained Bird, while completely ignoring the initial elbow strike by Bird that started the conflict.[17] CBS seemed to only amplify the racist resentments of the league's Black athletes.

The network's lack of confidence in the NBA and its problematic use of the broadcast rights, by criticizing the NBA's image while reinforcing negative stereotypes about its players, were not lost on the league. David Stern, who was tasked with overseeing business and legal operations as the NBA's executive vice president, realized that the NBA needed to "put out the fires."[18] Stern's proposed solution was NBA Entertainment, which would help to promote the league in-house and on its own terms. In Travis Vogan's examination of NFL Films, he argues that "football's meaning is pliable" and that, through their production division, "the NFL has developed various strategies to manufacture an image that sets the gridiron game apart from other sports and that distinguishes itself from other sports organizations."[19] In taking inspiration from NFL Films, the NBA's own entertainment division sought to do the same for basketball, distinguishing the sport and reframing its meaning. Steve Sabol, former president of NFL Films, described the football subsidiary as made up of "historians, storytellers, [and] mythmakers."[20] The same is true of NBA Entertainment, which allowed the league to take charge of its own promotional materials and to change the conversation by "focusing on the players, their talents on the court, their talents off the court, their sense of personality."[21] NBAE enabled the league to reimagine itself as a television program, emphasizing its characters and its narrative elements.

The NBA was well positioned to succeed in this pursuit. Sports scholars Todd Boyd and Kenneth L. Shropshire have described how, "unlike baseball and especially football, in basketball the players' faces are easy to see and thus easy to use in advertisements," which creates a "clearer identification between fans and individual players."[22] As a result, the NBA was more readily able "to utilize television as a key resource in changing the perception of the league and creating a new message," according to John Fortunato, who studied the league's use of media during the 1980s and 1990s.[23] In addition to the NBA's internal efforts to improve fan reception, CBS also began to evolve their approach by focusing on the rules of the game and the lives of the players, rather than on fighting and allegations of drug use. Mike Burks, CBS coordinating producer at the time, has explained their ultimate strategy as one of education: "how do we make a viewing audience understand the game, care about the people, and want to watch?"[24] Tommy Heinsohn, a former Boston Celtics forward and broadcaster, joined CBS for the playoffs in 1984 and became instrumental in teaching the production staff about the nuances of the sport.[25] NBA Entertainment remained fundamental to this pursuit by providing the network with supplementary programming, such as commercials and features that would "support NBA games through telling stories and personalizing players."[26]

The logic of advertising and marketing, moreover, increasingly guided programming decisions during this period, including those of the NBA. According to new media and marketing scholar Joseph Turow, advertisers increasingly moved away from demographics and began to focus instead on a "a soup of geographical and psychological profiles" called "lifestyles."[27] During the 1980s, new cable channels such as Nickelodeon and MTV served as ideal examples of "lifestyle-segmentation in action," by gearing their programming and branding toward children and teens in particular.[28] Television industry scholar John T. Caldwell has also described the resultant "aestheticization of television," the "visual sophistication," and "program individuation" that dominated the programming of the period.[29] "Advertising teaches television," Caldwell argues. "It is a hungry proving ground for new televisual production technologies; it is a leaky cache of creative personnel that denarrativizes television; it is an omnipresent aesthetic farm-system for primetime."[30] Sports television, as a particularly visual and flexible form, lends itself to these same aesthetic interests.

This was evident in NBAE's own promotional campaigns, which were more reflective of MTV and the televisual qualities of cable programming than of the broadcast networks. *That Championship Feeling*, on the Philadelphia 76ers' 1983 Finals win, would become the first major straight-to-video documentary produced by NBAE. Featuring popular music like Irene Cara's "What a Feeling," and taking advantage of the league's improved archive of game footage and highlights, the video was a step forward for NBA productions and the crystallization of their own style, distinct from the guts-and-glory mythological style of NFL Films.[31] Rather, the video reflected the populist leanings of Paul Gilbert and Don Sperling, who had been hired away from CNN, and Ed Desser, who understood the need to "do something different and create some programming that would be . . . better promotion for the league."[32] In one of NBAE's more playful promos from this era, for example, the sound of cannon fire was synced to highlights of buzzer-beating baskets being launched from half-court.[33] By capturing the televisuality of cable programming, the NBA sought to position itself as the young, hip, and fun sports league and move further away from its earlier reputation for violence and drug abuse.

With the NBA on the upswing entering the 1983–84 season, Larry O'Brien announced his resignation as commissioner, effective the following February. O'Brien recommended that the board consider David Stern for his replacement, and indeed, on November 15, 1983, Stern was officially voted the league's fourth commissioner.[34] Already evident in his creation of NBA Entertainment, Stern's taking office would greatly accelerate the league's investment in media production and distribution, as well as its overall conception of basketball as media content.

The "Less Is More" Strategy

The first major media strategy under the new tenure of David Stern became known within the league office as "less is more." Ed Desser, director of broadcasting at the time, explains the strategy as "let's not overexpose ourselves, let's try to make each telecast special." The goal, with the NBA still "fighting for ratings," was to use more measured exposure to improve the ratings average. "What's a more attractive thing for a television network," Desser asks, "one game that gets a ten rating, or five games that get a two rating?"[35] For the NBA at the time, the former scenario would allow the league to demonstrate more sustained interest and ratings growth, which would make their media product more attractive to prospective sponsors. At the annual meeting of the National Cable Television Association in June 1984, Stern announced a landmark cable deal with Ted Turner. For $20 million over two years, TBS would air fifty-five regular-season games and twenty playoff games, becoming the NBA's exclusive cable partner; previously, the NBA had aired games across multiple channels, including TBS, ESPN, and USA Network.[36] In a press release, Stern described the league's philosophy as privileging scarcity: "In reducing the number of games to be carried exclusively on one cable network, we are increasing dramatically the attractiveness of NBA basketball to both the viewer and the advertising community."[37] The "less is more" strategy thus reflected the league's deepening conception of basketball as a television program first and foremost, as well as its willingness to manipulate its mediation through executive decision-making to enhance its media value. At the same time, by lessening the overall number of games and increasing the number of prime-time offerings on cable, the NBA and NBAE were able to maintain greater control over storylines and narratives, building suspense for particular matchups and depicting players as characters in an ongoing soap opera. The NFL had successfully accomplished the same in its streamlined Sunday and Monday schedule. With *Monday Night Football*, Michael Oriard has explained, ABC Sports president Roone Arledge "brought to televised football the idea that the show, not the game, was what mattered."[38] The NBA translated this approach into the cable era.

The result of reducing the media exposure surpassed anyone's greatest expectations. By the mid-1980s, viewership for sports television had begun to decline—except for professional basketball. "Ratings for most major league sports have eroded in the last five years," wrote Amy Saltzman of *Adweek*, "and growing competition from national, regional and local cable outlets is likely to bring a continued decline." The NBA, which had reduced its broadcast coverage and invested in the burgeoning cable industry, was the only sport to have seen a ratings *increase* over the previous five years.[39] Indeed, since the Nielsen ratings low of 6.7 in 1981, the NBA Finals saw an average rating of 14.7 from 1986 through 1990, with a high of 16.7 in 1987.[40] Ahead of the 1984–85 season, the *Washington Post* also spotlighted the NBA's success by capitalizing on a "big event atmosphere" as a result of fewer telecasts. "Not so coincidently," wrote Anthony Cotton, "the league's upswing in attitude has coincided with the first year of David Stern's reign as NBA commissioner."[41] Part of the league's resurgence was, in fact, coincidental, timed perfectly with the popular rivalry between Larry Bird and Magic Johnson, the high-flying theatrics of former ABA stars like Julius "Dr. J" Erving and George "The Iceman" Gervin, and the rookie class from the 1984 draft, which featured the likes of Michael Jordan, Hakeem Olajuwon, Charles Barkley, and John Stockton. But Stern and NBA Entertainment also fully capitalized on these developments. By stockpiling archival footage and developing promotional campaigns in-house, the league was able to better define the identity of its own product.

The NBA thus continued to benefit from the flexibility offered by the cable industry and its turn toward niche programming. Robert V. Bellamy has referred to the "mutually beneficial relationship of the cable and sports institutions," in which cable gains "a source of popular programming" and the sports organizations acquire a new distribution outlet, "weaning" themselves from the major broadcast networks.[42] By 1987, for instance, cable would double its reach over the previous four years, "nourished by improved programming and by its physical expansion into half of all homes."[43] Journalist Ken Auletta, who chronicled the development, saw the process as democratization: viewers were being given more options, as the low overheads of cable companies could be "satisfied with small, targeted audiences." The advertising industry responded by "shifting from national advertising to targeted promotion budgets," thus turning away from the mass market to "hundreds of demographically distinct markets."[44] Sport offered the ideal conduit for the changes, as a genre of television that could reach mass and niche audiences alike. Sports television caters to the "ongoing interdependence of the broadcasting and cable industries," explains Victoria E. Johnson, as the media industries "strive to balance their portfolio of interests in order to engage *both* a broad(cast) audience and increasingly narrower niches within that audience."[45] The NBA capitalized on these industrial changes by investing more heavily in the sport's cable distribution and taking on greater production and promotional responsibilities.

By 1988, sports would account for 1,800 hours of programming on broadcast television in comparison with 5,000 hours on cable television.[46] Despite persistent fears of a glut of televised sports, NBA basketball continued to excel, especially during the early and midround playoffs on TBS. The 1988 Eastern Conference Finals between the Boston Celtics and Detroit Pistons managed to hit ratings of 8.1 and 8.8, setting a new cable record for the NBA.[47] When accounting for production costs and rights fees, moreover, basketball had easily become the most profitable sport. Cheaper to produce than both football and baseball, basketball was estimated to cost $512,000 per hour to produce in 1987, cheaper even than the average sitcom and dramatic series, at $800,000 and $900,000 per hour, respectively.[48] Although basketball's average prime-time rating of 6.2 still sat below baseball's 8.7 and football's 17.2, it was cost-effective programming and its ratings continued to steadily improve.[49]

At the same time, overseas opportunities continued to emerge for the NBA to expand its "Manifest Destiny" vision. After the 1985 rights negotiations with CBS that had allowed the NBA to take over its own international television distribution, taped telecasts now reached more than seventy countries, stretching as far as Hungary, Zambia, Nigeria, Luxembourg, and Greenland.[50] As the demand for US sports in Europe and Asia continued to grow, the NBA in particular had "reaped the largest economic harvest," as the *United Press International* reported.[51] The league had "jumped far ahead" of the NFL and MLB and was "slightly ahead" of the NHL. "It's easy to see why," noted Christine Brennan of the *Washington Post*. "Basketball is a very popular sport in many areas of Europe and the Americas. U.S. college players not quite good enough to play in the NBA go there. Italy, Spain and France have well-organized leagues."[52] The NBA had carefully cultivated the popularity of basketball abroad, moreover, and helped guide its international development throughout the 1980s through its overseas exhibitions and training camps, such as the Atlanta Hawks' Soviet Union tour and the McDonald's Basketball Open, as discussed in chapter 1.

The league amassed greater international control and found a niche where it could pull ahead of its US sport counterparts, but international revenues still generally lagged behind domestic revenues. The NBA's total international rights netted them only $4 million annually, against their $400 million in domestic grosses. "The important thing," noted Stern, "is that we've already laid the groundwork to take full advantage of any opportunities that come up."[53] Stern compared the investment to the league's investments in cable, via TBS, ESPN, and USA Network, which had helped to turn the league's fortunes around over the course of the 1980s: "In 1979, the NBA got $400,000 from network cable. In 1989, we'll get $27 million. International opportunities, though embryonic, show just as much potential."[54] The league's global groundwork would continue to evolve, hitting its next peak in 1992 with the Olympic "Dream Team" and leading to a new phase of international expansion, as discussed later in this chapter.

By June 1989, seventy countries were set to carry the NBA Finals either live or on a tape-delayed basis. One of the latter countries was the Soviet Union, which was set to air the Finals for the first time ever. Five countries—Italy, Spain, Greece, Brazil, and Denmark—went as far as to send their own television commentators to sit courtside for their live coverage.[55] The others would record voiceovers in their own home-country studios, a minor relinquishing of control back to the international broadcasters and away from NBAE.[56] At the same time, as NBA programming continued to explode, the prior eighteen months saw NBA International grow from a few part-time employees to seven full-time ones. Ed Desser, vice president for international broadcasting, reflected on the newfound global success of the once-fledgling organization: "It's no longer true that the first thing you do in the morning is reach for the sports page. Now I look at the world news page, to see what's going on in the markets we're distributed in."[57]

David Stern, who took over as commissioner during this period, downplayed his own role in the NBA's turnaround: "No fan has ever bought a ticket or watched a game on TV because of an owner, a general manager, or a commissioner. What is going to excite our fans are the great athletes and the breathtaking plays they make. It's my job to help provide a stage for that."[58] While the players indeed drove in the fans, Stern's administration worked to expand and alter the possibilities of that stage, by launching NBA Entertainment and investing in more flexible media distribution. The interests of the NBA, which desired a stronger media presence and stronger control over that output, had thus aligned with the evolving television industry, which required distinctive programming for an expanding number of channels. Through the NBA's in-house media operations, basketball had become firmly established as a media product. The process of mediatizing the sport only intensified by the end of the year, when the league left longtime broadcast partner CBS for NBC, which had offered the NBA greater oversight and involvement in the network's media operations. The next section, "NBA on NBC," presents the culmination of a nearly decade-long process of basketball's deepening mediatization.

Beyond Basketball: The NBA on NBC

By 1989, NBC Sports felt that it needed to make a splash, having lost the broadcast rights to MLB the year before. Dick Ebersol, in his first day running the division, called David Stern and made it clear that he desperately sought the NBA rights. After six months of back-and-forth communication, Stern and Ebersol were finally prepared to make the move to NBC happen. The NBA "knew that there was a lot of money on the table" that CBS, their incumbent partner, was not prepared to offer.[59] To NBC, the NBA was worth as much as $600 million over four years, that figure beating out offers by both CBS and ABC. The fact of a bidding war between networks was itself significant and was inspired by MLB's leaving NBC for CBS. MLB commissioner Peter Ueberroth and Bryan Burns, the league's head of broadcasting, had orchestrated a massive four-year $1.1 billion deal.[60] "They created a term sheet and gave it to the network and then said, 'that's what the deal is, do you want to bid on it?'" explained John Kosner, the NBA's director of broadcasting at the time, succeeding Ed Desser in the role.[61] Ueberroth and Burns's approach was completely different from the way renegotiations had traditionally been carried out. Previously, the network president might offer a slight raise over the current rate in exchange for some additional games. As a result, NBC was completely offended by the audacity of a league demanding anything of a network, as CBS would be when the NBA did the same.

The NBA, having spent a decade cultivating its in-house media operations, saw a valuable opportunity to expand the responsibilities of its executive office. John Kosner and Ed Desser began crafting the NBA's own version of the term sheet, which included a pregame studio show to be coproduced by NBA Entertainment. NBC's winning bid, in addition to offering the most money and a new pregame show, would offer four guaranteed seasons of an additional NBA-produced program to air on Saturday mornings. Ed Desser, reflecting on the move from CBS to NBC, explained how the CBS deal had been a largely traditional sports-rights deal: "Basically the network would say to the sports league, 'well, we know about television, you don't; you'll give us the rights, we'll give you a pittance and you'll thank us.' . . . NBC came along and it was a fundamental flipping of that."[62] The new arrangement with NBC thus created a lasting impact on the nature of sports-rights deals, as well as on the status of sports as media content, by enabling and empowering the NBA to create a vast amount of media content as a reputable television producer in its own right.

The NBA-NBC agreement was announced on November 13, 1989, and at $600 million over four years, the deal was a 241 percent increase over the NBA's deal with CBS. Through the use of weekend double-headers, the arrangement allowed for more games on television: twenty regular-season games, the All-Star Game, and up to thirty postseason games.[63] Included in the deal was the Saturday morning magazine show, which Dick Ebersol described at the time as "sort of an *Entertainment Tonight* for basketball fans."[64] The show, set to begin a week before the season opener in October and continue until a week after the July draft, would include behind-the-scenes features and player spotlights "instead of the usual NBA highlight and strategy shows found on three cable networks."[65] The NBA magazine show, now called *Inside Stuff*, would air out of NBA Entertainment's newly renovated 45,000-square-foot studio and production facility in Secaucus, New Jersey. From that studio, NBAE would also produce halftime features, advertisements and promos, and their usual slate of home videos.[66]

Now more extensively intertwined, the NBA and NBC began to work more closely together on game presentation than the league ever had with CBS. John Kosner remembered going to lunch with Ed Desser and Tommy Roy, the NBC producer in charge of professional basketball: "Poor Tommy, we had, like, three pages, single-spaced, of stuff to go through with him, of stuff that we wanted them to do."[67] After two years of working together, the organizations initiated a practice of weekly meetings. "Twelve to fourteen of us for lunch, once our season starts up, to discuss how we're promoting, how we're producing, what we're doing with features in the pregame, at halftime, what *Inside Stuff* is doing, our thoughts about the previous weekend," explained Ebersol at the time.[68] For a sports league to be contributing to a network's presentation of its games was unique at the time. When the NBA had earlier attempted the same with CBS, the network was "incredibly insulted," Kosner recalled.[69] The working relationship with NBC was thus a major step forward for the league's capability as an aspiring producer-distributor in its own right.

The league also expanded its cable arrangements. A few weeks after the NBC agreement, the NBA announced a new deal with Turner for

$275 million over four years. In an innovative agreement between the partners, the league agreed to move its cable telecasts from TBS to TNT once the latter channel's household penetration reached a large enough number.[70] TNT would carry fifty regular-season games and twenty-five playoff games per season, as well as the NBA draft, the All-Star Saturday festivities, and a new half-hour postgame show, *Inside the NBA*. David Stern also noted that TNT and NBC would be included in discussions of international television coverage, as the league continued to invest in overseas distribution.[71] NBC, in fact, had already secured the rights to air the 1990 McDonald's Open in Barcelona, a trial run for the synergistic potential of the upcoming 1992 Olympics.[72] The NBA's media-rights agreements were groundbreaking for the autonomy they provided to a sports league and reflected the deepening symbiosis between the sports and television industries. For NBC, basketball functioned as a premier television program and the NBA was accordingly treated as a genuine television production studio, transferring its show into the hands of the network for US distribution. The NBA spent the better part of the 1980s improving its media capabilities and creating an international media operation. Ultimately, NBC was able to trust the NBA's media expertise in the production of *Inside Stuff* and the studio pregame show.

At the same time, the NBA's increasing investment in national (and international) television prompted it to take issue with individual teams securing their own national contracts via "superstations," which were defined as "any commercial over-the-air television station whose broadcast signal is received outside of the local designated market area."[73] The NBA felt that the Atlanta Hawks on TBS, the Chicago Bulls on WGN, and the New Jersey Nets on WOR, for example, not only damaged "national television revenue and exposure" but "hindered the ability of local teams to sell their games."[74] As a result, the NBA reduced the number of games it allowed to air on superstations from twenty-five to twenty in 1990. TBS and WOR acquiesced, but WGN took the league to court in early 1991, challenging the organization on antitrust grounds. WGN won the lawsuit, which was upheld on appeal, allowing the station to quickly add five games to its schedule.[75]

While "the entire WGN lawsuit on the surface amounted to a dispute over the broadcasting of five games," NBA scholar John Fortunato argues that the lasting significance of the WGN dispute is in "the message of the NBA's need for the proper exposure of the product, its games, and the need to protect the largest revenue source—national television money."[76] The league's willingness to challenge a team and "to litigate to a great extent," moreover, "sent a clear signal to all the other NBA teams who might attempt to challenge the league's national television contract structure," according to Fortunato.⁷⁷ The NBA demanded control—over its national distribution partners and indeed over its own franchises. The league's actions reflect its increasing perception of itself as a media conglomerate, which felt its subsidiaries were acting counter to the best interests of the parent company.

After the resolution of the WGN lawsuit, the NBA signed a new round of rights agreements with NBC and Turner for a combined $1.1 billion over four years.⁷⁸ The Turner contract would include forty-five regulation season games and thirty-five playoff games on TNT, plus another twenty-five regular-season games and ten playoff games on TBS. As in the NBC deal, Turner would now share advertising profits with the league.⁷⁹ Soon thereafter, *Broadcasting and Cable* ran a cover story on the NBA's recent run of media success, featuring an image of a smiling David Stern holding a basketball. In the interview, the commissioner compared the NBA to Disney and the league's twenty-seven franchises to twenty-seven theme parks: "We very much think of ourselves as a global entertainment company."⁸⁰ Though the NBA had lost the conflict over the superstations, its vision of manifest destiny continued unabated.

New Frontiers: The NBA's International Offices

The NBA remained keenly aware of the potential value in privileging a global media marketplace as traditional Hollywood production studios did. Michael Curtin, writing in 1997 on the "neo-network" era of television, highlights the relationship between globalization and fragmentation, between "mass cultural forms aimed at broad national or global markets" and "forms targeted at niche audiences."⁸¹ The NBA's splitting its television packages—across a mass broadcast audience, a niche cable audience, and an international audience—reflects its engagement with these tendencies. As commercial television grew and satellite technologies evolved, the demand for cheap content greatly aided US suppliers, the NBA among them. As Silvio Waisbord has emphasized, "the fact that most systems shifted toward an 'American' model of television gave a substantial advantage to the industry that had invented it."⁸² The NBA, with basketball as its media product, was thus able to benefit from the global ecosystem as much as any Hollywood producer-distributor.

As a consequence, the NBA sought to consolidate and centralize its operations, taking on more production, distribution, and marketing responsibilities and growing a league-owned archive of materials that could aid in that process. By early 1992, David Stern made additional plans for a series of overseas satellite offices, which would give the NBA a more tangible foothold in international territories. The move was, in part, in anticipation of the global visibility that would come from the upcoming Summer Olympics in Barcelona, the first time that professional basketball players would be allowed to compete after the governing body, the International Basketball Federation, changed its rules.[83] During the commissioner's state-of-the-league address at the 1992 All-Star Weekend in February, Stern told the press that offices would be opening in the next ninety days in Hong Kong, Barcelona, and Melbourne.[84] The mandate was "to build popularity of the game of basketball and by doing so build the awareness of the NBA," using league operators to observe and more deeply imbricate themselves in the fabric of local life.[85] The overtones of imperialism were not lost on the Australian press, which sought to assuage criticism. "Fear not," explained the *Melbourne Herald Sun*, "There is no millionaire American coming to Australia to buy one of Melbourne's NBL clubs. . . . All the NBA wants is office space in Melbourne."[86]

The NBA's move reflected the increasingly commonplace approach of international television producers at this time. Jean Chalaby has examined the methods by which US-based channels, such as Discovery, National Geographic, and Bloomberg, sought to localize their offerings for international markets during the 1980s and 1990s. To find success overseas, companies relied on local offices with local staff that were well acquainted with the local media and cultural landscape.[87] The establishment of the NBA's local offices with similar market-priming responsibilities reinforces the status of basketball as a global television program and the NBA as a global television company. Simultaneously, the NBA was running advertisements in *Variety* for its international programming. "The Global Appeal of NBA Television" reads the banner across the top of one such advertisement, which features Michael Jordan leaping upward for a dunk, with a separate image of Magic Johnson driving toward the hoop. Colorful abstract lines around them indicate their motion.[88]

This global approach only intensified after the summer, when the Olympic Dream Team, which included the NBA's Magic Johnson, Michael Jordan, Charles Barkley, and Larry Bird, took home the gold medal in Barcelona.[89] After the Olympic success and the continuation of NBA's investments in global television, the media market saw a decline for all US sports except professional basketball. With the sales of licensed NBA products ballooning 103 percent in 1992, to $260 million, David Stern's vision of the NBA's global conquest went unabated. "There are 250 million potential NBA fans in the U.S., and there are 5 billion outside the U.S.," he told *Forbes* in June 1993. "We like those numbers."[90] Only a few months later, however, superstar Michael Jordan announced his retirement from basketball, after his Chicago Bulls had won their third consecutive championship over the Phoenix Suns, the first "three-peat" since Bill Russell's 1960s Boston Celtics. "It's time for me to move on to something else," Jordan told the *Chicago Sun-Times*.[91] Despite the setback of losing its most globally popular star, the NBA's expansion seemed to continue undeterred. A fourth office was opened in Geneva, which would serve as a European headquarters, while three ownership groups began to bid on a possible Toronto franchise.[92]

During the 1993–94 season, the NBA's global presence continued to grow. In February 1994, a Vancouver franchise was officially approved by the league, to be purchased by Arthur Griffiths.[93] NBA Properties, the league's marketing arm, remained heavily involved in the development of the team. Researchers hit the streets of New York, focus-testing groups of young people with a selection of colors, logos, and names. The proposed "Vancouver Mounties" eventually became the Vancouver Grizzlies, joined by the Toronto Raptors expansion team.[94] South of the United States border, the NBA also began to plan a series of exhibition games in Mexico City, which would help with the opening of a new regional office there.[95] Commissioner Stern had earlier made clear his intention to eventually open an NBA franchise in Mexico, which "would complete our North American agenda."[96] While Stern's ambition had still not come to pass as of this writing, the NBA has since added a team from Mexico to its developmental G-League, a significant step toward a professional franchise.[97]

The regional offices thus became essential to the league's expansion into markets beyond the United States, especially as international play became more commonplace. "Eventually it got to a point where it just was not humanly possible to be in two places at once," explains Terry Lyons, who became vice president of international public relations in 1993. "We're handing out rings in wherever, and the commissioner is there, and we're running Japan games an hour after that."[98] The regional offices were able to take on more of the planning burden by working closely with local interests, at which point the NBA could "bring in the troops for the event itself," Lyons added.[99] As the league has continued to expand in the twenty years since, the trend has remained the same. With more events, the various satellite offices have taken on more production and planning responsibilities and the global responsibilities of NBA Entertainment have receded, as discussed in chapter 1. Ultimately, the NBA functioned as a more globally diffuse organization, in much the same way as the "Disneys and Time Warners and Viacoms and Paramounts and Sonys" that it aspired to become.[100]

A Canadian box of Frosted Flakes® promotes the inaugural season of the Vancouver Grizzlies to young fans.

The early 1990s was thus an important transitional moment for the league office during which it hastened its transition into a full-fledged global entertainment conglomerate. Its physical operations expanded into a European headquarters in Geneva and a Latin American headquarters in Mexico City, in addition to the existing offices in Barcelona, Melbourne, and Hong Kong. The expansion of NBA play into Canada, via the Toronto Raptors and Vancouver Grizzlies, also served as an important league foothold north of the border. The satellite offices, as well as the new Canadian teams, held a twofold purpose. They allowed for a further increase in international events and they deepened the NBA's market research and localization efforts. The local knowledge gained, in turn, incentivized new and aggressive media investments. Following the success of the Olympics, the league was determined to find the best method for reaching an emerging and disparate international fan base, resulting in its more sustained investment in direct-to-consumer platforms such as the League Pass satellite service in 1994 and NBA.com in 1995. The launch of these distribution outlets, therefore, highlights the impact of the NBA's executive office on the contours of the league's circulation and the significance of basketball's mediation beyond its status as cultural pastime. The NBA remains valuable insofar as it can be successfully broadcast to audiences around the world.

Dunk Street: The NBA as Media Format

The initial expansion into Canada before the 1995 season started also served as a beachhead and a model for the sustained international expansion of the NBA's media product. The NBA had worked diligently to supplant the popularity of professional hockey and professional baseball in Canada by launching a show aimed at teens called *Dunk Street*.[101] "The content is split roughly fifty-fifty between stories produced in Canada and footage from the NBA's weekly international reel," explained Stuart Foxman of *Strategy*, a Canadian business magazine.[102] The show would ultimately succeed in providing the league with a valuable foothold on young viewers. Forty percent of the *Dunk Street* audience was eighteen years old and up, coinciding with an NBA survey that found that basketball had become the second-most-popular sport in Canada among eighteen- to twenty-four-year-olds, behind only hockey. "When the NBA launched in Canada, Commissioner Stern had said that our goal was to be the number two sport globally," said Ken Derrett, managing director of NBA Canada. "As we are the number two sport in the U.S., coming in second behind hockey in Canada would be a significant accomplishment."[103]

The Canada strategy, using localized television programs in combination with marketing research conducted by local offices, reflected the model for NBA operations around the world. Like Canada's *Dunk Street*, Japan aired a different NBA-produced version of the same program called *Fastbreak*; Mexico's was called *Rafaga*. While *Dunk Street* emphasized features and personal spotlights, *Fastbreak* contained more highlights in response to measured audience feedback and demand. Albert Moran explains the television format as containing "invariable" structuring qualities, "out of which the variable elements of an individual episode are produced."[104] Formats, such as the NBA's offerings, are a process. They remain "less than fully matured, incomplete, ever ready to incorporate further elements" that will "add, cumulatively, to its system of knowledge."[105] In addition to learning from the relative success or failure of the programs, elements are acquired from the efforts of the regional offices. Around the world, David Stern explains, NBA employees are deployed "on the ground, so that they can be part of the local scene and understand local television sponsorship, local licensing and retailing."[106] In this way, the NBA operates precisely as an international television format producer.

Formats, as the manifestation of these localization efforts, are thus inherently a kind of imperialist project. Operating in service of profit rather than conquest, formats function as an accumulation of knowledge that works to benefit the original copyright holder. Marcel Danesi has argued that global brands such as the NBA, "by co-opting local signification systems and blending them with more global ones," encourage individuals "to see themselves as members of local and global communities at once."[107] The NBA's own involvement in this process, editing and translating the programming themselves for international broadcasters, thus works to blend US and non-US interests in such a way as to craft a more marketable "global identity."[108] The NBA's formatting of its global youth programming, featuring its usual US sponsors, demonstrates an uneasy alliance between the NBA's earlier entrepreneurial efforts and a broader capitalist imperative to expand into new markets. The NBA's ability to control international programming through its international offices allows a much greater capacity for imperialistic behavior. Despite any dialogic cultural flows that may inform the NBA's actions, the accrued information simply becomes marketing research, which is fed back into the formula for the commercial benefit of the NBA and its sponsors.

The dynamic remains evident in the NBA's recent format approach, in which the league office has gone as far as to modify the sport's in-arena mise-en-scène in order to reflect international practices of fandom and improve the league's ability to adapt its telecasts to overseas contexts. During the 2007 Finals, for instance, fans in San Antonio were dressed in color-blocked white shirts to "white out" the arena, reminiscent of a passionate overseas soccer match.[109] *Sports Illustrated* took particular note of the phenomenon by 2013, using the soccer descriptor for the "sea of red" at Staples Center. In 2015, John Branch of the *New York Times* took the observation further, arguing that "with the proximity and visibility of fans surrounding a basketball court, NBA arenas . . . may represent the pinnacle, the

Game 1 of the 2007 Finals in San Antonio. The "white out" look, which has become increasingly commonplace at US sporting events, manipulates the arena space in a way that better addresses international television audiences.

near-perfect blend of allegiance, marketing and stagecraft."[110] Though the origin of this level of coordination is contested—some give credit to college football, others to hockey—its reminiscence to "the soccer model" of fandom is not.[111] Richard Giulianotti, for instance, has discussed such fan behaviors in its UK soccer context. He describes the "social solidarity" of this sort of fandom, and its enhancement of a "collective consciousness." By coordinating clothing or colors, a "display of visual solidarity," the act becomes "one of the few means by which fans scattered across the world may continue to signify their deep allegiance to a local team."[112] Douglas Kellner and Hui Zhang expand on the point in their discussion of global media spectacles. Sports fans, they argue, are "like a congregation and their cheers and boos are a form of liturgy."[113] As the NBA is broadcast globally, then, this visual solidarity becomes a spectacle to which faraway fans can connect. If the NBA perceives its sport as a media format to be adapted, such equivalences make the process easier.

Though the sport of basketball may be incorporating cultural practices from outside the United States, the league's ultimate motive remains revenue rather than genuine inclusion. This in keeping with Marwan Kraidy's concept of "corporate transculturalism," in which cultural hybridity merely serves "as an economic energy stream to be leveraged by transnational corporations and exploited by individual consumers."[114] Any genuine "progressive potential" is thus squandered by the strategic use of hybridity as a tool for economic gain.[115] The NBA, as one such corporation, has similarly sought to deploy internationalized content in order to accumulate profit on a global scale through a programming strategy that takes the television format as its guiding influence and uses flexible direct-to-consumer distribution that enables a multinational audience. While the multiculturalism of athletic competition has allowed various sports to benefit from this practice, arguably no entity has excelled more than the NBA, which has worked to cultivate a strong global presence for decades, first by embarking on overseas exhibition tours to expand its cultural footprint during the 1980s and later by opening multiple regional offices for year-round boots-on-the-ground engagement during the 1990s.

Over time, the NBA's global formatting efforts have also given way to a franchising of the NBA itself, a clear signal that the league has fashioned itself as a conglomerate large enough for multiple subsidiaries. The first instance came in June 1996, when the NBA and NBC jointly announced the Women's National Basketball Association (WNBA), which would launch the following year under a five-year revenue-sharing agreement. Featuring eight teams, playing from June to August, NBC agreed to televise ten Saturday afternoon games while ESPN and ESPN2 would each televise a game per week.[116] The WNBA thus functioned as an adaption of the NBA league format, which demonstrated the NBA's greater ambitions as a complete entertainment conglomerate as well as its continued perception of sport as media content.

A more experimental investment was for an NBA-operated football league in collaboration with Turner and NBC, who had both recently lost their NFL packages. While the NBA remained a somewhat silent partner, NBC and Turner announced the league in May 1998 at halftime of a Chicago Bulls playoff game with the NBA's full approval. The new league would feature ten to twelve teams and begin the following fall.[117] "When this new league begins it wouldn't surprise me if some NBA owners are owners of these teams," Stern coyly told the *New York Daily News*.[118] The NBA's version of a football league was eventually aborted because of the already-full plate of the WNBA and labor negotiations, but their initial involvement reflects a greater self-confidence in the NBA itself as format.[119] If the NBA's executive structure and media strategy could be translated and adapted into many different contexts, the international possibilities would become boundless. The possibilities are reflected in more recent examples of the NBA's becoming an investor and organizer in leagues around the world, including the Basketball Africa League and Brazil's Liga Nacional de Basquete, as discussed in chapter 2.[120]

Some of the NBA franchising included copycat leagues beyond their control. In China, a Hong Kong promotions firm launched the Chinese National Basketball Alliance, or CNBA. Using the NBA initials as well as NBA players in its advertising the CNBA was quickly sued by the NBA Asia office. The Chinese sports governing body had originally given permission for the CNBA to compete with the more established Chinese Basketball League (CBL), but it quickly rescinded its approval after angering the NBA and the CBL's backer, the US management company IMG.[121] Andy Jay, the chief operating officer of Spectrum, the CNBA's organizers and promoters, denied the accusation that he was copying the NBA: "Maybe we will benefit a little bit, but if you walked down the street and asked 100 people what the NBA was no one would know. It's not a household name in China."[122] The CNBA had nonetheless used English names and thirty-two US players. The NBA further clarified its stance, noting that its problem was not with the league itself but with the name alone. "We would support the development of basketball everywhere in the world. We've no problem with the league. Our problem is with the name," said Cheong Sau-ching, NBA Asia spokesperson.[123]

All the same, the CNBA name ultimately aids in the league's expansion. Ramon Lobato and Julian Thomas have noted that such informally produced instances "can extend market opportunities for brands, by making the brand visible in places where it might not otherwise be seen."[124] Like bootlegged NBA tapes that had helped the league in the Soviet Union in the 1980s, the CNBA thus provided an important "market-priming role" for the NBA.[125] As Cheong Sau-ching was suggesting, moreover, the development of NBA-caliber play only helped basketball succeed in those territories. This understanding results in the league becoming more proactive in international player development, launching a series of camps and later academies to train young athletes and prepare them for the NBA.

The NBA's youth programs can be described as a pyramid. At the bottom, Junior NBA features 60 million participants in seventy-two countries under the age of fourteen, as of the 2019–20 season.[126] Children can then advance into the NBA's more elite development programs, which includes the Basketball without Borders summer camp and the NBA Academies, of which there are now five, in China, India, Australia, Mexico, and Senegal.[127] Beginning in 2015, the NBA also launched a Basketball without Borders Global Camp to take place during All-Star Weekend, featuring the best players chosen by consensus from the training camps that occurred during the previous summer.[128] "We're identifying at a young age the top prospects in the world," explained Troy Justice, senior director of international basketball operations at the NBA. "All the NBA personnel, scouts, GMs, they're all there in the gym watching these kids, getting a chance to scout them."[129]

By any measure, then, the Global Camp and its broader international development pipeline have been an unqualified success for the NBA in cultivating a number of players that have kept the league's global engine running, including Joel Embiid, Pascal Siakam, and Danilo Gallinari.[130] The Global Camp aids the NBA's media efforts, as the internationalization of its "cast" of athletes allows the league to more easily appeal to prospective fans around the world, much as the traditional television format does, which is often "indigenized" through local actors.[131] By taking greater control over production and distribution, opening subsidiary satellite offices around the world, and formatting its programming as well as its own executive structure, the NBA established itself as a legitimate media conglomerate that prepared for many more years of international growth.

Conclusion: Cable and Control

In January 2002, the NBA officially left its decade-long partnership with NBC and announced its new deals with ABC/ESPN and Turner, totaling $4.6 billion over six years, which would allow the league to reach new heights as an integrated producer-distributor. Not only would the league be more heavily investing in cable distribution, via ESPN, but the deal included an unnamed new sports channel to be owned jointly by Turner and the NBA. ESPN would receive twenty-four playoff games, including one of the Conference Finals, as well as the NBA draft and draft lottery. As broadcast partner, ABC would air fifteen regular-season games, five early-round playoff games, and the NBA Finals. Turner, meanwhile, would take the All-Star Game from NBC, in addition to a massive increase in exclusive regular-season and postseason coverage.[132]

The deal signaled the launch of a new era for the NBA and the wider sports media industry. The joint move to ABC and ESPN, in addition to incumbent cable partner TNT, reinforced the further dominance of cable over broadcast television. The NBA's investments in the medium thus reflect an industry in transition. While the league still required the mass address that remained possible only on ABC, it also sought a more flexible schedule that only cable could provide. The new industrial implications were not lost on trade magazine analysts, who took the move as a broader indication that "sports television is definitely making its way from network TV to cable," though the NBA, in particular, was "unique in that the vast majority of the games will be on cable."[133] The $2.2 billion from AOL Time Warner and the $2.4 billion from Disney-ABC-ESPN, at roughly $765 million annually, also offered a 25 percent raise over NBC's final deal at $615 million per year.[134]

The money was certainly an incentive for the NBA's transition to cable, but so too was the opportunity for more extensive control within the league office. Russ Granik, deputy commissioner at the time, explained the relative inflexibility of broadcast television, which would "wait until Sweeps were over in June before you'd see an NBA game on a weekday night. . . . I think that was almost as important as dollars, was to try and get the games out there to more fans at more and more convenient times." In splitting the majority of the package between TNT and ESPN, "it gave us a lot more and better coverage of what were still to us important games," Granik noted.[135] This new cable-centric strategy is reflected in the 2002 deals, wherein the number of regular-season games on broadcast television was reduced from thirty-two to fifteen. They were replaced by a greater number of prime-time games on cable: TNT was set to air fifty-two games in prime time, in addition to the All-Star Weekend events and the first two rounds of the playoffs, while ESPN would air an additional seventy-five regular-season games, the NBA draft, and a variety of postseason play, before handing off responsibilities to ABC for the Finals.[136]

On the Turner side of the new television agreements, the NBA's level of input and control also continued to expand. Like the autonomy provided by NBC in 1989–90, as a product of the NBA's early success as a producer during the 1980s, Turner sought to become a more equitable and collaborative partner with the NBA office. Mark Lazarus, president of Turner Entertainment and later NBC's chairman of broadcasting and sports, witnessed the media innovations and aggressiveness of the league firsthand throughout the 1990s. "I really do think that they think of themselves as a content company, not as a sports league," he explained. "They really were the first sports league to see the value, I think, of controlling their content and having business not just in the rights-fee realm but in distributing their own content and being able to generate revenue from that."[137] Lazarus's confidence in the NBA's media savvy would even lead to the proposal of a new joint cable network to feature programming beyond basketball, tentatively titled the All Sports Network, which would draw from Turner's CNN and *Sports Illustrated* holdings, as well as possible rights deals with other professional sports leagues.[138] Though the plan would fall through by July 2002, the arrangement reflected the NBA's growing media ambitions and its capabilities as a media producer-distributor. Ultimately, AOL Time Warner chose to invest instead in the NBA's own established digital cable channel, which would be renamed NBA TV from the unwieldy NBA.com TV, at $45 million for a 10 percent stake.[139] The NBA was now playing in the big leagues of television.

With the streaming revolution steadily brewing in the background by the early 2000s, cable distribution had more publicly ascended over broadcast television. By the 2003–4 television season, basic cable finally overtook network television in the percentage of households viewing in primetime, a gap that continued to grow in cable's favor over the next several years.[140] In adding more of its programming slate to cable, the NBA contributed to this transition by further enhancing the medium's distinct offerings. Where once sport was a hallmark of network television, as exemplified by *Monday Night Football* and *The Wide World of Sports*, the NBA helped lead the charge onto cable television, where sports could fill more hours of the schedule at more favorable times. CBS and NBC relegated the NBA to weekend afternoons, as they had for most sports, but ESPN and TNT could continue to air NBA games in prime time throughout the week. When *Monday Night Football* left ABC for ESPN after the 2005 season, the move was part of a trend demonstrated earlier by the NBA.[141] Sport and cable continued to grow together, the latest iteration of the "symbiosis" proposed by Robert McChesney, whose ambitions remained aligned to the pursuit of profit.[142] Cable could use prime-time sporting events to compete with broadcast programming, while sports leagues gained more extensive oversight of their product, more prestigious time slots, and greater leverage in rights negotiations.

The NBA's deepening investment in cable distribution over broadcast thus reflects scholarship that describes the period as the post-network era. I follow Amanda D. Lotz's timeline, in particular, which effectively periodizes television as consisting of a network era (1952 to mid-1980s), multichannel transition (mid-1980s through mid-2000s), and post-network era (early 2000s onward), the last of which is defined by its nonlinearity and viewer control. The character of the post-network era emerged out of the programming multiplicity and audience fragmentation of the multichannel transition (i.e., cable and satellite) and intensified with the aid of advanced computing power and bandwidth. The post-network era, with "new tools" and an audience "fractured among different channels and devices" is thus "profoundly different" in nature from the network era.[143] It was in the early 2000s, then, that the NBA's executive office truly emerged as a genuine media conglomerate. The NBA's cultivation of internet and cable distribution, through League Pass, NBA.com, and NBA TV, presented the possibility for direct and simultaneous programming that could successfully reach viewers around the world within a fractured media landscape, outside the strictures of a traditional network-driven ecosystem. As the number of digital platforms and devices have expanded, so too have the NBA's ambitions and its capabilities. In the next chapter, the home viewing space offers an increasing number of opportunities for global direct-to-consumer programming, as the NBA and its peers evolve into an era of streaming television, social media, and sports betting.

CHAPTER 5

The Couch

At-Home Sport Spectatorship and the Multiplatform Viewing Environment

Before the 2017–18 NBA season, the league decided to cut the number of timeouts per game from 18 to 14 and also reduced the number of timeouts during the final two minutes from three to two. In the announcement, Commissioner Adam Silver, who succeeded David Stern during the 2013–14 season, said the move was designed to improve "the pace and the flow of the game."[1] While Silver's statement was certainly true, there was more motivation behind the decision. Internal research by the NBA had indicated that during timeouts, viewers often switched the channel and never returned.[2] Moreover, in order to accommodate the demands of advertisers, the league eliminated the use of "short" twenty-second timeouts and "full" hundred-second timeouts, replacing them with uniform seventy-five-second timeouts, which would allow for the more consistent use of commercial time for the television audience. While the execution of these mandates were worked out in collaboration with the league's Basketball Operations department, the decision followed from the demands of the sport's media presentation first and foremost.[3]

As the industrial forces of sports media move from the court, into the arena, through the wires, and across the floors of the NBA's corporate offices, they ultimately settle into viewers' homes, driving a vast multi-platform media ecosystem of televisions, smart devices, and video-game consoles. The flow includes a fan sitting on the couch watching a game on television while posting about it to Twitter on a smartphone. It includes out-of-home viewers like the fan making the daily commute on the train while catching highlights on the House of Highlights social media pages, operated by Bleacher Report, which is owned by Turner. It also includes someone placing bets on FanDuel, the NBA's official betting partner, while watching a mobile-view stream from the NBA platform operated in partnership with Turner. As the home viewing space has become increasingly fragmented, the NBA's various multiplatform investments have prepared it to succeed in the competition for attention. The present chapter highlights the NBA's historical use of digital means to cultivate viewership, as well as the modern media ecosystem, in which sports leagues and their media partners draw on social media, statistics, news, and betting to drive viewers to telecasts, whether on cable or on dedicated streaming services.

Ultimately, the endless hours of live sports, highlights, and analysis have enhanced the synergistic potential for large conglomerates such as Disney (ESPN) and AT&T (Turner). It has also sustained a seemingly endless number of upstart streaming services, such as DAZN and fuboTV and driven ongoing investments by Amazon in the live sports landscape, which purchased the exclusive rights to the NFL's *Thursday Night Football*, the Women's National Basketball Association (WNBA), and a select package of New York Yankees games.[4] Revenues from streaming still lag behind revenues from cable television, but the gap between them has considerably narrowed since 2010.[5] By the close of 2018, ESPN was down nearly 15 million cable and satellite subscribers from 2011, equating to an estimated $1.44 billion in lost revenue.[6] Streaming services, meanwhile, have excelled. The combined number of worldwide streaming subscriptions, an estimated 613 million, finally exceeded the 556 million global subscribers of cable television in 2019.[7] ESPN launched a standalone streaming service, ESPN+, hoping to capitalize on the trend and make up for lost revenue.[8] After five months of operation, the service had already reached one million paid subscribers and, after another five months, the total had doubled to two million.[9]

The push toward streaming and multiplatform viewing, of course, is not merely about following audiences but about the industrywide initiative toward the most lucrative possible outcome. Viewers on streaming platforms can be much more easily tracked by platform managers, who provide valuable consumer data to content providers. As discussed in chapter 3, Endeavor Streaming, which manages international streaming platforms for the NBA, NFL, and UFC, regularly provides information on audiences that enables their clients to create strategic pricing models designed to extract the maximum possible revenue. As discussed in chapter 1, moreover, the niche address of particular teams, such as the Sacramento Kings' push into India and the Houston Rockets' historical success in China, creates lucrative global opportunities for advertisers via streaming. As a result of streaming's ability to reach increasingly fragmented audiences, many major cable providers have since launched or are set to launch streaming services of their own, including the aforementioned ESPN+ as well as HBO Max and NBC Peacock, rearranging their revenues as cable subscriptions continue to decline.

At the same time, the spontaneity and mass address of sport has helped to keep linear television alive, since major sporting events regularly draw the largest possible audiences for live viewing and thus the largest payouts from advertisers. Sports leagues, therefore, exist in a dialectical relationship with their audiences. The NBA, for instance, wants its media content to be accessible wherever there are the most viewers but, at the same time, viewers can watch only where the NBA is made available. As viewers cut their cable subscriptions en masse, the NBA has expanded the reach of its streaming service, going as far as to sign a deal with Amazon to make League Pass available on the Prime platform.[10]

Steve Hellmuth, NBA's executive vice president of media operations and technology, explained that since the early days of the internet, a sports website's most important services have been the *schedule* and the *scores*: "When can I watch and what's the score?"[11] News, features, and highlights offer additional context, which can be useful in drawing more viewers to the actual games. "All of those things, to us, were engagement tools to get people to watch more TV, what we were really monetizing," Hellmuth notes of the NBA's original website.[12] The approach has remained consistent while incorporating social media platforms that can similarly direct attention to the telecasts on ABC/ESPN, TNT, or the league's own streaming service. The trajectory of this chapter follows from Hellmuth's assertion by examining the various aspects of *television* (both linear and nonlinear), *numbers* (i.e., statistics and gambling), and *news* (especially via social media) that regularly engage viewers. In doing so, the chapter highlights the increasingly global nature of media viewership and sports spectatorship as they converge and adopt a more international address across a multitude of media platforms within the space of the home.

Hoop Heaven: Sports Television as Multiplatform Multiplex

The television ecosystem of the 2010s and 2020s has been increasingly driven by the principles of "connected viewing," which Kevin Sanson and Jennifer Holt have defined as an initiative "across the media industries to integrate digital technology and socially networked communication with traditional media practices."[13] The landscape is characterized by "the continued marriage of hardware and software into one ecosystem," as streaming platforms, linear television, and social media become integrated across television sets, smartphones, and laptops.[14] There are now more than three hundred streaming services available in the United States, for instance, which only stands to multiply as the COVID-19 pandemic has led to a substantial increase in the number of hours that viewers spend streaming content in the safety of their homes.[15] "If every streaming launch or direct-to-consumer pivot was a preamble teasing what streaming could do," argues Julia Alexander in *The Verge*, "our reality right now is a clear depiction of what it's like when more people are forced to rely on entertainment they can access inside their homes."[16]

While the current streaming boom may last, or could recede along with the pandemic, the increase still reflects a longer ongoing trend toward web-based television. Forecasts by *Digital TV Research* in late 2020 predicted that global revenues from cable and satellite will fall to $152 billion by 2025, down from a peak of $202 billion in 2016.[17] Global revenues for subscription streaming services still follow behind at about $50 billion, but the number is expected to double to $100 billion by 2025.[18] One medium is declining as the other is expanding; a clear power shift has taken hold. Concurrent with the rise of streaming, the nature of internet use has also changed substantially, shifting from web browsers and desktop and laptop computers to dedicated mobile applications and smart devices.[19] This affects how and where media companies seek to monetize. Connected viewing, as a strategy for producer-distributors, can reach fragmented audiences who are split across all the available devices and platforms by presenting "the promise of constant connectivity," which is especially useful in keeping sports fans engaged with one another and with their teams.[20]

As traditional television and the web converge onto the same platforms, viewers increasingly act as users, choosing the platforms and services that they want to watch and when they want to watch. The NBA provides an important precedent for the connected multiplatform ecosystem in its cable investments during the mid-1990s, which highlight a transition from an approach that privileged the artificial scarcity of programming to one that valued the circulation of as much content as possible across as many channels as possible. The "multiplex," as it was called, was inspired by an initial experiment by HBO in 1991 unrelated to sport at all. In May, HBO announced plans to "multiplex" its HBO and Cinemax channels, in which programming would now be spread out over several channels, such as an East Coast and West Coast feed, in order to present subscribers with as much variety as possible without actually expanding their content holdings.[21] The test started small, in Texas and Kansas under the management of the TeleCable Corporation, though multiple-system cable operators expressed an interest in participating in the experiment.[22] After a successful initial run, HBO continued its multiplex experiment, to the chagrin of competing cable channels, including Showtime and Encore, who feared that subscribers would drop their channels in favor of the fuller HBO slate. Within a year, in fact, Nielsen ratings had shown HBO viewership up by as much as 80 percent. John Billock, HBO executive vice president of sales and marketing, refuted the concerns of competitors, explaining that "HBO has no hidden agenda. Multiplexing is not exclusive to HBO."[23] Before long, other cable channels indeed began to take HBO up on this offer.

The NBA and its cable partner Turner, which owned and operated both TBS and TNT, would be one such entity. After HBO's strategy demonstrated that total programming hours could be far more profitable for the NBA than a more selective slate of games, the league would launch an NBA postseason multiplex across TBS and TNT. This evolving strategy was a major shift from the "less is more" approach that brought the league ratings legitimacy in the 1980s. Instead of thinking about cannibalization, John Kosner and Ed Desser combined their insights from the Broadcasting and TV Ventures departments and began to value *cumulative* ratings. "It was unheard of, prior to that time, for anyone to have multiple games on at the same time," explained Desser. "You're going to cannibalize your own rating, that isn't going to be a good idea."[24] Inspired by HBO's success, the NBA adopted an altogether new perspective.[25] If a single game airing unopposed at 8 pm were to average a 3 rating, as opposed to two games head-to-head averaging 1.9 and 1.7 ratings, the cumulative rating would add up to a 3.6 rating versus a 3.0 rating—more people, in total, would be watching the games. "The idea of getting more games created more value and it all came back to that first premise: let's put our most valuable stuff on television," recalled John Kosner.[26] The introduction of the multiplex was thus a major step forward in the NBA's overall media strategy, reflecting the additional introduction of a satellite service, a cable channel, and a website. The more NBA content on the air, and the more total consumers and viewers, the better—concerns about ratings cannibalization were an issue of the past. It was a media strategy ideally suited to the burgeoning digital age.

In April 1994, the NBA officially began its multiplex coverage of the playoffs, splitting games across TBS and TNT. Though the idea originated with HBO, news coverage credited NBA and Turner with the invention. "Turner is calling this concept 'multiplexing,'" reported the *Atlanta Journal and Constitution*, which also noted that the order came from the NBA league office and Turner had simply obliged them.[27] "Multiplex," reported the *San Diego Union-Tribune*, is "the name David Stern & Co. came up with" to air forty playoff games across the channels. The next year's postseason in 1995 would finally feature every single NBA playoff game on television, across NBC, TNT, and TBS.[28] On Thursdays and Fridays, TBS would air games at 7 pm and 9:30 pm and TNT games would begin at 8 pm and 10:30 pm.[29] By the close of 1996, led by the success of its NBA programming, TNT would finish first in the prime-time cable ratings for the first time ever, surpassing USA Network's 2.0 ratings average with a 2.1.[30]

The NBA's multiplex thus encouraged a more active viewer, who could jump across two channels to watch simultaneous programming, seeking out the best games. While the NFL had aired games head-to-head across its broadcast partners since 1970, when it signed deals with CBS and NBC, the NBA's approach was unique in that it actively marketed to viewers the sheer tonnage of programming and the ability to switch between games.[31] A 1997 commercial for the playoffs on TNT and TBS, for instance, sold viewers on "40 games in 30 nights," imploring them, "don't miss a game."[32] Don Maguire, senior vice president and executive producer for Turner Sports, even marketed the idea of viewer choice and switching between channels: "Instead of having us making the decision in the studio as to which game you can see," he explained, "it goes to the control of the consumer who can make his choice with a flick of the wrist in his living room."[33] Soon thereafter, the emergence of the internet and streaming as viable distribution technologies only expanded the global possibilities of the original multiplex strategy. The launches of NBA.com and NBA League Pass in 1995 and the NBA's broadband service in 2007 offered the ability to disseminate games to everyone, everywhere, all at once. The league's aggressive approach to programming set a precedent for cross-platform connectivity and engagement that other organizations would be forced to follow.

The institution of multiple media platforms and their opportunities for twenty-four-hour programming thus reflect a transition to a contemporary post-network concept of media flow. For Bernard Miège, flow is continuous and requires daily contact and entails "the development of audience loyalty" and a "wide variety of consumption preferences."[34] Miège's definition is especially reflective of contemporary media viewing habits, which exist "outside prime time or overlap and stretch prime time's borders in unpredictable ways."[35] The NFL's Game Pass service, the NBA's League Pass service, and the MLB.TV service, for example, all address an imagined multinational audience, who can watch any game at any time. Victoria E. Johnson, moreover, argues that "the expansion of digital broadcast, satellite

A 1997 print advertisement for the NBA's forty games in thirty nights across TNT and TBS, encouraging viewers to switch channels and maximize the action.

television providers, and the growth of digital tier and streaming services," which began in the mid-1990s, "saw the flourishing of out-of-market sports league subscription packages," including the NFL's Sunday Ticket and MLB's Extra Innings as well as NBA League Pass.[36] These services also created new viewing possibilities for audiences outside the boundaries of the home. More than five thousand bars and restaurants, for instance, subscribed to NFL Sunday Ticket in 1995, the first season that the package was available to DirecTV subscribers.[37] The 2019 measurements demonstrated that

71 percent of adults 25 to 34 years old had viewed sport in a bar or restaurant, followed by the 18–24-year-old demographic at 70 percent, and viewers over 35 years old at 63 percent. More than 30 percent of 18–24-year-old respondents, moreover, noted that they watched games at a gym or fitness center, and an average of 53 percent of respondents, across all demographics, noted that they had viewed games in someone else's home. (Out-of-home viewing numbers inevitably declined later, during the COVID-19 pandemic's lengthy global quarantines.)[38]

Whether inside or outside one's own literal "home," the results are in keeping with the multiplex media strategy that emerged during the 1990s, in which sports leagues leveraged new distribution opportunities to solicit more viewers in more places. Cumulative ratings became more important than single measurements, a small step toward the contemporary valuation of combined metrics like "engagement" that prioritize clicks and eyeballs in various forms. As Johnson explains, the multiplatform era of television is defined by "hybridity," with which sports programming is particularly compatible, in that "consumers are encouraged to seek out new information and make connections among dispersed media content."[39] Where the original cable multiplex primarily valued cumulative television ratings, the modern multiplatform iteration has added measurement tools such as clicks, shares, and viewing time to determine audience interest across devices. By engaging those same kinds of programming strategies and consumption patterns, the establishment of the NBA multiplex helped to position the league for the multiplatform era to come.

Numbers Games: Fantasy Sport and Sports Betting

NBA.com was conceptualized as a direct-to-consumer platform that could direct fans' attention through real-time statistics in order to create additional value for telecasts, as Steve Hellmuth noted.[40] As profit models continued to coalesce and shift within the online media landscape, fantasy sports emerged as another important aspect of the digital space. By the mid-1990s, competition intensified. A variety of fantasy sports websites had launched, some independent and some with large institutional backing. Sites such as Internet Baseball League, Cheesesteak League, CyberSoccer, Alpha Sim, Gametime Challenge, and Small World all began to compete for a piece of the growing fantasy sports business.[41] Fox Sports signed a deal with MCI Communications to help develop its fantasy sports services, and NBC signed a deal with Microsoft on an NFL-specific venture. The Starwave-programmed fantasy sport services for the ESPN website, meanwhile, continued to set the industry pace, achieving a reported two thousand users at $40 per premium subscription.[42]

The act of transforming fantasy sport from a pen-and-paper pastime into an internet-driven service was not without conflict, as fantasy sports drew on the same real-time statistics that sports leagues sought to control and leverage. Thus, as online fantasy sport was becoming increasingly popular and online statistics increasingly important, sports leagues opted to fight against media providers such as Fox and ESPN, who had begun hosting their own fantasy sport services outside the leagues' purview. In the summer of 1996, a legal opportunity presented itself. The NBA sued Motorola and its partner Sports Team Analysis and Tracking Systems (STATS) over a special pager service called SportsTrax, which transmitted live scores of NBA games.[43] The NBA, hoping to maintain greater control over what was becoming a fundamental media asset, argued that because game scores and data simulated NBA action, these statistics should be considered its intellectual property.[44] The defendants, meanwhile, contended that their services transmitted only "bare-bones facts" of the game, with no real sense of the plays being made.[45]

Comprehending the massive First Amendment implications for the future of the media landscape, the *New York Times* and the *Associated Press* both filed briefs in support of Motorola, while the NFL, MLB, NHL, and even NBA broadcast partner NBC filed in support of the NBA.[46] Robin Bierstedt, the deputy general counsel for Time Inc., which had decided to sit out the case, explained to the *New York Times*, "A basketball game is news, not a performance, and as such should not be subject to a proprietary interest of a party."[47] In September 1996, the district court ruled in favor of the NBA, by which point the league had already gained enough confidence to pursue an additional lawsuit against AOL, which had also been working with STATS to provide real-time score updates on its web platform.[48] Motorola appealed the decision, of course, and in January 1997, the ruling was overturned in the US Court of Appeals for the Second Circuit. "With regard to the NBA's primary products—producing basketball games with live attendance and licensing copyrighted broadcasts of those games—there is no evidence that anyone regards SportsTrax or the AOL site as a substitute for attending NBA games or watching them on television," argued Ralph K. Winter Jr. on behalf of the circuit court judges.[49] While this remained true as of 1996, that statistical updates could not replicate the experience of an actual game, Winter's point would be put to the test in the years that followed, as media organizations saw an opportunity to craft ever-more advanced visualizations of sporting

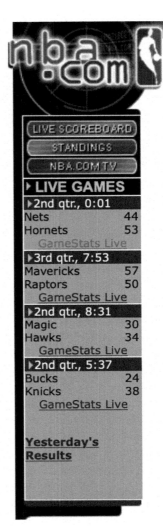

Live scores on the NBA website c. 2001, which the league hoped would direct fans' attention to exciting games on television.

events using only "bare-bones facts," in the parlance of Motorola's defense attorneys.

The decision explicitly protected media providers from further lawsuits involving the transmission of basic facts and numbers, such as scores and time remaining in the game, which was the foundation of the growing fantasy sports industry. With freely available and updated statistics, participants could seamlessly follow their players, teams, and matchups in a single accessible platform.[50] In the wake of the decision, without any need for licensing fees or rights negotiations with the major sports leagues, fantasy sports exploded more widely than ever before. By the summer of 1997, CNN/Sports Illustrated made a stronger push into online distribution, including online fantasy sports, an area where the company felt it could defeat ESPN by undercutting ESPN's prices.[51] ESPN had since reduced the cost of its own premium options to $29.95 for a season pass, down from $40, to stay competitive. Fantasy football remained the website's single most popular option, at fifty thousand participants, though the company claimed to have exceeded six figures in overall registrations for its fantasy offerings.[52] Small World, meanwhile, continued to emerge as a fantasy competitor, signing an agreement to provide more robust fantasy programming on the Fox Sports website, before also signing with CNN/SI in 1999.[53] By then, an estimated four million users were thought to be playing fantasy sports online, double the total from 1996, not long after ESPN and the NBA launched their original web ventures with Starwave.[54] Only a year later, the estimate had risen to somewhere between 10 and 20 million users, as people increasingly used the internet to seek advice and track statistics.[55]

As the number of fantasy sport participants skyrocketed, so did the number of news features showcasing the game's ascent from novelty to the mainstream, many of which drew attention to the significance of real-time statistics for the success of the enterprise. In *USA Today*, for instance, columnist Michael Hiestand described how "web sites have simplified fantasy sports" with their "automated databases," thus "making them appealing to fans that don't have time to slog through box scores."[56] In the *New York Times*, too, writer Tom Watson colorfully described how "complex corporate computer networks and high-speed Net connections will be used to track the progress of teams like Jimbo's Bombers and the Amazin' Jakes as executives sweat the decision to drop $11 million in funny money on Mark McGwire while leaving the bullpen to the likes of Turk Wendell."[57] Through real-time statistical updates, websites such as ESPN, Small World, CBS Sportsline, CNN/SI, and Fox Sports simplified the experience of fantasy sports for its participants by integrating fantasy sports services, sports news, and statistical databases. In early 2000, with the increasingly fundamental role of online statistics in the success of fantasy sport, Fox's parent company, News Corp., purchased STATS in order to bring those operations in-house and better position Fox Sports as the leading online provider of real-time statistics.[58]

The fact that *NBA v. Motorola* has continued to be upheld has not stopped other professional sports leagues from trying to privatize their statistics, nor has it stopped media organizations from trying to push the boundaries of what might be considered public information in a court of law. ESPN, for instance, launched its first "gamecast" visualization as early as August 20, 1997, for the ongoing baseball season—only a few months after Motorola's successful appeal—which featured a "diamond view" graphic, pitch-by-pitch updates, and "mouse over" indicators for base runners and fielders.[59] Without any intellectual property barriers, descriptive play-by-play updates became integral to the execution of fantasy sport platforms, allowing participants to follow the games and their own teams in extreme detail. In 2006, MLB made one last significant bid for the league control of statistics and by extension fantasy sport, by ignoring the ruling altogether and requiring compensation for such data. When MLB was successfully sued for its actions by CBC Distribution and Marketing, the decision crucially served to affirm and modernize the NBA case on the legal grounds of players' "right of publicity." US District judge Mary Ann Medler argued in her ruling, however, that "the names and playing records of MLB players as used by CBC in its fantasy baseball games are akin to the names, towns and telephone numbers in a phone book, to census data, and to news of the day."[60] Crucially, explained Medler, "even if the players have a claimed right of publicity, the First Amendment takes precedence over such a right," echoing the earlier victory of Motorola over the NBA.[61] Through the case of *CBC v. MLBAM*, the *NBA v. Motorola* decision was updated and upheld in a more advanced media environment, which had since come to include even more detailed representations of sports information.

By 2017, an estimated 59.3 million people were playing fantasy sports, up from 12.6 million people in 2005 when CBC sued MLBAM, and up from the 1 to 3 million annual participants from 1991 to 1994, according to the Fantasy Sports and Gaming Association.[62] In the nascent internet economy, companies such as ESPN and Fox Sports were able to flourish online by relying on publicly available information while privatizing their particular iterations of fantasy sports services. The leagues, of course, still retained media rights and all other sorts of licensing revenues, but fantasy sports and statistics were left to external firms in the wake of the aforementioned court battles. By maintaining sports statistics as fact-based news, the ruling in *NBA v. Motorola* removed the NBA and its peers as potentially major impediments to the proliferation of fantasy sport.

More recently, the creation and widespread legalization of daily fantasy sports (DFS) has altered the possibilities of the relationship between leagues, fantasy sport, and sports television. Considered by most states to be a game of skill, rather than gambling, services like FanDuel (launched in 2009) and DraftKings (launched in 2012) prompt users to draft specifically priced players of their choice under an imposed salary cap. The partnership between FanDuel and the NBA, in particular, most profoundly points the path forward for the possibilities of an integrated media ecosystem, which encompasses betting, television, and the internet. The NBA, which has an equity arrangement with FanDuel, offered a free-to-enter "prop bet bingo" during the 2018 All-Star Game's Saturday night skill challenges.[63] Using the FanDuel website or mobile app, the first to call "bingo" by pressing a designated button was awarded $1,000. Second through tenth place received $200, then $100 through twentieth place, down to $2 for those between 2001st and 4725th. The props, like an appearance by rapper Drake or a LeBron James commercial, affected how fans engaged the festivities by making them wait for specific occurrences. The NBA's ultimate goal is to boost viewership by raising the stakes for fans, encouraging people to watch games that they might not ordinarily watch. A late-season game without any playoff implications suddenly matters to anyone wagering on DFS. Accordingly, all NBA contests on FanDuel feature a banner that encourages fans to follow along live by signing up for its streaming service, League Pass. More betting equals more viewers, which results in higher advertising rates and higher revenues. "When consumers engage with fantasy sports, they consume more sports content," explained Mike Raffensperger, chief marketing officer for FanDuel.[64]

All-Star Bingo highlights the synergistic potential between the NBA and FanDuel, encouraging greater attention to games through financial incentives for viewer participants.

The strategy has only expanded as the DFS industry has transitioned into proper sports betting. In May 2018, in the case of *Murphy v. National Collegiate Athletic Association*, the US Supreme Court ruled unconstitutional the Professional and Amateur Sports Protection Act of 1992, which had effectively banned sports betting nationwide. In overturning the law, the Supreme Court allowed states to decide whether to legalize the activity.[65] By the close of 2020, twenty-six states had either legalized sports betting or made plans to do so. Some states will allow only in-person betting, but many will allow individuals to place wagers through their digital devices.[66] The most popular platforms for sports betting, moreover, are operated by DraftKings and FanDuel, which have quickly expanded their business models to become fully functional sportsbooks in their own right, competing with legacy companies like MGM and Caesar's. In July 2018, FanDuel opened its first physical location in New Jersey, and DraftKings became the first to offer mobile betting in the state in August, in partnership with Resorts Casino Hotel in Atlantic City.[67] The paradigm developed by DFS thus points to an even deeper integration of television and betting, wherein fans can watch live games on television or streaming while wagering throughout on their smart devices.

Over time, leagues beyond the NBA have seen gambling as an opportunity to improve fan interest and improve ratings. FanDuel, for instance, signed a leaguewide partnership with the NHL as well as deals with specific teams, such as the NFL's Denver Broncos and the NBA's Memphis Grizzlies.[68] "FanDuel is going to be a pretty significant part of the broadcasting presence when fans are watching games on Fox Sports Southeast," explained Anthony Macri, vice president of partnership marketing for the Grizzlies. "Not just the branding of being on-screen, but they're going to find ways to enhance our broadcast and make it better for betting fans and also the average fans looking to find information on other teams, players, and games around the league." Other NBA teams, such as the Philadelphia 76ers, Boston Celtics, and Indiana Pacers, signed similar agreements with DraftKings, which also agreed to a leaguewide partnership with the NFL.[69] These collaborations have extended to television providers as well. After Sinclair Broadcast Group purchased twenty-one regional Fox Sports networks from Disney in 2019, the channels were relaunched in March 2021 as Bally Sports Networks, in partnership with Bally's Corporation, a casino operator with properties in seven states.[70] The same month, Dish Network and DraftKings came to a landmark agreement that will allow Dish subscribers to place bets through their television set-tops.[71] By integrating gambling into leagues' media output, sportsbooks are able to funnel interest from the game into their dedicated digital platforms, and a greater interest in one's wagers is thought to improve television ratings for both local and national telecasts. During the 2019 NFL season, for instance, the league saw its ratings increase by 5 percent on linear television and 45 percent on digital platforms over the previous season. While it is not clear how large a role legalized betting played in such increases, many attributed the improvement to gambling, including New York Giants co-owner Steve Tisch.[72]

After the *NBA v. Motorola* decision, which helped fuel the rise of online fantasy sport by ensuring the free, public availability of real-time statistics, the establishment of DFS and the legalization of sports betting have offered sports leagues a way to reacquire control over the domestic viewing space. Victoria E. Johnson has described how, in the post-network era, sports television has come to be "characterized by individuated modes of address and à la carte packets of information and alerts delivered to the desktop, laptop, or hand-held mobile media device."[73] Ethan Tussey, in his work on the procrastination economy and workplace media, similarly uses the example of Fox Sports' *Lunch with Benefits* midday slate to highlight sports' ability "to provide snackable content" and take advantage of the "versatility of mobile devices."[74] Fantasy sports, and now sports betting, have become a driving force of this sports media ecosystem across its vast multiplatform network of mobile apps, websites, YouTube channels, and television programs. Using real-time statistical updates and real-money wagers, the fantasy and betting landscape has allowed leagues to drive even greater attention to their sports and telecasts, fulfilling the goal of NBA.com as a direct-to-consumer tool and monetizing viewers' sustained attention more effectively than ever before.

Houses of Highlights: Digital News and Social Media

In January 2019, ESPN basketball writer Zach Lowe appeared on *The Full 48* podcast, produced by *Bleacher Report* and hosted by sportswriter Howard Beck, after a nighttime news cycle that saw a viral video of Houston Rockets star James Harden being hit in the face by the ball. In response, Lowe posited, "I think the NBA, the less it becomes about the game, I think at some point the NBA is going to have to look at itself in mirror and say, are we about basketball or are we about player movement and three screens and Twitter and all this stuff, or . . . do we care about the actual on-court product and people understanding it? . . . It's less about the game than ever before and it just trends more and more in that direction."[75] Lowe's sentiment reflects the expansion of the league's media ambitions beyond its interest in the sport of basketball. There is irony, however, in its airing on *The Full 48* podcast, whose producer, *Bleacher Report*, is owned by the NBA's longtime cable and digital partner Turner Broadcasting System—one of the most significant contributors to the transformation of sport into media content first and foremost. Over time, the journalistic qualities of organizations like *ESPN*, *Sports Illustrated*, and *Bleacher Report* have increasingly receded, functioning more like statistics, fantasy sport, and sports betting, in building storylines and drama that will enhance the stakes of games and direct viewers' attention to telecasts on partner networks.

The relationship between sports leagues and the press underwent a substantial shift during the 1990s, especially in the NBA, as reporters were moved back from courtside in favor of more valuable seats for paying spectators. "The newspapers became less important to the league to sell the product," recalled Harvey Araton, longtime sports columnist for the *New York Times*, and so "the owners decided, why the heck are we using that space where the reporters are sitting, when we don't really care where they sit anymore. We can sell those for thousands of dollars to people who can afford it."[76] Marc Spears, an NBA writer for *Yahoo! Sports*, recalled another diminishment of reporters' role: the "minders" who began to police postgame interviews with players. "It's almost like, 'Ok, we can't censor you, but we're going to make you uncomfortable and make the player uncomfortable, too, so you don't [get] anything [he] shouldn't say.'"[77] Such policies, of course, did not apply to reporters from the NBA's own media partners, such as ESPN or Turner. "Whoever pays the broadcast rights to a sport receives the better treatment," notes sportswriter Mike Freeman, adding that "it is common for ESPN reporters covering professional football to receive access print reporters can only dream of."[78]

Such preferential treatment ensures a more favorable depiction of the NFL or NBA by its partners and more effectively promotes the sport on those networks. Such a relationship thus raises significant questions about the journalistic profile of an organization like ESPN. Many have been particularly critical of ESPN's coverage of concussions in the NFL. In August 2013, ESPN coproduced a docuseries with PBS on the NFL's inadequate handling of head trauma, *League of Denial*, before abruptly removing their name from the project. A report in the *New York Times* alleged that ESPN caved in to pressure from the NFL after a "combative" lunch meeting in which the league expressed "irritation with the direction of the documentary."[79] In October, though, the accompanying *League of Denial* book, written by two ESPN reporters, was nonetheless heavily promoted by ESPN across its web platform and television offerings, perhaps as an attempt to correct the narrative that the network was abiding by the NFL's demands.[80]

The preferential approach to the NFL is reflected in the league's other partners as well. In 2015, after Greg Hardy was suspended for four games for assaulting his ex-girlfriend and returned to the NFL as a member of the Dallas Cowboys, CBS commentator Phil Simms made it a point during the broadcast to focus on "how good he is," calling him a "dynamic player" and noting that "everybody deserves a second chance."[81] In the network's interview with Jerry Jones, owner of the Dallas Cowboys, there were no follow-up questions on Jones's assertion that "I have a complete sensitivity toward domestic violence," despite the implication to the contrary in his hiring of Hardy.[82] Sports media scholar Travis Vogan has argued that the *League of Denial* incident, in particular, "usefully illustrates the limits of ESPN's cultural aspirations," since the company's "decision to end its partnership with PBS was almost certainly an effort to protect its relationship with the National Football League, which it pays roughly $2 billion a year for the rights to *Monday Night Football*."[83] The journalistic aspirations of organizations such as ESPN or CBS may be sincere, but commercial incentives will always win out in a profit-driven enterprise.

The NBA was largely spared from high-profile controversies for the majority of its partnership with ESPN. In 2012, however, rumors began to circulate that Stan Van Gundy, former head coach of the Orlando Magic, had been in advanced negotiations to join the network as a studio analyst before NBA commissioner David Stern prevented ESPN from making the hire.[84] Stan Van Gundy himself perpetuated the idea at the time. "No one at ESPN will tell us what happened," he told Dan Le Batard on his Miami radio show. "We actually did agree on a role, but then [ESPN] came back and pulled that. That's when we knew something was up."[85] Jeff Van Gundy, employed as ESPN's lead analyst, came to his brother's defense and supported the theory. "There's certainly circumstantial evidence that something from the outside—presumably the NBA—changed [ESPN's] thinking," he told *USA Today*, while raising pertinent ethical concerns, ESPN "is an organization that's treated me great. But this raises interesting questions about what a (league-network) partnership means. . . . It seems like there are certain people in each sport that (TV) can't criticize, or you can't criticize the league itself."[86] The hiring of a particular analyst is undoubtedly more minor a concern than concussion issues in the NFL, but the Van Gundy situation further reveals a dynamic between the ESPN and its content providers, in which leagues play a major role in the depiction of the sport, despite the journalistic posture of the network.

The ESPN-NBA relationship experienced more high-profile and widespread controversy following a tweet by Houston Rockets general manager

Daryl Morey, which expressed support for the sovereignty of Hong Kong against the Chinese government, a longtime ally of the NBA. On October 4, 2019, Morey tweeted an image with the slogan "Fight for Freedom, Stand with Hong Kong." Chinese government officials called for Morey's firing and banned all NBA games from airing in the country.[87] The NBA responded by supporting Morey's freedom of expression, though the league stood to lose "hundreds of millions" of dollars from the fallout.[88] By October 2020, NBA games returned to Chinese television.[89] While the NBA was able to successfully weather the turbulent situation, ESPN was heavily criticized for its own handling of the controversy, in which it attempted to walk an apolitical line and avoid taking any side. An internal memo by Chuck Salituro, ESPN's senior news director, mandated that any story on Morey avoid discussion of China, Hong Kong, and the details of the political landscape there.[90] ESPN commentators such as Stephen A. Smith even went on the air to admonish Morey. "You don't just think about yourself before you act," Smith said of the tweet. "That's what boys and girls do. That's what children do."[91] At the same time, when NBA reporter Zach Lowe attempted to interview an expert on China from the Council on Foreign Relations, he was forced to cancel the appearance. Many public figures spoke publicly to condemn ESPN's attempt at an apolitical stance, including Republican senators Josh Hawley and Rick Scott.[92]

More recently, the same ESPN investigative reporters who wrote the *League of Denial* book, Steve Fainaru and Mark Fainaru-Wada, published an exposé on the NBA's youth academies in China in July 2020, reporting that Chinese coaches had been physically abusing young players and failing to provide any schooling, which was a fundamental component of the program. The NBA disclosed that the Xinjing academy, where the worst violations took place, had been shut down in 2019, but multiple complaints went back to the opening of the facility in 2016.[93] Other major news publications, including the *New York Times*, quickly picked up the story.[94] Yet the report received no promotion by ESPN, despite its being a significant journalistic success for the organization. *Get Up*, *First Take*, *SportsCenter*, *The Jump*, *Jalen & Jacoby*, *Around the Horn*, and *Pardon the Interruption* all failed to even acknowledge the story. Only *Highly Questionable*, which is known for more political content, spent time discussing the story and its horrific details. "You have these kids in these camps who are being physically abused—child abuse—within the basketball context, with the NBA logo on all of this," noted cohost Pablo Torre—"That's worrisome."[95] As with *League of Denial*, the NBA Academy story highlights the duality of ESPN or any other "news" organization with a commercial interest in the topics on which it reports. ESPN maintains immense journalistic capabilities, as the story demonstrates, but they are often rendered immobile by the interests of its media partners, including the NFL, the NBA, and others, who stand to benefit from the suppression of negative press coverage.

This relationship goes both ways, however, as the NBA has also sought to ensure that its players are as cooperative as possible with the news outlets that cover the sport. During the preseason "rookie orientation," in which the rookies meet with veteran players to learn the ins-and-outs of the league, the NBA began to include a "media relations instructional video" in 1992.[96] During the Tournament of Americas in Portland ahead of the 1992 Olympics, the NBA had approached stars such as Larry Bird, Magic Johnson, and Karl Malone, as well various news media personnel, to record answers, tips, and explanations to instruct rookies in how to treat and interact with media coverage before, during, and after games. "It was instead of suits teaching you how to deal with yes and no," recalled Terry Lyons, the NBA's director of media relations at the time, who executive produced the video, "it was Larry Bird saying, 'Hey, Jeff Twist my PR guy is my best friend. Every time I had a problem, I'd bounce it off of Jeff.' Magic Johnson saying the same thing. 'Hey, I know it's not my favorite thing, especially after a tough loss, but these guys are going to judge you on whether you're there if you win or lose.'"[97] Hosted by Rolando Blackman, the vice president of the players' association at the time, the video was designed to encourage players to cooperate with the news media and instruct them in how to best navigate those situations, from their peers rather than from executives in suits.[98] The video demonstrates the fundamentality of the sports-media relationship in putting players in the position of working with the press to generate consumable content to promote the sport on a global scale. Ultimately, media partners like ESPN may compromise on journalistic aspirations in order to serve the interests of content providers like the NBA, and it is likewise in the interest of sports leagues to fully participate in those media practices that will ensure the most positive depiction of the sport and its players.

This kind of sports-media synergy is even more evident in the NBA's relationship with Turner, which extends beyond any journalistic rigor in that the two collaborate closely on production, distribution, and promotion. The synergy includes the extensive incorporation of the social media landscape, where sports leagues such as the NBA are able to exert more direct control over the release of information. In 2012, Turner purchased Bleacher Report (B/R), a sports news website that had been grown considerably in popularity since its launch in 2005. By the time Turner purchased it for an estimated $200 million, B/R was averaging ten million unique monthly views, which

Turner hoped would buoy the company's digital sports footprint after losing control of *Sports Illustrated* to Time Inc., a corporate sibling within the Time Warner hierarchy.[99] In the years since, Turner has driven B/R deeper into the mobile and social media landscape. In 2016, the company purchased the rights to House of Highlights (HoH), an Instagram account that posts highlights from across the sports world, ranging from the impressive to the humorous. Launched in July 2014 by Omar Raja, then a sophomore at the University of Central Florida, HoH reached half a million followers in only nine months of operation. "I kind of said to myself, these are videos I share with my friends," Raja recalled. "Why has no one put them together in one spot?"[100] Since being folded into B/R's operation, HoH has reached 21 million followers on Instagram and expanded to 2.85 million subscribers on YouTube.

Moreover, about 75 percent of all clips on HoH are related to the NBA.[101] The least cynical interpretation of this fact would posit that it is highly convenient for B/R and its parent company, Turner, which is able to effectively promote the sport for which it holds extensive multiplatform media rights. The most cynical interpretation would propose that the HoH account heavily promotes only those sports from which Turner has the most to gain financially. It is difficult to attribute the proper degree of intentionality, lacking a direct admission, but it is undoubtedly true that B/R's purchase and integration of HoH has been a significant success. By October 2019, when Raja left B/R and HoH for a multimillion-dollar deal at ESPN to steer its own social media strategy, Raja's creation had grown to account for 10 percent of B/R's overall revenue.[102] Unlike ESPN, which still aspires to be perceived as a legitimate news organization, Turner and B/R seem far more content with attracting eyeballs, monetizing clicks, and promoting telecasts.

Sports media scholar Michael Serazio has examined how "the accelerated interplay of sources, platforms, and audiences" driven by digitization has since "restructured how reporters go about gathering and disseminating sports news," pushing news professionals to produce "*more* and *faster*" content.[103] "The entire journalistic edict has changed," Bonnie Bernstein, formerly of ESPN and more recently vice president of content and brand development for Campus Insiders, tells Serazio. "Now the bosses are saying: tweet first, blog second, write your article third."[104] Social media have become important direct-to-consumer outlets, driving the dissemination of both news and highlights. As of 2016, an estimated 2 percent of linear television programming consisted of sports content, yet approximately 60 percent of conversations on Twitter were sports-related.[105] While the advertising and subscription revenues of linear television ensure that it remains more profitable than social media, sustained user engagement on Twitter and Instagram remain highly valuable in its ability to direct viewers to monetizable content, whether it is a telecast or a dedicated mobile app. This approach is reflected in B/R's overall media strategy. By 2019, B/R's dedicated mobile app accounted for 50 percent of the company's traffic and overall revenue, including $80–$100 million in advertising sales.[106] In its pitch to prospective advertisers, moreover, B/R promotes its "unrivaled social engagement," including a "205M Global Facebook Reach," "26M Total Twitter Interactions—more than the next 20 top sports publishers combined," "B/R Instagram is No. 1 among all sports publishers with 202M interactions," and "100MM social interactions a month."[107] Given the multinational status of such platforms, social media remain especially valuable as direct-to-consumer tools for integrated media companies, as exemplified here by the Turner-B/R-HoH activities.

The NBA, too, has been able to succeed on social media with its own league-operated accounts.[108] On Twitter, for instance, the NBA's 32.3 million followers pace the NFL's 26.2 million and, on Facebook, the NBA's

Kenny Beecham of House of Highlights appears on TNT's NBA postgame show, which was then edited and posted to the HoH YouTube channel in an effort to address a wider audience across shared media properties.

The Couch 157

39 million followers are more than double the NFL's 17 million. The splits are even more drastic on Instagram, where the platform's younger user base is more reflective of the NBA's target audience.[109] As of 2020, the NBA maintains 54 million followers, in contrast with the NFL's 20 million, MLB's 7 million, and the NHL's 4.5 million. The NBA was especially prepared to excel on social media through its historical investment in self-distribution, including the establishment of NBA Entertainment as an in-house production company in 1982 and the launch of NBA.com in 1995. "What we really never anticipated, what's really changed a lot, is that back then most of this stuff was for highlight packages the next day, or for videotapes that would be produced at the end of the season, or for features that would be on an NBC *Game of the Week*," recalled Steve Hellmuth, who helped develop the NBA website in his role as vice president at NBA Entertainment before becoming executive vice president of media operations and technology in 2007. "But now all the logging and all the work that we do here is focused on turning stuff around immediately into social media channels, into the NBA app."[110] As in the early years of the NBA website, most of the NBA's social media strategy interest is driven by the NBA's distinct use of highlights.

Since 2014, the NBA's efforts have been heavily aided by its agreement with WSC Sports, an Israel-based technology company that creates readily shareable video highlights through automation. Using machine learning, WSC's software processes telecasts by drawing on visual and audio cues, such as crowd noise and movement, to identify the most significant moments in each game, producing video clips at a far faster rate than any human editor.[111] "Previously, it could take an hour to cut a post-game highlights package," explained Bob Carney, the NBA's senior vice president of social and digital strategy. "Now it takes a few minutes to create over 1,000 highlight packages."[112] After signing with the NBA, WSC Sports has gone on to obtain contracts with Major League Soccer, the PGA Tour, Cricket Australia, Germany's Bundesliga, and Japan's J1 League, as well as media companies such as Amazon, which tasked WSC with creating content for its Premier League broadcasts.[113] WSC's technology enables clients such as the NBA to post videos of big moments to its social media accounts almost immediately after they occur, a highly effective tool in drawing viewers to ongoing telecasts, which remains the NBA's main priority.

Because the league's goal is eyeballs, attention, and/or engagement, the NBA often allows fans to share their own highlights and clips that demonstrate the excitement of the sport. The original HoH account on Instagram, for instance, was able to post a substantial number of NBA highlights without any copyright issues, despite having no formal agreement with the league. "We have always believed that fans sharing highlights via social media is a great way to drive interest and excitement in the NBA," notes Mike Bass, the league's executive vice president of communications.[114] Indeed, since the early days of NBA.com, Adam Silver, in his role as the president of NBA Entertainment, had felt "if some kid's going to stay up all night to edit his tribute to Kobe Bryant, I'm not going be the guy that pulls it down," recalled Steve Hellmuth.[115] With Silver installed as NBA commissioner, this philosophy has continued into the social media era, informing the league's approach to fan-shared clips on Facebook, Twitter, and Instagram. "When other leagues were pulling material off of YouTube," notes Hellmuth, the league decided that such material could instead "live side-by-side with the stuff that we're editing on NBA.com."[116] Leagues such as the NFL, for instance, have much more aggressively policed social media accounts for violations of intellectual property law. In 2015, the NFL filed complaints with Twitter against popular websites *Deadspin* and *SB Nation* for sharing clips of NFL action, which led to the deactivation of their Twitter accounts.[117] The NFL's strict copyright enforcement prevents the kind of free-flowing exchange that has been beneficial for the NBA, and the latter's approach has allowed it to excel on social media, where fan-generated and league-generated highlights coexist, creating a wider ecosystem that boosts overall engagement and drives attention to the league's product.

Ultimately, the NBA's global reach is the result of a careful and sustained investment in digital platforms, including the league's in-house Game Distribution Center and its agreement with WSC Sports, which allows the posting of video highlights to social media accounts at a rapid pace. The emphasis on social media allows entities like the NBA or B/R to maximize control and direct viewers' attention to the most desired platforms, whether that is ESPN, TNT, NBA League Pass, or HoH. Fulfilling a role similar to that of the initial iteration of NBA.com and other early sports websites, social platforms allow leagues to boost viewership of particular games through targeted highlights, to promote positive headlines, and to circumvent negative news coverage by eschewing traditional press outlets in favor of league collaborators or league-owned platforms.

Conclusion: Bringing It All Back Home

While the NBA continues to benefit from both broadcast and cable, the league's investment in an in-house digital pipeline has prepared it to succeed as a self-sufficient media empire. The point is especially important to note as cable ratings and subscriptions continue to fall. "I'm not surprised that our ratings are down thus far," NBA commissioner Adam Silver told the *Washington Post* in December 2019, before the onset of the coronavirus pandemic dropped ratings even lower. "I'm not concerned, either. In terms of every other key indicator that we look at that measures the popularity of the league, we're up. We're up in attendance over a record-setting high from last year. Social media engagement remains in the magnitude of 1.6 billion people on a global basis. Our League Pass viewership is up. Our merchandising sales are up. The issue then, for me, is that we're going through a transition in terms of how [the league] is distributed to our fans, particularly our young fans."[118] These kinds of metrics, such as social media engagement and streaming viewers, thus remain crucial to pitching advertisers and media partners on the viability of the NBA as a content provider, even if traditional television ratings have declined.

The NBA's peers have seen similar decreases. The NFL, for instance, averaged 15.4 million traditional television viewers during the 2020 season, a 7 percent drop from the previous year.[119] Cancellations and postponements due to COVID-19 only strengthened the trend, as viewership for the Stanley Cup Finals fell by 61 percent over the previous season, the NBA Finals fell by 49 percent, and the World Series was the least watched on record.[120] Some have argued that the drop is temporary, a result of cannibalization as every major sport returned at the same time and aired important playoff games in the middle of the day.[121] Yet there is clear evidence of an ongoing shift away from linear television, and overall cable viewership was declining even before the pandemic. According to a *Variety* survey of the most watched networks in 2019, Nick at Nite was down by 24 percent among total viewers, AMC by 22 percent, FX by 21 percent, USA by 19 percent, TBS by 16 percent, and TNT by 14 percent.[122] As the television audience increasingly shifts streaming platforms, most of the major conglomerates have sought to follow them. In a decision more significant than Disney's launch of ESPN+, NBC announced in January 2021 that it would be shutting down its dedicated NBC Sports cable network, shifting its existing contracts to the USA Network while investing more heavily in its Peacock OTT service.[123] Cable remains viable for now, but the medium continues to decline as streaming continues to expand.

As a result, sports leagues like the NBA have also rearranged their priorities, making greater efforts to integrate their social, mobile, streaming, and linear television offerings. At the 2019 NBA All-Star Game in North Carolina, for instance, the league drew on Turner's resources in B/R and HoH for a large "fan activation" showcase called B/R x NC at the local Music Factory in Charlotte, featuring two full-length basketball courts, a concert stage, and a live programming studio. The site was designed to serve as the operations center for all B/R social content during All-Star Weekend, drawing on B/R talent and video created and posted by fans. "We're building a physical set to entertain consumers on the ground but, more important, to capture, create, shoot, and push content out to the 100 million social followers that we have across all areas," explained Howard Mittman, chief marketing officer and chief revenue officer at B/R. "I don't know that it's possible to engage modern consumers, especially the millennial and Gen Z consumers that we deliver to, in a way that deepens our connection with them better than video does."[124] Ultimately, these videos were able to enhance Turner's linear programming around All-Star Weekend, especially the more shareable and spreadable events like the Dunk Contest, Three-Point Contest, and Skills Challenge, which all air on TNT.

The success of the showcase encouraged the NBA and Turner to continue their push into social media integration. In January 2020, they announced a special Tuesday night edition of *NBA on TNT*, hosted by Dwyane Wade, Candace Parker, Shaquille O'Neal and Adam Lefkoe, that would focus on more than basketball by "touching on entertainment, business, lifestyle, fashion and social activism," according to Craig Barry, Chief Content Officer at Turner Sports.[125] This includes a more extensive use of social-driven segments, such as "Fit Watch with B/R Kicks," which looks at players' outfits, "Flash it Forward," which spotlights an uplifting story that has gone viral, as well as an overall greater use of TikTok challenges and fan polling. The endeavor has proven successful, as the NBA and TNT announced plans to continue the special Tuesday edition of *NBA on TNT* for the 2020–21 season.[126] The sporting elements of basketball continue to recede as the NBA and its media partners more heavily emphasize its circulation as multiplatform content.

The launch of a separate B/R Live mobile app in April 2018, moreover, has allowed for even greater synergy across Turner's platforms.[127] The company can use the B/R name and user base to charge access to on-demand games, leveraging the preexisting media rights agreements with entities like the NBA, MLB, and the PGA. Using a "micro-transaction" model, the B/R Live service enables viewers to pay for access to telecasts on a per-minute basis.[128] In November 2019, however, the standalone B/R Live app was absorbed into the broader one, which Turner Sports general manager Hania Poole explained was always going to be the plan. "Because of this need to speed to the market, we needed to be quick and launched two separate experiences," Poole told *Sports Business Journal*. "Now we're in the mid stages of integrating those two experiences together under the Bleacher Report brand."[129] The app's live offerings have continued. In November 2020, TNT aired a celebrity gold showdown called *The Match: Champions for Change*, which featured a "House of Highlights Showdown" pre-event competition exclusively on the B/R report app, a full coordination the company's social, digital, and linear platforms.[130]

At least ten million users, moreover, are signed up for B/R's push alerts, which CEO Howard Mittman believes is critical for the emerging possibilities of real-time sports betting and its integration with linear and streaming television. "Our alerts are fast," Mittman explained to *Axios*. "You'll get them anywhere between 1 minute and 7 minutes faster than any other subscription alert service. Speed is the key performance indicator that we monitor in terms of alerts."[131] In keeping with its investment in betting as an emerging source of engagement, B/R signed an agreement in February 2019 with casino operator Caesars Entertainment to develop Caesars-branded sports betting content for the B/R platform, while also constructing a B/R-branded studio inside Caesars Palace in Las Vegas. "Gaming content will be a key driver for increasing fan engagement across all platforms, including time spent watching live sporting events and other criteria that impact television viewership," noted Turner Sports president Lenny Daniels.[132] The NBA, especially, seems to agree. As part of the NBA League Pass app, which is managed by Turner, the league launched a special "NBABet Stream" option for the 2020 season restart and the 2020–21 season that offers on-screen betting lines as well as gambling analysis provided by experts from B/R, the Action Network, and Yahoo Sports.[133] "We view these telecasts as a great way to engage on a deeper level with our fans who are watching the game through a sports betting lens," explained Scott Kaufman-Ross, the NBA's head of fantasy and gaming.[134] Such specialized feeds are more easily possible in an expansive multiplatform ecosystem, which allows content providers to host alternative direct-to-consumer offerings without cannibalizing the main telecast. While Turner can air a golf tournament on TNT, for instance, it is able to enhance the event's reach through social media and streaming platforms.

NBA commissioner Adam Silver has made it clear that, while new opportunities have emerged for sports leagues like the NBA, far greater competition for attention within the home viewing space had occurred. "This notion that the Pelicans are just competing against the Knicks or the Lakers or the Thunder, they're competing against every other form of entertainment out there in the world," Silver explained in an interview with *The Ringer*'s Bill Simmons in May 2019. "That has to be my mind-set, . . . that we're an entertainment product competing against an infinitesimal [*sic*]

The NBA's "betstream" feed, which features gambling odds from MGM and commentary from B/R's Cabbie Richards and Kelly Stewart, demonstrates the full integration of sports, betting, news, and television.

number of opportunities for people to do other things with their time."[135] This mind-set is reflected in the NBA's endeavors over many years, in the launch of a cable multiplex to enhance viewer choice, in early online fantasy sport to drive an emerging dot-com ecosystem, and in the recent investment in betting and the NBABet Stream feed to try to enhance the real-world stakes of its games. It is also reflected in other ancillary media like the NBA 2K video game franchise and the recent launch of NBA Top Shot, a block-chain-based platform that allows users to trade collectible video highlights, which saw $500 million in sales in only its first six months of operation.[136] Like social media, real-time statistics, and news, which can generate some amount of revenue for themselves, these efforts also serve to bring more viewers to the telecasts, which for now remain the most lucrative endeavor.

Just as the NBA invested more heavily in cable television in its 2002 contracts with Turner and ESPN/Disney, as the medium was ascending over broadcast television, the NBA's investment in internet distribution since the 1990s positioned the league to excel within a media industry dominated by streaming video. The NBA has demonstrated an aggressive effort to make itself available wherever the most viewers are congregating, in all possible nations and on all possible devices. This approach once meant a cable multiplex and a web homepage, but it has evolved to include social media platforms and mobile apps such as Twitter, B/R, and League Pass. Such efforts have further warped the relationship between sports leagues and news outlets, like ESPN.com and B/R, which are often obliged to function as partners in the promotion and profitability of particular sports. In 2019, ESPN analyst Zach Lowe questioned the extent to which the competitive elements of basketball mattered at all anymore, whether the NBA had simply come to operate as a viral media machine. As the NBA invests even more heavily in its streaming and social media distribution in conjunction with Turner, and sports betting in collaboration with FanDuel, Lowe's provocation has only become more valid. Arguably, the NBA's near-monopolistic control over professional basketball in the United States is simply the most profitable path forward as the demand for media content continues to grow with the number of personal media devices. As the home viewing space has become increasingly fragmented, the NBA is prepared to succeed in the competition for attention, with basketball highlights, statistics, news, and telecasts able to circulate across the variety of screens and services that make up the multiplatform media economy.

CONCLUSION

The House That Hoops Built

The NBA's "bubble" postseason, which ran from July to October 2020 as a result of the COVID-19 pandemic, demonstrated the contemporary state of the global sports media ecosystem in action. The NBA invited twenty-two teams to finish out regular-season play, in order to most effectively whittle down the competition to sixteen playoff contenders.[1] Hosted at Walt Disney World in Orlando, Florida, the event featured three basketball courts, a two-hundred-thousand-square-foot broadcast production complex, 436 miles of fiber cable, thirty-six contact microphones, seventeen-foot-tall wraparound LED video boards, and more than twenty cameras, including a new rail cam at courtside that could move laterally to follow the game action more closely than ever before.[2] "We had dreamed about all these things and being able to do these things in NBA buildings but were prevented by fans," explained Steve Hellmuth, the NBA's executive vice president of media operations and technology. "But now there are no fans. We knew exactly where we wanted to put the cameras."[3] As a made-for-television event, designed first and foremost for viewers at home, the bubble made the relationship between sport and media more transparent than ever before.

To aid in the production of the live event aspects, the NBA partnered with Fuse Technical Group, a live events specialist. "Our largest challenge was understanding how to adapt 22 different teams' shows for this new environment," noted Charles Dabezies of Fuse Technical Group.[4] The effort required the coordination of four production teams across the three courts, often with simultaneous action, including thirty-three scrimmage games, eighty-eight regular-season "seeding" games, and eighty-three playoff games, in which the LeBron James–led Los Angeles Lakers would defeat the Miami Heat to become 2020 NBA Finals Champions.[5] Around the courts, LED screens were installed to approximate the appearance of fans, aided by a database of reaction shots to make games feel as "normal" as possible, for both players and at-home viewers.[6] The NBA also hired Firehouse Productions to assist with audio components, having used the company for the draft, Hall of Fame Ceremonies, and the previous nine All-Star Games. "When the idea of playing in empty arenas was floated, I saw LeBron (James) interviewed and he said he'd never play without fans," recalled Mark Dittmar, vice president at Firehouse and the sound designer for the Bubble project. "I woke up the next morning thinking, 'What if he didn't feel like there were no fans? What if we could replicate it so well, it would seem normal to everyone?'"[7] In turn, Firehouse installed a sound system of 130 speakers for each court to create as normal an atmosphere as possible for the players, while a separate system was provided for the television broadcasts and at-home viewers.[8]

For each game, sound producers from Firehouse worked in collaboration with an NBA game director, an arena DJ, and two additional audio technicians operating the soundboards. Much as in a typical live event, the DJ was responsible for music and audience cues like chants of "de-fense!"[9] The game director, moreover, monitored the games and directed the audio in real time, working like a conductor to sync the sounds of the digital crowd with the pace of the game. "How do you make the crowd have all the appropriate reactions?" explains Dittmar, of the job of the game director. "If the shot hits the rim, circles around and then falls off, you'll have a big cheer, an 'Ahhh,' then disappointment, and then cheers for the other team as the ball is rebounded and going the other way."[10] To aid in this challenge, designated soundboards featured prerecorded sounds numbering in the thousands, from both previous NBA games and the NBA 2K video games, which could be accessed through multiple sixty-four-button color-coded controllers.[11] Navigating the contradictory possibilities of crowd noises was a complicated task for the sound teams, but they were equipped to handle the new responsibilities by drawing from their extensive experience with the live production of NBA games.

Meanwhile, the NBA's telecast partners, Turner and ESPN, worked in collaboration in order to most effectively disseminate the games to audiences around the world. Unlike a typical NBA game, which might use one production truck with ten personnel, games in the bubble featured two per network for each of the courts, resulting in thirteen trucks, thirty-one office trailers, and twenty power generators.[12] Speaking to the massive scale of the production, ESPN used both its EN2 and its EN3 mobile units. While EN3

NBA and Firehouse audio personnel work together to monitor games and insert the proper crowd sounds.

The House That Hoops Built 167

has been the primary NBA unit since its 2018 launch, EN2 has been used for both *Sunday Night Baseball* and ESPN International's broadcast of the Super Bowl.[13] In conjunction, ESPN was able to provide an improved broadcast, especially from a video standpoint. "We've boosted a lot of our regular cameras to high frame rate for better clarity. . . . We also had an opportunity to try out some new lenses," including both close-up handheld angles and those on robotic cameras, noted Eddie Okuno, ESPN senior remote operations specialist.[14] Because of the new safety protocols, moreover, regional sports networks were not allowed into the bubble, so those responsibilities fell to ESPN. For each game, the network would edit and distribute a clean feed, which featured video and audio without any commentary or graphics, to the NBA's production headquarters in Secaucus, New Jersey. From there, the league would digitally insert the agreed-upon digital arena advertising before rerouting the feed to the appropriate regional sports network (RSN) to insert its own announcer audio and graphics for television distribution.[15]

Within the telecast itself, the NBA's emphasis remained on a transnational audience, which was aided by invoking stars with overseas appeal, including Luka Dončić, LeBron James, and Giannis Antetokounmpo. The NBA's senior vice president of global media distribution, Matt Brabants, noted in 2016 that game producers "are constantly seeking out replays featuring international players that fans from overseas are tuning in to see."[16] The feat is accomplished largely by featuring those same marketable players in both feeds. During game 5 of the 2020 NBA Finals from the bubble, for instance, the CC television-5 broadcast featured the same close-ups and replays of LeBron James and Jimmy Butler as the ABC/ESPN feed in the United States.[17] The CCTV feed, in fact, is essentially equivalent to the US product, including the English-language scoreboard and its ESPN and NBA Finals logos. The only distinguishing features are arguably the Chinese-language commentary and the CCTV-5 logo in the upper-left corner.[18] The same is true of prior broadcasts on CCTV, which are drawn from the clean feeds that air on ESPN, TNT, or RSNs, with local producers overlaying text and commentary to make the telecasts more easily legible to local fans. Overlays can include, for example, an additional Chinese-character scoreboard in the upper-right corner, the upcoming schedule on Chinese television, and scrolling text of player statistics (some of which remain in English).[19] Besides such minor distinctions, however, the game is identical to the one being aired in the United States.

To further cultivate such media efficiencies, the bubble also saw the use of staggered early start times for games, which enhanced the primetime viability of the television product in time zones outside the United

States, just like 8 pm Eastern Time start times that try to maximize ratings in conjunction with a 5 pm Pacific Time start time. While games in the United States were often relegated to afternoons, where they suffered rating declines, the bubble saw more games air overseas in prime time than ever before during such a short period.[20] As a result, the NBA excelled on international television. Through the first two weeks of the bubble, ratings increased by 325 percent in the Philippines, 130 percent in Spain, 88 percent in Mexico, 79 percent in Lithuania, and 29 percent in Italy, in comparison with their average regular-season ratings.[21] Moreover, this strategy was not a fluke, as the NBA continued the start-time experiment after the bubble. For the final two days of the 2020–21 regular season, for instance, the NBA started half of its twenty-one games between 1 pm and 3:30 pm Eastern Time, providing prime-time viewing for a large percentage of Europe.[22]

In general, the domestic television ratings were the NBA's least successful metric during the bubble. The Finals averaged 7.45 million viewers, below the previous low of 9.29 million in 2007, in which the San Antonio Spurs swept the Cleveland Cavaliers.[23] Yet the numbers showed more promise in the NBA's key demographics, featuring a median viewer age of 46.1 years, far younger than the 2020 NHL Stanley Cup Final at 54.5 years or the previous MLB World Series at 56.9 years.[24] The age of the NBA's audience was

During game 5 of the 2019 Eastern Conference Finals between the Toronto Raptors and Milwaukee Bucks, the CCTV-5 broadcasts features the TNT feed with a Chinese-character scoreboard and text inserts laid on top of it.

The House That Hoops Built

also reflected in huge boosts to the league's social media presence across Facebook, Instagram, TikTok, Twitter, and YouTube, which gained 3.3 million new followers and generated 5.3 billion video views.[25] Much of the increase in engagement came from outside the United States. For instance, after Luka Dončić's game-winning basket to give the Dallas Mavericks a game 4 overtime victory over the Los Angeles Clippers, highlights of the buzzer-beater trended in fifteen countries: Argentina, Brazil, Canada, Chile, Colombia, Dominican Republic, France, Greece, Indonesia, Ireland, Italy, Mexico, Panama, Turkey, and Venezuela.[26] Through a combination of linear television, streaming distribution, and social media, the NBA cultivated an efficient media ecosystem, drawing on international stars and shared telecasts to create equivalencies and connections across multiple markets.

In trying to attract as wide a television audience as possible, the NBA's decisions have thus impacted the performance, production, circulation, and consumption of the sport. During the bubble, in particular, the NBA offices were the ultimate arbiter, serving as both the central decision-making entity and the switchboard between the event's various game feeds. Through the $180 million cost of the event, the league was able to save an estimated $1.5 billion, though it still lost approximately $695 million from the 258 regular-season games that were canceled from March 2020 on. "Our No. 1 priority was health and safety and from a business standpoint, it was important that we would finish the 2019–2020 season, crown a champion and be able to include our business and media partners and develop a plan to bring our fans courtside," said Kelly Flatow, NBA executive vice president of global events.[27] Much of the lost revenue was made up through the digital advertisements and sponsorships that the league oversaw from Secaucus, as featured on the courts or on the video boards. Michelob Ultra, for instance, sponsored a Courtside Club that drew sixty thousand virtual fans. For the NBA Finals, YouTube TV also received a large logo at center court because of its status as a presenting partner.[28] The sponsorships were disseminated to homes, televisions, and digital devices across the 215 countries where games were made available, through international broadcast partners such as CCTV (China), TV Band (Brazil), Viasat Sport (Russia), Cosmote TV (Greece), and Ruutu (Finland), as well as the NBA's own transnational streaming platform in League Pass.[29]

Ultimately, the confined space of the bubble demonstrates even more strongly the ways in which the NBA administers control over basketball as both sport and media program by funding the enterprise, overseeing the cables into and out of the space, and dictating the sponsorships and advertising that circulates within the program. As an event constructed primarily for the NBA's television audience and media partners, the bubble made more transparent the various mechanisms that inform and structure the live performance of sport. The easy virtualization of fans and crowd noise, for instance, highlights the ways in which even flesh-and-blood spectators are there to play a particular role for the media production of sport. While gate revenue still provides a substantial portion of the NBA's profits, the entertainment of in-person fans is important insofar as it signals the necessary excitement to at-home fans. The construction of the arena space, moreover, is designed to maximize engagement that can be transported outside its physical walls, through dedicated mobile apps and ever-closer cameras (like the rail cam) that bring fans nearer to the game action. The bubble thus offers the latest example of sporting spaces being modified by media interests, which can be traced back to the NBA-NBC collaborative reconstruction of modern arenas.

While the most straightforward approach to understanding the NBA's production, distribution, and consumption may be a linear one, moving through each subsequent space as the live event travels from the court into viewers' homes, these industrial forces frequently overlap and collide, calling attention to the multidirectional relationships between the event, the arena, the wires, the office, and the home. The demands of one space often affect the outcome of the other, as mediated elements travel backward and

The NBA's rail cam includes a view of the massive LED screens, which can feature digital advertisements whenever necessary.

The House That Hoops Built   171

forward along their course, from Orlando to Secaucus to Atlanta or Bristol and back to Secaucus again. The global appeal of NBA events, for instance, encourages the expansion of streaming distribution, which affects how the live event itself is conceived, which opens new possibilities for game broadcasts that will air on a local, regional, and global scale. The NBA thus illuminates a fundamental dialectic between globalization and digitization, as new technologies facilitate a vaster distribution potential and in turn encourage a more substantial global address. While each of these spaces has its own history, influences, and demands, they combine to reflect a broader mediatization and marketization of sport, following the emergence of sport as modern media content in the 1980s and the ascent of sports leagues as media conglomerates during the 1990s.

The multidirectional nature of the sports-media relationship thus reflects the evolution of the sports media industry itself, which features a history of stops, starts, and what ifs. By the 2000s, as cable expanded and streaming distribution became more reliable, sports media institutions were able to favor untapped global audiences over an established domestic audience. For the NBA, the investment was made easier by the overseas offices that it established in the early–mid-1990s in anticipation of Olympic success in 1992. By the 2010s, the overseas offices would play an even more central role in the internationalization of the NBA's live events, given the extensive local knowledge of the personnel there. This approach was inspired by the television-format trade of the 1990s, such as the NBA's various international versions of *Inside Stuff*, which similarly utilized a boots-on-the-ground strategy to more effectively adapt programming to local tastes. Since then, the league has worked to bring local basketball cultures in line with a more uniform global NBA culture by investing in international sporting infrastructures that give the NBA a stronger year-round presence, as in Brazil's LNB and the African BAL. These efforts have a precedent in the league's investments in the Soviet Union during the 1980s in collaboration with Turner, in which the partners sought to establish the country as a major media market for basketball. The altruism of the NBA's social programs and educational endeavors, then, remains complicated by the league's commercial incentives as a global entertainment conglomerate.

The NBA, as the most aggressive and experimental sports organization in terms of its global and multiplatform media distribution, thus provides the ideal object for examining the contemporary state and historical development of the sports-media relationship. The continued success of streaming platforms and the development of a post-network media ecosystem has enabled a league such as the NBA to become a fully integrated and transnational media empire, while also opening up global opportunities for its individual franchises such as the Houston Rockets, the Sacramento Kings, and the Milwaukee Bucks. The NBA, of course, is not the only league to benefit from the post-network ecosystem and its demand for lucrative and exclusive sports programming. In March 2021, the NFL signed a new round of eleven-year rights agreements with Fox, ESPN, NBC, CBS, and Amazon for a total of $10 billion per season. While the linear television aspects remain essentially the same as in the past, Amazon now holds the exclusive rights to *Thursday Night Football* and the streaming rights for the networks' affiliated platforms have expanded, including NBC's Peacock, Fox's Tubi, CBS's Paramount+, and ESPN+.[30]

In keeping with the greater synergy between linear and streaming sports distribution, the NHL signed its own round of seven-year media contracts in April 2021 with ESPN and WarnerMedia totaling $625 million per season. While TNT will air three of the seven possible Stanley Cup Finals, half of the postseason, and up to seventy-two regular-season games, part of the deal includes live programming on the HBO Max streaming platform and supplementary coverage through Bleacher Report, much as in the company's approach to the NBA.[31] The league's influence, therefore, remains apparent, as a clear incentive for the NHL was to partner with the longtime digital and cable partner of the NBA. "That's what we're excited about," noted Gary Bettman, the longtime NHL commissioner, after WarnerMedia News and Sports Chairman Jeff Zucker explained that the company's "style

The NBA Top Shot digital marketplace, in which users are able to buy and sell limited-edition collectible highlights, sometimes at astoundingly high prices.

and approach" with the NHL product will be similar to the one they have with the NBA.[32]

Ultimately, the NBA's aggressively global and digital approach remains a meaningful influence on the sports and media landscape, extending to its strategic use of virtual and augmented reality, sports betting through its equity arrangement with FanDuel for both daily fantasy sports and traditional wagering, and nonfungible tokens (NFTs) such as NBA Top Shot in collaboration with Dapper Labs. After the NBA's early success with the block-chain-based trading-card endeavor, which allows users to buy and sell digital video highlights, MLB followed in April 2021 with the launch of its own line in partnership with Topps.[33] In September 2021, the NFL announced its own NFT agreement with Dapper Labs.[34] These initiatives can be understood as efforts to boost and monetize engagement with viewers outside the boundaries of linear television. In May 2019, in fact, NBA commissioner Adam Silver expressed concern for the long-term viability of cable at the MIT Sloan Sports Analytics conference: "From 2010 to 2018, among 18- to 34-year-olds—and that's our core audience, it's an incredibly attractive young audience—their viewership on pay TV is down almost 50 percent. . . . So, I think we're going to have to figure this out with ESPN, and with now our new partners at AT&T and WarnerMedia, how the new world looks."[35] As the NBA comes to function as a media empire in its own right, with offices spanning the world and divisions with various responsibilities, the league is well positioned to take on even greater distribution responsibilities and expand its capabilities as a media company.

The NBA has not yet taken the step of promoting other sports or media properties within their institutional network, but the notion continues to seem plausible. That step had been the plan, after all, for their aborted partnership with Turner Entertainment on a CNN/SI channel.[36] Although the NBA continues to entrust Facebook, Twitter, Tencent, Turner, and Endeavor to administer the various properties that the NBA has provided them, the league could very easily take on those distribution responsibilities themselves, should the benefits ever outweigh the costs. As streaming revenues continue to rise while traditional linear television declines, it seems increasingly possible that the NBA would intervene and take greater control over its own distribution, as lucrative opportunities continue to emerge for streaming sport. In addition to Amazon's aggressive pursuit of the space, NBC used the launch of Peacock to invest more heavily in English Premier League Soccer while fending off competing bids from ESPN and ViacomCBS.[37] ESPN also announced the acquisition of the rights to the Spanish soccer league, La Liga, despite interest from ViacomCBS for its Paramount+

service.[38] Audiences and markets thus continue to converge as streaming becomes more viable as the primary mode of media distribution. The ongoing transnational success of formerly national programming, such as European soccer or US basketball, has created opportunities for sports leagues to become more self-sufficient than ever before.

Other major sports leagues beyond the NBA, therefore, require further inquiry as media companies. In *Fighting Visibility: Sports Media and Female Athletes in the UFC* (2021), for instance, Jennifer McClearen interrogates the operation of Ultimate Fighting Championship (UFC) as a media entity and highlights the company's leveraging and exploitation of gender for profit. In *Keepers of the Flame: NFL Films and the Rise of Sports Media* (2014), for another instance, Travis Vogan examines the NFL's internal media division, NFL Films, which is similar to the discussion here of NBA Entertainment.[39] The NHL and MLB, too, warrant further comprehensive study of their strategic investments in the digital space for the past few decades. MLB, for instance, launched BAMTech, arguably the most successful streaming intermediary service in the world, and NeuLion/Endeavor Streaming had its origins as the in-house intermediary of the NHL. All these professional leagues, as well as supposedly amateur organizations like the NCAA, call for large-scale surveys of their evolution as genuine media companies, given the profound influence of those operations on the sports themselves. Much scholarship has been conducted on the cultural impact of these sports and their governing bodies, but the media industrial forces that guide leagues' decision-making must be taken more fully into account.

Media scholarship, then, is important for illuminating the whole range of forces that determine the contours of sport, and sports scholarship is important for excavating the full cultural impact of what has become a fundamental media asset during the multiplatform era of television. With the projected economic growth and deeper integration of the sports and media industries, scholars must remain attentive to their ongoing globalization and digitization, as outlined in the chapters of the present work, including the simultaneous address of streaming platforms, the effect of such possibilities on programming choices, the engagement with global media brands from local perspectives, and the growing interest of digital distributors in sports programming. Ultimately, these two businesses, sports and media, are part of a single integrated ecosystem with major transnational institutions that have stakes in both worlds. The late former NBA commissioner David Stern argued as much when I spoke with him in early 2018, as he looked back on his responsibilities running the league from 1984 to 2014: "It's really being the CEO of a far-flung entertainment and media conglomerate that has not just television relationships, for games and for other things, but for assisting the teams with respect to the sales of their tickets in their buildings and their game presentation, and presiding over a [consumer] products business that's billions of dollars, and a sponsorship business . . . and all of that on a global basis."[40] I hope that the particular case of the NBA, as it transforms into a media conglomerate that sees basketball as multiplatform media content with transnational appeal, provides a sturdy foundation for further research on the global sports media industry.

Notes

Introduction

1. Daniel Holloway, "TV Ratings: NBA Finals Is Most Watched since 1998," *Variety*, June 13, 2017.

2. Matt Moore, "He Plays for Who Now? Recapping the Wildest Offseason in NBA History," *CBS Sports*, September 25, 2017, https://www.cbssports.com/nba/news/he-plays-for-who-now-recapping-the-wildest-offseason-in-nba-history/.

3. Steve McClellan, "NBC-NBA Deal: $750 million + Revenue Sharing," *Broadcasting and Cable*, May 3, 1993, 14; "Turner Broadcasting and the National Basketball Association Broaden Partnership with Digital Rights Agreement," *Business Wire*, January 17, 2008.

4. Brian Windhorst and Zach Lowe, "A Confidential Report Shows Nearly Half the NBA Lost Money Last Season. Now What?" *ESPN.com*, September 19, 2017, https://www.espn.com/nba/story/_/id/20747413/a-confidential-report-shows-nearly-half-nba-lost-money-last-season-now-what.

5. Russ Granik, telephone conversation with the author, March 22, 2018. Emphasis in original.

6. Ibid.

7. David DuPree, "Strike Is Averted as NBA, Players Agree in Principle," *Washington Post*, April 1, 1983, https://www.washingtonpost.com/archive/sports/1983/04/01/strike-is-averted-as-nba-players-agree-in-principle/dda33961-9ec7-42b7-ae20-0316a9333d9e/; Larry Coon, "Breaking Down Changes in New CBA," *ESPN.com*, November 28, 2011, https://www.espn.com/nba/story/_/page/CBA-111128/how-new-nba-deal-compares-last-one.

8. Elizabeth Comte, "How High Can David Stern Jump?" *Forbes*, June 7, 1993.

9. Christina Gough, "NBA Regular Season Ticketing Revenue as Share of Total Revenue 2010–2020," *Statista*, February 17, 2021, https://www.statista.com

/statistics/193410/percentage-of-ticketing-revenue-in-the-nba-since-2006/; Christina Gough, "Total Broadcasting Rights of the NBA by Sector in 2019/20," *Statista*, March 5, 2021, https://www.statista.com/statistics/1120204/broadcasting-rights-nba-by-sector/.

10. Sam Amico, "NBA Lucrative Deal with China-Based Tencent May Be in Jeopardy after Trump Order," *Sports Illustrated*, August 12, 2020, https://www.si.com/nba/cavaliers/nba/cavaliers/nba-amico/wechat-app-tencent-basketball-trump-order.

11. Michael Colangelo, "The NFL Made Roughly $16 billion in Revenue Last Year," *USA Today*, July 15, 2019, https://touchdownwire.usatoday.com/2019/07/15/nfl-revenue-owners-players-billions/; Jabari Young, "Major League Baseball Revenue for 2019 Season Hits a Record $10.7 billion," *CNBC*, December 22, 2019, https://www.cnbc.com/2019/12/22/report-mlb-revenue-for-2019-season-a-record-10point7-billion.html.

12. Barry M. Bloom, "NBA Returns with Fans in Some Arenas and Shortfalls Nearly Everywhere," *Sportico*, December 22, 2020, https://www.sportico.com/leagues/basketball/2020/nba-opens-season-revenue-shortfall-1234618855/; Mike Ozanian, "Why the NBA Still Has Potential for Big Revenue Growth outside the US," *Forbes*, October 23, 2019, https://www.forbes.com/sites/mikeozanian/2019/10/23/why-the-nba-has-potential-for-big-revenue-growth-outside-us/?sh=5199fd88232e; Christina Gough, "Total Broadcasting Rights of the NFL by Sector in 2019/20," *Statista*, March 5, 2021, https://www.statista.com/statistics/1120226/broadcasting-rights-nfl-by-sector/; Ronald Blum, "AP Exclusive: MLB Projects $640K per Game Loss with No Fans," Associated Press, May 16, 2020, https://apnews.com/article/75087708a030c20637c5ea25b5c99c40.

13. Zak Garner-Purkis, "Don't Be Fooled by the Premier League's $1 billion Predicted Revenue Drop," *Forbes*, June 11, 2020, https://www.forbes.com/sites/zakgarnerpurkis/2020/06/11/dont-be-fooled-by-the-premier-leagues-1bn-predicted-revenue-drop/?sh=7b525f7f237e.

14. David Hesmondalgh, *The Cultural Industries*, 3rd ed. (Los Angeles: Sage, 2013), 128.

15. Terry Flew, "The 'Theory' in Media Theory: The 'Media-Centrism' Debate," *Media Theory* 1, no. 1 (2017): 51.

16. John Goldlust, *Playing for Keeps: Sport, the Media, and Society* (Melbourne, Australia: Longman Chesire, 1987), 145.

17. Robert McChesney, "Media Made Sport: A History of Sports Coverage in the United States," in *Media, Sports, and Society*, ed. Lawrence Wenner (Newbury Park, CA: Sage, 1989), 49.

18. Sut Jhally, "Cultural Studies and the Sports/Media Complex," in Wenner, *Media, Sports, and Society*, 80.

19. Lawrence A Wenner, "Playing the MediaSport Game," in *MediaSport*, ed. Wenner (New York: Routledge, 1998), 4.

20. Kirsten Frandsen, *Sport and Mediatization* (New York: Routledge, 2020), 11.

21. Douglas Kellner, "The Sports Spectacle, Michael Jordan, and Nike: Unholy Alliance?" in *Michael Jordan, Inc.: Corporate Sport, Media Culture, and Late Modern America*, ed. David L. Andrews (Albany, NY: SUNY Press, 2001), 66–67.

22. David L. Andrews, *Sport-Commerce-Culture: Essays on Sport in Late-Capitalist America* (New York: Peter Lang, 2006), 9.

23. Ed Desser, telephone conversation with the author, May 9, 2017.

24. Mark Lazarus, telephone conversation with the author, April 18, 2017.

25. Ramon Lobato, *Netflix Nations: The Geography of Digital Distribution* (New York: NYU Press, 2019), x.

26. Ibid., 160. Emphasis in original.

27. Benjamin Rader, *In Its Own Image: How Television Has Transformed Sports* (New York: Free Press, 1984), 94.

28. Ibid., 113, 101, 121–122.

29. Ibid., 125.

30. Tom Tolnay, "Pro Basketball on Verge of Tapping in TV $$," *Back Stage*, April 18, 1969, 2–3.

31. Hazel Hardy, "The Many Slices of the Sports TV Pie," *Broadcasting*, December 1, 1969, 46–47.

32. "ABC's Arledge Places $16-Mil Bet on Pro Basketball in 3-Year Deal," *Variety*, February 18, 1970, 1.

33. "ABC Goes to Court to Get Back NBA Rights," *Broadcasting,* March 12, 1973, 61.

34. "ABC Loses Basketball Suit," *Broadcasting,* August 6, 1973, 23.

35. Adam J. Criblez, *Tall Tales and Short Shorts: Dr. J, Pistol Pete, and the Birth of the Modern NBA* (Lanham, MD: Rowman and Littlefield, 2017), 174.

36. Criblez, *Tall Tales*, 168; Leonard Koppett, "N.B.A. Merger Off, A.B.A. May Try Law-Court Press," *New York Times*, January 3, 1974, 47.

37. Sun-Telegram Wire Services, "Watch Out NBA! You've Been Raided Again," *Evening Telegram,* September 12, 1969, D4.

38. Criblez, *Tall Tales*, 171.

39. Ibid., 174.

40. Pete Croatto, *From Hang Time to Prime Time: Business, Entertainment, and the Birth of the Modern-Day NBA* (New York: Atria, 2020), 20.

41. Sam Goldaper, "N.B.A. Gets Merger 'Spur,'" *New York Times*, May 25, 1976.

42. Two other ownership groups also benefited, despite not joining the league. Kentucky Colonels owner John Y. Brown received $3.3 million for folding his team, and Spirits of St. Louis owners Danny and Ozzy Silna earned $2.2 million plus a percentage of NBA television revenue in perpetuity, which would have amounted to nearly $1 billion before the two sides agreed to close the arrangement in January 2014 (Criblez, *Tall Tales*, 174–75.

43. David Klatell, "NBA Aim: No Network Tangle while Untangling Cable," *Washington Post*, July 22, 1979.

44. David Dupree, "NBA: Red Ink and a Bleak Future," *Washington Post*, March 15, 1983.

45. Criblez, *Tall Tales*, 172.

46. Alvin P. Sanoff, "Even Bigger Bucks Ahead for Pro Sports," *U.S. News and World Report*, October 11, 1982, 74.

47. Gerald Eskenazi, "Familiar Foes in NBA Talks," *New York Times*, October 24, 1982.

48. For more on the original proposal, see Ed Garvey, "Union Goal for '80s: Greater Share of Gross Revenues," *Washington Post*, February 11, 1979.

49. Jeff Hasen, United Press International, March 28, 1983.

50. BRI would become a contentious term in the subsequent decades, and disputes over its meaning would play a major role in the NBA's four labor strikes to come (in 1995, 1996, 1998, and 2011).

51. David Dupree, "NBA, Players Put Faith, Hope in Parity," *Washington Post*, April 2, 1983.

52. "Basketball," *Washington Post*, December 21, 1985.

53. Mike Prada, "NBA to Announce 9-Year, $24 billion TV Deal with ESPN, Turner," *SB Nation*, October 5, 2014.

54. Meg James, "The Rise of Sports TV Costs and Why Your Cable Bill Keeps Going Up," *Los Angeles Times*, December 5, 2016.

55. While the names of the latter two services have since changed to HBO Max and Paramount+, the point remains valid. Ennel van Eeden and Wilson Chow, "Perspectives from the Global Entertainment & Media Outlook 2018–2022," *Pricewaterhouse Coopers*, June 2018, 10, 16, https://www.pwc.com/gx/en/entertainment-media/outlook/perspectives-from-the-global-entertainment-and-media-outlook-2018-2022.pdf.

56. "At the Gate and Beyond: Outlook for the Sports Market in North America through 2022," *PricewaterhouseCoopers*, November 2018, https://www.pwc.com/us/en/industries/tmt/library/sports-outlook-north-america.html.

57. Frank Fitzpatrick, "A Wide World of Sports Fans," *Philadelphia Inquirer*, October 17, 2005.

58. Mark Koba, "US Pro Teams Give 'Away Game' a Whole New Meaning," *CNBC*, October 10, 2013.

59. Timothy Havens, *Global Television Marketplace* (London: BFI, 2006), 17, 27.

60. Ibid., 37.

61. Hesmondalgh, *Cultural Industries*, 128, 137, 151.

62. Jennifer Holt, *Empires of Entertainment: Media Industries and the Politics of Deregulation, 1980–1996* (New Brunswick, NJ: Rutgers University Press, 2011), 10.

63. Brett Hutchins and David Rowe, *Sport beyond Television: The Internet, Digital Media and the Rise of Networked Media Sport* (New York: Routledge, 2012), 9.

64. Victoria E. Johnson, "Everything New Is Old Again: Sport Television, Innovation, and Tradition for a Multi-platform Era," in *Beyond Prime Time: Television Programming in the Post-network Era*, ed. Amanda D. Lotz (New York: Routledge, 2009), 133.

65. Johnson, "Everything New," 115–16.

66. Travis Vogan, *Keepers of the Flame: NFL Films and the Rise of Sports Media* (Urbana: University of Illinois Press, 2014), 2.

67. Victoria E. Johnson, "Historicizing TV Networking: Broadcasting, Cable, and the Case of ESPN," in *Media Industries: History, Theory and Method*, ed. Jennifer Holt and Alisa Perren (Malden, MA: Blackwell, 2009), 61.

68. David Z. Morris, "NFL vs. NBA: Which Will Be America's Biggest Sport 10 Years from Now?" *Fortune*, May 26, 2018, https://fortune.com/2018/05/26/nfl-vs-nba-americas-biggest-sport/.

69. Dan Wolken, "Falling TV Ratings across Most Sports? Here Are Four Reasons to Explain Drop during Pandemic," *USA Today*, October 8, 2020, https://www.usatoday.com/story/sports/media/2020/10/08/pandemic-why-tv-ratings-sports-have-been-down-since-returning/5913720002/.

70. Adrian Wojnarowski and Zach Lowe, "NBA Revenue for 2019–20 Season Dropped 10% to $8.3 billion, Sources Say," *ESPN.com*, October 28, 2020, https://www.espn.com/nba/story/_/id/30211678/nba-revenue-2019-20-season-dropped-10-83-billion-sources-say; Chris Bumbaca, "With Start of NHL Season Approaching, Commissioner Gary Bettman Says League Losses Will Eclipse $1 billion," *USA Today*, January 11, 2021, https://www.usatoday.com/story/sports/nhl/2021/01/11/2021-nhl-season-gary-bettman-losses/6632033002/; Jenna Ciccotelli, "Rob Manfred Says MLB Teams Combined for $3 billion in Losses amid COVID-19," *Bleacher Report*, October 20, 2020, https://bleacherreport.com/articles/2914363-rob-manfred-says-mlb-teams-combined-for-3-billion-in-losses-amid-covid-19.

71. Associated Press, "NFL Teams Lost Almost $4 billion in Revenue due to Coronavirus Pandemic," CBS News, January 29, 2021, https://www.cbsnews.com/news/nfl-pandemic-billion-revenue-loss/.

72. Shlomo Sprung, "NBA TV Ratings on TNT, ESPN, ABC Up 34% from Last Year, per Nielsen," *Forbes*, January 21, 2021, https://www.forbes.com/sites/shlomosprung/2021/01/21/nba-tv-ratings-on-tnt-espn-abc-up-34-from-last-year-per-nielsen/?sh=6dccbd294ddc; John Ourand, "National Hockey League Viewership Numbers Off to an Impressive Start," *Sports Business Journal*, February 18, 2021, https://www.bizjournals.com/newyork/news/2021/02/18/nhl-viewership-numbers-off-to-an-impressive-start.html.

73. Jonathan Berr, "NFL, TV Networks Sign $105 billion Broadcast Rights Deals," *Forbes*, March 18, 2021, https://www.forbes.com/sites/jonathanberr/2021/03/18/nfl-tv-network-sign-105-billion-broadcast-rights-deal/?sh=582832b84e0a; "NHL Back on ESPN with 7-Year Multiplatform Deal," *ESPN.com*, March 10, 2021, https://www.espn.com/nhl/story/_/id/31039351/nhl-back-espn-7-year-multiplatform-deal.

74. Michael Curtin, *Playing to the World's Biggest Audience: The Globalization of Chinese Film and TV* (Berkeley: University of California Press, 2007), 215.

75. Lobato, *Netflix Nations*, 108.

76. Richard Lapchick, "The 2015 Racial and Gender Report Card: National Basketball Association," *Tidesport.org*, July 1, 2015, https://static.ecestaticos.com/file/c01/981/d07/c01981d07e3019b279279eaed8ad56f9.pdf.

77. Meredith Cash and Shayanne Gal, "NBA's Trend of Increasing Number of International Players Appears to Be Slowing Down, *Business Insider*, October 16, 2018, https://www.businessinsider.com/growing-number-of-foreign-born-players-in-nba-slows-2018-10.

78. Jonathan Abrams, "NBA Imports Euro Step and Other Moves of a Global Game," *New York Times*, November 17, 2010.

79. Jake O'Donnell, "The NBA's Vice President of Global Merchandising Reached Out to Set the Record Straight about Short Sleeve Uniforms," *SportsGrid*, January 24, 2014.

80. Michael McCarthy, "NBA's Silver: Ads on Player Jerseys Are 'Inevitable,'" *Advertising Age*, March 19, 2014.

81. Brian Mahoney, "NBA to Begin Selling Jersey Sponsorships in 2017–18," *NBA.com*, April 15, 2016.

82. Lobato, *Netflix Nations*, 160. Emphasis in original.

83. Chuck Tryon, *On-Demand Culture: Digital Delivery and the Future of Movies* (New Brunswick, NJ: Rutgers University Press, 2013), 47–48.

84. Albert Moran, *Understanding the Global TV Format* (Portland, OR: Intellect, 2006), 20.

85. Ibid., 25.

86. The Euro step is a specific move popularized by European players that entered the NBA in the early 2000s, which is now commonplace throughout the league. For more, see Jonathan Abrams, "NBA Imports Euro Step and Other Moves of a Global Game," *New York Times*, November 17, 2010.

87. Paul S. N. Lee, "The Absorption and Indigenization of Foreign Media Cultures," *Asian Journal of Communication* 1, no. 2 (1991): 65.

88. Michael Keane, Anthony Y. H. Fung, and Albert Moran, *New Television, Globalisation, and the East Asian Cultural Imagination* (Hong Kong, PRC: Hong Kong University Press, 2007), 74.

89. Tony Schirato, "Television Formats and Contemporary Sport," in *Global Television Formats: Understanding Television across Borders*, ed. Tasha Oren and Sharan Shahaf (New York: Routledge, 2012), 56–58.

90. Marwan Kraidy, *Hybridity, or the Cultural Logic of Globalization* (Philadelphia: Temple University Press, 2005), 1.

91. John Tomlinson, *Cultural Imperialism: A Critical Introduction* (London: Continuum, 1991), 175. Emphasis added.

92. Daya Kishan Thussu, "Mapping Global Media Flow and Contra-flow," in *Media on the Move: Global Flow and Contra-flow*, ed. Daya Kishan Thussu (London: Routledge, 2007), 23, 28.

93. Thomas Lamarre, "Regional TV: Affective Media Geographies." *Asiascape: Digital Asia* 2 (2015): 94, 109.

94. Silvio Waisbord, "McTV: Understanding the Global Popularity of Television Formats," *Television New Media* 5, no. 4 (November 2004): 371, 380.

95. Michele Hilmes, *Network Nations: A Transnational History of British and American Broadcasting* (London: Routledge, 2011), 310.

96. Toby Miller, Geoffrey Lawrence, Jim McKay, and David Rowe, *Globalization and Sport: Playing the World* (London: Sage, 2001), 4.

97. Raymond Boyle and Richard Haynes, *Power Play: Sport, the Media, and Popular Culture*, 2nd ed. (Edinburgh: Edinburgh University Press, 2009), 44, 144.

98. Michael Serazio, *The Power of Sports: Media and Spectacle in American Culture* (New York: NYU Press, 2019), 17.

99. Soheil Daulatzai, "View the World from American Eyes: Ball, Islam, and Dissent in Post-race America," in *Basketball Jones: America above the Rim*, ed. Todd Boyd and Kenneth L. Shropshire (New York: NYU Press, 2000), 198.

100. Ibid., 199.

101. Jhally, "Cultural Studies," 82.

102. Victoria E. Johnson, *Sports TV* (New York: Routledge, 2021) 14. Emphasis in original.

103. Ibid., 15.

104. Jennifer Holt and Alisa Perren, "Introduction: Does the World Really Need One More Field of Study?" in *Media Industry Studies: History, Theory, and Method*, ed. Holt and Perren (Malden, MA: Blackwell, 2009), 8–9.

105. Timothy Havens, Amanda D. Lotz, and Serra Tinic, "Critical Media Industry Studies: A Research Approach," *Communication, Culture and Critique* 2 (2009): 238, 246, 249.

106. Todd Gitlin, *Inside Prime Time* (Berkeley: University of California Press, 1983), 14.

107. The other colocation is Turner's Techwood campus in Atlanta, Georgia, from which Turner operates the NBA's domestic League Pass streaming service.

108. John Thornton Caldwell, *Production Culture: Industrial Reflexivity and Critical Practice in Film and Television* (Durham, NC: Duke University Press, 2008), 4.

109. Yago Colás, *Ball Don't Lie! Myth, Genealogy, and Invention in the Cultures of Basketball* (Philadelphia: Temple University Press, 2016), 12.

Chapter 1. The Court

1. Scott Davis, "TV Viewing Habits Show How the NFL Is Still as Dominant as Ever," *Business Insider*, January 5, 2019.

2. Anne Wright, telephone call, August 16, 2017.

3. Bernard Miège, *The Capitalization of Cultural Production* (New York: International General, 1989), 144. Emphasis in original.

4. Robert McChesney, "Media Made Sport: A History of Sports Coverage in the United States," in *Media, Sports, and Society*, ed. Lawrence Wenner (Newbury Park, CA: Sage, 1989), 49.

5. "Goodwill Games Roundup: Soviet Union Beats United States by 99 Medals," Associated Press, July 21, 1986.

6. The XFL did not receive any up-front rights fees from ESPN/ABC or Fox; instead, the partners agreed to a split of advertising revenue beyond an undisclosed amount, and the networks agreed to cover any television production costs. For the networks, then, the arrangement was fairly low-risk and allowed the XFL to use its airtime to establish an audience that could then be leveraged into a more lucrative agreement. Because the Big3 contract lacked concrete figures, a similar type of arrangement seems most likely (Michael Colangelo, "The XFL Isn't Getting Any Money from ESPN or FOX for Its TV Rights," *USA Today*, May 7, 2019, https://touchdownwire.usatoday.com/2019/05/07/xfl-espn-fox-abc-fs1-tv-rights-television-rights-broadcast/; Dade Hayes, "CBS Sports and Big3 Set Exclusive TV Deal for 3-on-3 Basketball Summer Season," *Deadline*, April 4, 2019).

7. Daniel Dayan and Elihu Katz, *Media Events: The Live Broadcasting of History* (Cambridge, MA: Harvard University Press, 1992), 1, 4–5.

8. Ibid., 54.

9. Mike Chant, telephone communication, November 13, 2017.

10. Margaret Morse, "Sport on Television: Replay and Display," in *Regarding Television: Critical Approaches—an Anthology*, ed. E. Ann Kaplan (Los Angeles: American Film Institute, 1983), 48.

11. Ibid.

12. John Goldlust, *Playing for Keeps: Sport, the Media, and Society* (Melbourne, Australia: Longman Chesire, 1987), 91.

13. Ibid., 147–48.

14. Raymond Boyle and Richard Haynes, *Power Play: Sport, the Media and Popular Culture*, 2nd ed. (Edinburgh: Edinburgh University Press, 2009), 55.

15. Cornwell, T. Bettina, Clinton S. Weeks, and Donald P. Roy, "Sponsorship-Linked Marketing: Opening the Black Box," *Journal of Advertising* 34, no.2 (2005): 23, 36.

16. Ibid., 36.

17. Ibid., 27, 35–36.

18. Ibid., 35–36.

19. Ibid., 39.

20. Sports Video Group, "SVG Summit: Keynote Conversation with Dick Ebersol and David Stern," YouTube video, 41:34, posted June 1, 2015.

21. "Basketball," *Washington Post*, December 21, 1985, B2.

22. Ed Desser, telephone conversation with the author, May 9, 2017.

23. Associated Press, June 9, 1987.

24. Brian Moran, "Big Mac, NBA Court Soviets," *Advertising Age*, June 1, 1987, 1.

25. Michael Hiestand, "The NBA Hustles a New Event," *Adweek*, October 12, 1987.

26. Moran, "Big Mac, NBA Court Soviets."

27. Hiestand, "NBA Hustles."

28. Ibid.

29. Ettore Frangipane, "Basket: Milwaukee Bucks—Tracer Milano 1987—Commento di Dan Peterson—Torneo McDonald's Open," YouTube, 1:20:44, posted October 9, 2019, https://www.youtube.com/watch?v=qB1whjIh8_Q.

30. Doug Smith, "Championship Series Hooks the World's Attention," *USA Today*, June 5, 1989, 5C.

31. Richard Tedesco, "Finding NBA Highlights Is Easier with Computer," *Electronic Media*, March 14, 1988, 24.

32. Desser discussion.

33. *Electronic Media*, January 4, 1988, 156.

34. Marianne Paskowski, "U.K. Firm Backs Off from Showtime," *Electronic Media*, April 28, 1989.

35. Jay Weiner, "Baseball Is Getting Worldly; Sport Starting to Catch Overseas," *Minneapolis Star Tribune*, October 20, 1991, 6C.

36. Michele Hilmes, *Network Nations: A Transnational History of British and American Broadcasting* (London: Routledge, 2011), 301.

37. Timothy Havens, *Global Television Marketplace* (London: BFI, 2006), 27.

38. Colin Hoskins and Stuart McFadyen, "The U.S. Competitive Advantage in the Global Television Market: Is It Sustainable in the New Broadcasting Environment?" *Canadian Journal of Communication* 16, no. 2 (1991): 207–24.

39. Desser discussion.

40. United Press International, April 8, 1988.

41. Skip Myslenski, "TBS Ready to Roll with Goodwill Epic," *Chicago Tribune*, June 29, 1986, https://www.chicagotribune.com/news/ct-xpm-1986-06-29-8602160411-story.html.

42. Lindsay Gaze, "Courtside," *Sydney Herald*, May 24, 1988.

43. Jack McCallum, "Rare Birds Sighted," *Sports Illustrated*, August 8, 1988.

44. Julia Greenberg, "What the NBA Knows about China That Silicon Valley Doesn't," *Wired*, June 1, 2016, https://www.wired.com/2016/06/nba-knows-china-silicon-valley-doesnt/.

45. Kim Bohuny, telephone communication, September 22, 2017.

46. Ibid.

47. Richard Lorant, Associated Press, October 8, 1988.

48. Larry Siddons, Associated Press, November 11, 1988.

49. "Greek Satellite Experiment Launched to Test Response to Original Eurofare," *Variety*, May 10, 1989, 382.

50. B. Samantha Stenzel, "Greek Exhibs Fight to Survive as Admissions Fall Alarmingly," *Variety*, September 28, 1988, 28.

51. "International Ratings," *Broadcast*, March 10, 1989, 26.

52. David Aldridge, "Stern Adds Worldwide Concept," *Washington Post*, February 12, 1989, D4.

53. Among those players were Utah Jazz teammates Karl Malone and John Stockton. "If he comes over and wins, a lot of guys are guying to be teed off," said Malone

(Michael Wilbon, "Once a Long Shot, Soviet in 3-Point Contest Aid International NBA," *Washington Post*, February 12, 1989).

54. "Coverage of 2017 NBA Global Games in Mexico City and London," *ESPN.com*, January 20, 2017.

55. Ruben Carbajal, telephone conversation with the author, October 20, 2017.

56. Mojie Crigler, telephone conversation with the author, June 15, 2017.

57. Ibid.

58. Carbajal discussion.

59. Anne Wright, telephone conversation with the author, August 16, 2017.

60. Ibid.

61. Dallas W. Smythe, "On the Audience Commodity and Its Work," in *Media and Cultural Studies: KeyWorks*, rev. ed., ed. Meenakshi Gigi Durham and Douglas M. Kellner (Malden, MA: Blackwell, 2006), 242.

62. Cornwell, Weeks, and Roy, "Sponsorship-Linked Marketing," 23, 35–36.

63. Albert Moran, *Understanding the Global TV Format* (Portland, OR: Intellect, 2006), 20.

64. Ibid., 65.

65. "NFL Announces Five 2019 International Games," *NFL.com*, January 21, 2019; Associated Press, "MLB Nixes Games in Mexico, Puerto Rico; Cards Games in London Still on Slate," *Fox Sports*, March 19, 2020.

66. Wright discussion.

67. Anne Wright, telephone conversation with the author, August 16, 2017.

68. Crigler discussion.

69. Daya Kishan Thussu, "Mapping Global Media Flow and Contra-flow," in *Media on the Move: Global Flow and Contra-flow*, ed. Daya Kishan Thussu (London: Routledge, 2007), 23, 28.

70. Roland Robertson, *Globalization: Social Theory and Global Culture* (London: Sage, 1992); Silvio Waisbord, "McTV: Understanding the Global Popularity of Television Formats," *Television and New Media* 5, no. 4 (November 2004): 378.

71. Marwan Kraidy, *Hybridity, or the Cultural Logic of Globalization* (Philadelphia: Temple University Press, 2005), 14, 95–96.

72. Peter Burke, *Cultural Hybridity* (Malden, MA: Polity, 2009), 53.

73. Waisbord, "McTV," 378.

74. Ramon Lobato, *Netflix Nations: The Geography of Digital Distribution* (New York: NYU Press, 2019), 108.

75. Tanner Mirrlees, *Global Entertainment Media: Between Cultural Imperialism and Cultural Globalization* (New York: Routledge, 2013), 199.

76. Ibid., 199.

77. Chuck Tryon, *On-Demand Culture: Digital Delivery and the Future of Movies* (New Brunswick, NJ: Rutgers University Press, 2013), 47–48.

78. Danny Meiseles, telephone conversation with the author, September 22, 2017.

79. Ibid.

80. Chant discussion.

81. Kerry Kolasa-Sikiaridi, "Greek Fans Send Giannis Antetokounmpo Best Wishes for the All-Star Game," *Greek Reporter*, February 15, 2017.

82. Lobato, *Netflix Nations*, 160–61. Emphasis in original.

83. Demetrius Bell, "Sacramento Kings Bring International Flavor to the Alternative Court Design," *Forbes*, September 15, 2017.

84. Sacramento Kings executive (anonymous by request), personal communication, Sacramento, California, May 29, 2018.

85. Greg Wissinger, "The Kings 'City' Jersey Has Leaked and It's Really Bad," *Sactown Royalty*, December 14, 2017.

86. Kevin Fippin, "Kings 2018 City Jerseys Revealed," *Sactown Royalty*, November 7, 2018.

87. Andrew Nicholson (vice president of digital and content, Sacramento Kings), email message to the author, June 11, 2018.

88. SI Wire, "Kings Launch First Hindi Website in NBA 'to Become India's Home Team,'" *Sports Illustrated*, July 22, 2014.

89. Matt Young, "A Look at Every Team's NBA 'City' Uniforms This Season," *SF Gate*, November 18, 2018.

90. "Knicks Announce Schedule of Theme Nights for 2018–19 Season," *NBA.com*, August 28, 2018.

91. Chant discussion.

92. Marcel Danesi, *Brands* (New York: Routledge, 2006), 122.

93. Ibid., 122.

94. Candice Avila-Garcia, "Spurs Go 'Puro San Antonio' with Creative Version of Schedule," *San Antonio Express-News*, August 28, 2019.

95. Goodnight&GoSpursGo, "The Spurs Loteria Cards Are Just as Amazing as Advertised," *SB Nation: Pounding the Rock*, October 27, 2019, https://www.poundingtherock.com/2019/10/27/20935210/the-spurs-loteria-cards-are-just-as-amazing-as-advertised.

96. Jamie Dejesus, "Brooklyn Nets Pay Tribute to Bed-Stuy, Notorious B.I.G. with New City Edition Uniforms," *Brooklyn Reporter*, November 29, 2019.

97. Chant discussion.

98. Waisbord, "McTV," 380.

99. Danesi, *Brands*, 122; Kraidy, *Hybridity*, 95.

Chapter 2. The Venue

1. Karen Hogan Ketchum, "One Season Down, Sacramento Kings' Golden 1 Center Remains Tops in Tech," *Sports Video Group*, May 18, 2017, https://www.sportsvideo.org/2017/05/18/one-season-down-sacramento-kings-golden-1-center-remains-tops-in-tech/.

2. Chintan Patel, interview by Taylor Bloom, "Bridging the Physical and Digital Worlds," *SportTechie*, March 26, 2020.

3. Andrew Shannon, interview by Taylor Bloom, "Bridging the Physical and Digital Worlds," *SportTechie*, March 26, 2020.

4. Ian Bogost and Nick Montfort, "Platform Studies: Frequently Questioned Answers," *Proceedings of the Digital Arts and Culture Conference*, University of California–Irvine, 2009.

5. Tarleton Gillespie, "The Politics of 'Platforms,'" *New Media and Society* 12, no. 3 (2010): 348.

6. Ibid.

7. Greg Siegel, "Disneyfication, the Stadium, and the Politics of Ambiance," in *Rethinking Disney: Private Control, Public Dimensions*, ed. Mike Budd and Max H. Kirsch (Middletown, CT: Wesleyan University Press, 2005), 303–4.

8. Ibid.

9. Göran Bolin, "Spaces of Television: The Structuring of Consumers in a Swedish Shopping Mall," in *Mediaspace: Place, Scale and Culture in a Media Age,* ed. Nick Couldry and Anna McCarthy (New York: Routledge, 2004), 127.

10. Holly Kruse, *Off-Track and Online: The Networked Spaces of Horse Racing* (Cambridge, MA: MIT Press, 2016), 5.

11. Fiona Allon, "An Ontology of Everyday Control: Space, Media Flows and 'Smart' Living in the Absolute Present," in Couldry and McCarthy, *Mediaspace*, 267.

12. Ibid., 271.

13. Nick Couldry and Anna McCarthy, "Orientations: Mapping MediaSpace," in Couldry and McCarthy, *Mediaspace*, 1.

14. Andrew Ross, "Dot.com Urbanism," in Couldry and McCarthy, *Mediaspace*, 146.

15. "Basketball Takes $600 million Bounce to NBC," *Broadcasting and Cable*, November 13, 1989.

16. Brandon Costa, "Specialty Cameras, Positions Highlight Coverage of CBS Sports' 31st Consecutive Final Four," *Sports Video Group*, April 7, 2021, https://www.sportsvideo.org/2013/04/07/specialty-cameras-positions-highlight-coverage-of-cbs-sports-31st-consecutive-final-four/.

17. Sports Video Group, "SVG Summit: Keynote Conversation with Dick Ebersol and David Stern," YouTube, 41:34, posted June 1, 2015, https://www.youtube.com/watch?v=X6zAFPu74sU.

18. John Fortunato, *The Ultimate Assist: The Relationship and Broadcast Strategies of the NBA and Television Networks* (Cresskill, NJ: Hampton, 2001), 111.

19. Ibid., 105.

20. Ibid.

21. Ibid., 106–8.

22. Ibid.

23. Brandon Costa, "NBA Returns: League, ESPN, Turner Unveil Preliminary Production Plans for the Disney Bubble," *Sports Video Group*, July 24, 2020, https://www.sportsvideo.org/2020/07/24/nba-returns-league-espn-turner-unveil-preliminary-production-plans-for-the-disney-bubble/.

24. Sports Video Group, "SVG Summit."

25. Ibid.

26. Ibid.

27. Zach Spedden, "NBA Arenas Oldest to Newest: 2020 Update," *Arena Digest*, January 8, 2020, https://arenadigest.com/2020/01/08/nba-arenas-oldest-to-newest-2020-update/.

28. John Siegfried and Andrew Zimbalist, "The Economics of Sports Facilities and Their Communities," *Journal of Economic Perspectives* 14, no. 3 (2000): 96.

29. Ibid.

30. Roger I. Abrams, *Playing Tough: The World of Sports and Politics* (Boston: Northeastern University Press, 2013), 210.

31. Neil deMause and Joanna Cagan, *Field of Schemes: How the Great Stadium Swindle Turns Public Money into Private Profit*, rev. ed. (Lincoln: University of Nebraska Press, 2008), 31.

32. Ibid. 48–55.

33. Ibid., 57–58.

34. Ibid., 34–35.

35. Ibid. 37.

36. George Lipsitz, *How Racism Takes Place* (Philadelphia: Temple University Press, 2011), 73.

37. DeMause and Cagan, *Field of Schemes*, 236.

38. Lipsitz, *How Racism Takes Place*, 78.

39. Howard Frank, Sandra Lopez, and Sonia Santana, "Old before Their Time: The Shortened Lifespan of Professional Athletic Venues and Its Implication for Public Subsidy," *Public Administration Quarterly* 22, no. 3 (1998): 390.

40. Ibid., 384, 397.

41. DeMause and Cagan, *Field of Schemes*, 65.

42. Ibid., 230.

43. Frank, Lopez, and Santana, "Old before Their Time," 395.

44. Ohm Youngmisuk, "MSG Shows Off New Features," *ESPN.com*, October 24, 2013, https://tv5.espn.com/new-york/nba/story/_/id/9874414/madison-square-garden-unveils-new-features-part-1-billion-renovation.

45. Kevin Seifert, "With $6.7 billion in Public Money, NFL Closes Stadium Era," *ESPN.com*, March 28, 2017, https://www.espn.com/blog/nflnation/post/_/id/234573/with-6700000000-in-public-money-nfl-stadium-era-closes.

46. Davide Dukcevich, "The NBA Is Blowing It," *Forbes*, December 18, 2001, https://www.forbes.com/2001/12/18/1218nba.html?sh=44295af343f1.

47. Robert Siegel and Stefan Fatsis, "NBA's Difficulties Renegotiating Television Contracts in the Wake of Decreased Viewership and a Soft Ad Market," *All Things Considered*, National Public Radio, February 9, 2001.

48. Steve Wyche, "Jordan Makes It Official: He's a Wizard," *Washington Post*, September 25, 2001.

49. Mike Penner, "NBC Exit Strategy Begins NBA Spin," *Los Angeles Times*, December 18, 2001.

50. Jay Posner, "Disney-AOL In, NBC Out in New NBA TV Accord," *San Diego Union-Tribune*, January 23, 2002.

51. Paulsen, "ABC's NBA Season Is Lowest Rated Ever on Broadcast TV," *Sports Media Watch*, April 14, 2017.

52. Michael Wilbon, "NBA Lockout Will Dwarf the NFL Strife," *ESPN.com*, July 1, 2011, https://www.espn.com/espn/commentary/news/story?page=wilbon-110630.

53. Mike Prada, "NBA to Announce 9-Year, $24 billion TV Deal with ESPN, Turner," *SB Nation*, October 5, 2014.

54. Larry Coon, "Breaking Down Changes in New CBA," *ESPN.com*, November 28, 2011.

55. Brian Windhorst, "No Teams for Sale as TV Deal Looms," *ESPN.com*, September 10, 2013; Kurt Badenhausen, "Record $550 million Milwaukee Bucks Sale," *Forbes*, April 17, 2014.

56. Kurt Badenhausen, "As Stern Says Goodbye, Knicks, Lakers Set Record," *Forbes*, January 22, 2014.

57. Nick Schwartz, "Steve Ballmer Explains Why He Paid $2 billion for the Clippers," *USA Today*, August 12, 2014.

58. Kurt Badenhausen, "New York Knicks Head the NBA's Most Valuable Teams," *Forbes*, January 20, 2016.

59. Jack Baer, "Get Used to It, Baseball: NBA Teams Pass MLB in Average Value for First Time Ever," *Yahoo! Sports*, April 11, 2019.

60. Mark McClusky, "Techies Are Trying to Turn the NBA into the World's Biggest Sport," *Wired*, May 31, 2016.

61. Bruce Schoenfeld, "What Happened When Venture Capitalists Took Over the Golden State Warriors," *New York Times*, March 20, 2016.

62. Ben Cohen, "The Golden State Warriors Have Revolutionized Basketball," *Wall Street Journal*, April 6, 2016.

63. Schoenfeld, "What Happened."

64. Eric Malinowski, *Betaball: How Silicon Valley and Science Built One of the Greatest Basketball Teams in History* (New York: Atria, 2017), 4.

65. Fitz Tepper, "The Sacramento Kings Just Held the NBA's First Startup Pitch Competition," *TechCrunch*, April 7, 2016.

66. Mary Milliken and Eric Kelsey, "At L.A. Clippers, Steve Ballmer Prizes Team Tested by Adversity," *Reuters*, September 25, 2014.

67. Ari Levy, "How the Golden State Warriors Tap Silicon Valley Tech for that Extra Edge," *CNBC*, February 13, 2017.

68. National Basketball Players Association, "NBPA to Hold Inaugural Technology Summit, Led by VP Andre Iguodala," *NBPA.com*, July 5, 2016.

69. Sam Amick, "Stern Q&A: Saving the Kings and Post-retirement." *USA Today*, October 3, 2016.

70. Taylor Soper, "Sacramento Kings Will Become First NBA Team to Use Chatbots," *GeekWire*, June 1, 2016.

71. Tim Bajarin, "Meet Levi's Stadium," *Time*, August 14, 2014.

72. Sacramento Kings executive (public relations), personal communication, Sacramento, California, May 29, 2018.

73. Associated Press, "New LA Clippers Arena Approved by Inglewood City Council," *NBA.com*, June 15, 2017.

74. Sam Riches, "This Man Wants to Make the NBA a Social Network—and Take It Global," *Wired*, December 26, 2013.

75. Ibid.

76. CBS Sacramento, "Golden 1 Center Opening Just a Week Away." YouTube, 3:16, posted September 27, 2016.

77. KCRA News, "Kings Owner Vivek Ranadive Gives Exclusive Tour," YouTube, 4:34, posted September 27, 2016, https://youtu.be/Kc77rakvRA4.

78. Ibid.

79. Ibid.

80. John Gaudiosi, "Why the Sacramento Kings Are Investing in VR," *Fortune*, October 28, 2015.

81. "NBA Digital and NextVR to Deliver One Live Game per Week in Virtual Reality," news release, *NBA.com*, October 20, 2016.

82. Tom Simonite, "The Sacramento Kings' New Stadium Is Wired for Virtual Reality," *MIT Technology Review*, June 20, 2016.

83. Ibid.

84. Eric Fisher, "Intel Signs Deal to Acquire VR Company Voke, Furthering Interest in Sports," *Sports Business Journal*, November 3, 2016, https://www.sportsbusinessdaily.com/Daily/Issues/2016/11/03/Finance/Intel-Voke.aspx.

85. "Sacramento Kings and Intel Launch NBA's First R&D Site at Golden 1 Center," *NBA.com*, https://www.nba.com/kings/news/sacramento-kings-and-intel-launch-nbas-first-rd-site-golden-1-center.

86. Lisa Fernandez, "Demolition of Candlestick Park Underway; New Development to Replace Old Stadium," *NBC Bay Area*, February 4, 2015, https://www.nbcbayarea.com/news/sports/demolition-of-candlestick-park-underway-new-development-replacing-stadium/114347/.

87. Editorial Board, "What Should Happen in Natomas as Old Arena Closes," *Sacramento Bee*, December 15, 2016.

88. Fernandez, "Demolition of Candlestick Park."

89. Siegel, "Disneyfication," 304–5, 308–9.

90. Ibid. 316.

91. Wendy Chun, *Updating to Remain the Same: Habitual New Media* (Cambridge, MA: MIT Press, 2006), 1–2.

92. David Pierce, "The Highest-Tech Stadium in Sports Is Pretty Much a Giant Tesla," *Wired*, June 3, 2016.

93. KCRA News, "Kings Owner."

94. Pierce, "Highest-Tech Stadium."

95. Ibid.

96. Soper, "Sacramento Kings."

97. Jeff Mosier and Lloyd Brumfield, "Texas Rangers Stadium Vote Passes in Landslide," *Dallas Morning News*, November 6, 2016.

98. Jenna Johnson, "Scott Walker Approves Spending $250 million," *Washington Post*, August 12, 2015.

99. "NBA and Brazil's LNB Announce Groundbreaking Partnership," press release, *NBA.com*, December 11, 2014.

100. Zach Lowe, "What the NBA's Partnership with Brazil Means," *Grantland*, October 27, 2014.

101. Lucas Shaw, "Netflix Wants the World to Binge-Watch," *Bloomberg*, January 12, 2017.

102. "Jeunesse Arena," http://www.jeunessearena.com.br/en/menu/about.

103. "NBA House Presented by Budweiser Returns to Brazil to Celebrate Basketball with Interactive Experience for Fans in Sao Paulo," *NBA.com*, March 25, 2019, https://pr.nba.com/nba-house-brazil/.

104. "NBA Seals Free-to-Air Brazilian Platform with Band," *SportBusiness Media*, October 16, 2019, https://media.sportbusiness.com/news/nba-seals-free-to-air-brazilian-platform-with-band/.

105. Ibid.

106. Chuck Culpepper and Jacob Bogage, "Belgium Leaves Brazil Reeling and Raving, Another World Cup Giant on the Side of the Road," *Washington Post*, July 6, 2018.

107. Ewan MacKenna, "Brazil's Soccer Prowess Has Been Consumed by Years of Neglect," *New York Times*, June 2, 2016.

108. Donna Bowater, "Growing Basketball in Brazil's Favelas," *Vice*, December 22, 2015.

109. Rahul Lal, "Explore the Streets in NBA LIVE 19: Rio Favela," https://www.ea.com/en-au/news/explore-the-streets-rio-favela.

110. Bowater, "Growing Basketball."

111. "Ministry of Education in China, NBA Join Forces," press release, *NBA.com*, October 17, 2014.

112. Terry Lyons, personal communication, New York, December 20, 2017.

113. Shaw, "Netflix Wants the World."

114. Robert Edelman (professor of Russian history, University of California–San Diego, and translator for the 1988 Atlanta Hawks Soviet Union tour), telephone conversation with the author, August 17, 2017; Julia Greenberg, "What the NBA Knows about China That Silicon Valley Doesn't," *Wired*, June 1, 2016.

115. Ailene Voisin, telephone conversation with the author, February 25, 2018.

116. Ennèl van Eeden and Wilson Chow, "Perspectives from the Global Entertainment & Media Outlook, 2018–2022," *PricewaterhouseCoopers*, June 2018, https://www.pwc.com/gx/en/entertainment-media/outlook/perspectives-from-the-global-entertainment-and-media-outlook-2018-2022.pdf.

117. Jeff Zillgitt, "NBA, FIBA Launching 12-Team League in Africa; Barack Obama to Have Hands-on Role," *USA Today*, February 16, 2019.

118. "Basketball Africa League Postpones Start of Inaugural Season," *NBA.com*, March 4, 2020, https://www.nba.com/news/basketball-africa-league-postpones-start-inaugural-season.

119. "NBA G League Expands to Mexico City with Landmark Partnership with Capitanes," press release, *NBA.com*, December 12, 2019, https://www.nba.com/news/nba-g-league-expands-mexico-city-official-release.

120. "Everything to Know about the NBA's 22-Team Restart at Walt Disney World," *ESPN.com*, July 29, 2020, https://www.espn.com/nba/story/_/id/29256449/everything-know-nba-22-team-restart-walt-disney-world.

121. Nick Greene, "How Fake Crowds Know When to Cheer," *Slate*, September 18, 2020, https://slate.com/culture/2020/09/all-of-your-nba-playoffs-broadcasting-questions-answered.html.

122. Ibid.

123. Ibid.

124. Jay Peters, "NFL Games Will Have Artificial Crowd Noise Specific to Each Stadium," *The Verge*, September 10, 2020, https://www.theverge.com/2020/9/10/21430974/nfl-games-artificial-crowd-noise-stadium-specific.

125. "Nicolás Rivero, "How the NBA Is Using Virtual Fans to Make Games Feel Normal," *Quartz*, August 14, 2020, https://qz.com/1891805/how-the-nba-is-using-virtual-fans-to-make-games-feel-normal/.

126. Ibid.

127. Ibid.

128. Bogost and Montfort, "Platform Studies."

129. Gillespie, "Politics of 'Platforms,'" 348.

130. Chintan Patel, interview by Taylor Bloom, "Bridging the Physical and Digital Worlds," *SportTechie*, March 26, 2020.

131. John Branch, "The End of the Warriors as We Know Them," *New York Times*, May 10, 2019, https://www.nytimes.com/2019/05/10/sports/basketball/warriors-oakland-san-francisco.html.

132. Jason Owens, "Clippers Unveil Plans for Privately Financed L.A. Arena Next to New NFL Stadium," *Yahoo!*, July 25, 2019, https://sports.yahoo.com/clippers-unveil-plans-for-privately-financed-la-arena-next-to-new-nfl-stadium-022554849.html.

133. Erik Spanberg, "Hornets Rolling Out New Mobile-Ticketing Policy This Season," *Charlotte Business Journal*, September 25, 2019, https://www.bizjournals.com/charlotte/news/2019/09/25/why-the-hornets-just-joined-a-trend-sweeping-the.html.

134. "Cavaliers and Rocket Mortgage FieldHouse Announce Health and Safety Protocols and Procedures for Start of 2020–21 Season," *NBA.com*, December 4, 2020, https://www.nba.com/cavaliers/safety-protocols-201204; Angie Treasure, "Vivant Arena to Reopen with Limited Number of Fans at Utah Jazz Games," *NBA.com*, November 24, 2020, https://www.nba.com/jazz/news/vivint-arena-reopen-limited-number-fans-utah-jazz-games; "Rockets and Toyota Center Announce Arena Protocol for Your Safety: 2020–21 NBA Season," *NBA.com*, December 17, 2020, https://

www.nba.com/rockets/rockets-and-toyota-center-announce-arena-protocol-your-safety-2020–21-nba-season.

135. Bill Shaikin, "Ballmer Hopes New Stars Will Build Buzz around Clippers," *Los Angeles Times*, July 27, 2019.

136. Ben Golliver, "Inside Chase Center, the Warriors' Billion-Dollar, Privately Financed San Francisco Arena," *Washington Post*, March 6, 2019.

137. Scott Davis, "Warriors President Rick Welts Explains Why Their New $1.4 billion Self-Financed Stadium Was a One-of-a-Kind Situation Other Teams Can't Replicate," *Business Insider*, March 28, 2019, https://www.businessinsider.com/how-chase-center-built-warriors-cost-perfect-storm-2019-3.

138. Golliver, "Inside Chase Center."

139. Bloomberg, "Warriors Make $2 billion from New Arena Even Before Doors Open," *Fortune*, March 28, 2019, https://fortune.com/2019/03/28/warriors-make-2-billion-new-arena/.

140. Johnson, "Scott Walker Approves"; Dale Kasler, "Sacramento Completes Kings Arena Financing with $272.9 million Bond Sale," *Sacramento Bee*, September 24, 2015.

141. Richard N. Velotta, "Don't Count on Raiders Reimbursing Any Public Money for Stadium," *Las Vegas Review-Journal*, September 22, 2019, https://www.reviewjournal.com/business/business-columns/inside-gaming/dont-count-on-raiders-reimbursing-any-public-money-for-stadium-1854372/.

142. Phil Matier and Andy Ross, "Muni Metro Stop at Warriors' New SF Arena Is One Pricey Platform," *San Francisco Chronicle*, April 2, 2018, https://www.sfchronicle.com/bayarea/matier-ross/article/Muni-Metro-stop-at-Warriors-new-SF-arena-is-12797596.php.

143. Steven Sharp, "Details Emerge for Proposed Inglewood People Mover," *Urbanize*, August 12, 2020, https://urbanize.city/la/post/details-emerge-proposed-inglewood-people-mover.

144. Associated Press, "LA Clippers Get Final City Approval to Build Inglewood Arena," *USA Today*, September 8, 2020, https://www.usatoday.com/story/sports/nba/2020/09/08/la-clippers-get-final-city-approval-to-build-inglewood-arena/42399987/.

Chapter 3. The Wires

1. Sarah Perez, "BAMTech Valued at $3.75 billion following Disney Deal," *TechCrunch*, August 8, 2017.

2. Joshua Braun, "Transparent Intermediaries: Building the Infrastructures of Connected Viewing," in *Connected Viewing: Selling Streaming, and Sharing Media in the Digital Era*, ed. Jennifer Holt and Kevin Sanson (New York: Routledge, 2014), 125.

3. Liana B. Baker and Carl O'Donnell, "Exclusive: Crown Castle in Bid to Buy Lightower Fiber Networks," *Reuters*, July 14, 2017, https://www.reuters.com/article

/us-lightower-m-a-crown-castle/exclusive-crown-castle-in-bid-to-buy-lightower-fiber-networks-sources-idUSKBN19Z2JD.

4. Jim Hayes, "Dark Fibers Lie in Wait," *Electrical Contractor*, https://www.ecmag.com/section/systems/dark-fibers-lie-wait.

5. Jason Dachman, "NBA Season Tip-Off: New Replay Center Set to Revolutionize Officiating, Video Ops," *Sports Video Group*, October 28, 2014.

6. Brian Larkin, *Signal and Noise: Media, Infrastructure, and Urban Culture in Nigeria* (Durham, NC: Duke University Press, 2008), 5.

7. Ibid., 6.

8. Lisa Parks, "Stuff You Can Kick: Toward a Theory of Media Infrastructure," in *Between Humanities and the Digital*, ed. Patrik Svensson and David Theo Goldberg (Cambridge, MA: MIT Press, 2015), 356.

9. Sports Video Group, "SVG Summit: Keynote Conversation with Dick Ebersol and David Stern," YouTube, 41:34, posted June 1, 2015, https://youtu.be/X6zAFPu74sU.

10. Ibid.

11. Ed Desser (president, Television and New Media Ventures, NBA), telephone conversation with the author, May 9, 2017.

12. Ibid.

13. Bill Carter, "With America Well Wired, Cable Industry Is Changing," *New York Times*, July 9, 1989.

14. Jennifer Holt, *Empires of Entertainment: Media Industries and the Politics of Deregulation, 1980–1996* (New Brunswick, NJ: Rutgers University Press, 2011), 15.

15. Steve Hershey, "Cable TV: Medium's Message May Be Solvency for NBA," *Washington Post*, October 25, 1981.

16. Steve Hershey, "Utah-Denver Merger Denied; NBA Signs Cable Contracts," *Washington Post*, January 31, 1982.

17. Terry Lyons, "30 Years of NBA Success: Started in a CBS Sports Truck in '83," *Huffington Post*, April 16, 2014.

18. "Sports Served Up," *Broadcasting,* June 20, 1983, 10.

19. Bob Johnson, "NBA to Join Rank of Computerized Sports," *Computerworld*, July 11, 1983.

20. Ibid.

21. Richard Tedesco, "Finding NBA Highlights Is Easier with Computer," *Electronic Media*, March 14, 1988.

22. E. M. Swift, "From Corned Beef to Caviar," *Sports Illustrated*, June 3, 1991.

23. Multichannel News Staff, "DirecTV First 10 Years," *Multichannel News*, March 29, 2018; US Government Accountability Office, *Direct Broadcast Satellite Subscribership Has Grown Rapidly, but Varies across Different Types of Markets*, GAO-05-257 (Washington, DC: US Government Accountability Office, 2005), 6–8.

24. Desser discussion.

25. Ibid.

26. Joe Flint, "Sat Dish Christmas Wish," *Variety,* December 20, 1994.

27. Thomas Walsh, "Satellite Sports: Stealthy Sidebar?" *Variety*, January 16, 1995, 33, 36.

28. Mike Slade, telephone conversation with the author, September 12, 2017.

29. Ibid.

30. Ibid.

31. Debra Aho Williamson, "Score One for ESPN, Starwave," *Ad Age*, October 2, 1995.

32. Bill King, "The Mouse That Roared," *Sports Business Journal*, March 10, 2008.

33. Paul Andrews, "NBA Junkies to Get Their Fill," *Seattle Times*, October 23, 1995.

34. Ibid.

35. "Welcome to the New, Improved Home of the NFL," *NFL.com*, July 25, 2017.

36. P. Andrews, "NBA Junkies."

37. Mark Berniker, "NBA Gets on Web with Starwave's ESPN SportsZone," *Broadcasting and Cable*, October 20, 1995.

38. Richard Tedesco, "NBA Web Sites Warm Up for Finals," *Broadcasting and Cable*, June 3, 1996.

39. Sallie Hofmeister and Jane Hall, "Disney to Buy Cap Cities/ABC for $19 billion, Vault to No. 1," *Los Angeles Times*, August 1, 1995.

40. Paul Farhi, "Time Warner, Turner Talking about Merger," *Washington Post*, August 31, 1995.

41. Paul Farhi, "Time Warner, TBS Agree on $7.5 billion Merger; Deal to Create World's Largest Media Company," *Washington Post*, September 23, 1995.

42. Holt, *Empires of Entertainment*, 165–66.

43. "Disney Wishes on Starwave," *CNN Money*, April 30, 1998.

44. Michael Stroud, "Disney Reportedly in Talks to Buy Stake in Starwave," *Daily News of Los Angeles*, February 14, 1997.

45. Slade discussion.

46. Richard Tedesco, "NBA Sells 'Net Game Packages," *Broadcasting and Cable*, November 3, 1997.

47. Mark Alesia, "Planet NBA League Cashes on Global Boom," *Chicago Daily Herald*, October 16, 1997.

48. Steve Hellmuth, telephone conversation with the author, June 28, 2018.

49. Desser discussion.

50. Richard Tedesco, "NBA.com Lets Fans Take Shots Online," *Broadcasting and Cable*, June 8, 1998.

51. Scott D. Pierce, "Broadcasters Transmit Finals to 175 Countries," *Deseret News*, June 5, 1998.

52. The Finals averaged an 18.8 rating and a 33 share, a number that no playoff series since has approached. The single-game high of 35.89 million viewers, however, was nearly matched by game 7 of the 2016 Cavaliers-Warriors Finals, at 30.8 million (Richard Deitsch, "NBA Finals Game 7 Delivers Huge Audience for ABC," *Sports Illustrated*, June 20, 2016).

53. Michael Stroud, "NBC Investing in NBA Futures," *Broadcasting and Cable*, June 22, 1998.

54. Michael Hiestand, "Jordan's Possible Retirement Permeates NBC Shows," *USA Today*, February 9, 1998.

55. Stefan Fatsis, "NBA Bravely Plans for the Day When Michael Jordan Retires," *Wall Street Journal*, February 6, 1998.

56. David Stern, "Is the NBA Hurt by Player Misconduct?" Lou Dobbs interview, *CNN Moneyline*, February 3, 1998.

57. John Dempsey, "Basketball Abort," *Variety*, October 14, 1998.

58. Kent McDill, "Is NBA Really Thinking the Unthinkable?" *Chicago Daily Herald*, December 9, 1998.

59. Richard Tedesco, "NBA.com Pushes Streaming, Nostalgia," *Broadcasting and Cable*, November 2, 1998.

60. Richard Sandomir, "'Inside Stuff' Succumbs to Old Stuff," *New York Times*, December 29, 1998.

61. Harry Berkowitz and Steve Zipay, "Now, Only Time Will Tell; NBA Lockout May Have Cost League More Than Money," *Newsday*, January 7, 1999.

62. Stephen Wade, "Jordan Creates Global Splash," Associated Press, January 13, 1999.

63. Richard Justice, "Jordan Announces Retirement," *Washington Post*, January 14, 1999.

64. David DuPree and Tom Pedulla, "Fans Still Sold on NBA; Excited Crowds Welcome Return of Game," *USA Today*, January 8, 1999.

65. Michael Hiestand, "Crews' Inside Position Adds Spin," *USA Today*, June 25, 1999.

66. Ed Sherman, "NBA Trying to Morph Web Site into Television," *Chicago Tribune*, December 17, 1999.

67. Desser discussion.

68. Richard Tedesco, "NBA Cross-Media Fast Break," *Broadcasting and Cable*, November 1, 1999.

69. Scott Hettrick, "NBA.comTV Will Tip Off Nov. 2," *Hollywood Reporter*, September 24, 1999.

70. Sherman, "NBA Trying to Morph."

71. Richard Tedesco, "NBA Drives Direct to Fans," *Broadcasting and Cable,* September 27, 1999.

72. Tedesco, "NBA Cross-Media Fast Break."

73. Sherman, "NBA Trying to Morph."

74. "Programmers Pump Up Net," *Broadcasting and Cable*, December 13, 1999.

75. Marcia C. Smith, "Cameras and Mics Help Market the NBA's Stars and Stories," *Orange County Register*, June 7, 2000.

76. Chris Jenkins, "NBA Decides It Will Take It to the Net," *USA Today*, September 19, 2000.

77. Annette John-Hall, "NBA Entertainment Racking Up Wins Worldwide," *Philadelphia Inquirer*, June 15, 2001.

78. "NBA Launches New Interactive Talk Show to Be Simulcast on NBA.com TV and NBA.com," *Business Wire,* October 24, 2000.

79. Richard Tedesco, "Playing in the Big Time," *Broadcasting and Cable*, December 11, 2000.

80. John-Hall, "NBA Entertainment."

81. Richard Tedesco, "Back to the Future: Internet TV," *Broadcasting and Cable*, January 31, 2000.

82. Rachel Alexander, "Take Me Out to the Web Site," *Washington Post,* May 14, 2000.

83. Richard Sandomir, "CBS Will Pay $6 billion for Men's N.C.A.A. Tournament," *New York Times*, November 19, 1999.

84. "RealNetworks Teams with NBA.com on Video Deal," *Brandweek*, January 29, 2001.

85. "NBA to Webcast First-Ever Live Game on NBA.com and REAL.com," *Business Wire*, April 9, 2001.

86. Alan Schwarz, "Take Me Out to the Web Site!" *Newsweek,* October 14, 2002.

87. Ibid.

88. LA Lorek, "High-Tech NBA Helps the World Tune in Video via Cell Phones," *Knight-Ridder Tribune*, June 11, 2005.

89. Richard Sandomir, "Baseball's Web Site Is Big Business," *New York Times*, April 2, 2006.

90. David Lieberman, "Can the Future of TV Be Seen on the Web?" *USA Today*, July 13, 2005.

91. Lorek, "High-Tech NBA."

92. Lieberman, "Can the Future of TV Be Seen?"

93. "American Basketball Comes under Scrutiny," *Contra Costa Times*, June 11, 2006.

94. "2007 NBA Finals by the Numbers," *NBA.com*, June 6, 2007.

95. Michael Lee, "For Spurs, a Familiar Ring," *Washington Post*, June 15, 2007.

96. "NBA Launches NBA League Pass Broadband on NBA.com," *Business Wire*, January 23, 2006.

97. Anick Jesdanun, "40 Live NBA Games Coming to the Internet," Associated Press, October 13, 2006.

98. "NBA.com to Feature Full Season of Live Webcasts as Part of New Site Launch," *Business Wire,* October 16, 2006.

99. R. Thomas Umstead, "NBA Takes It to the 'Net: 'League Pass' Subs Will Get Free Access to Game Streams," *Multichannel News*, October 16, 2006.

100. R. Thomas Umstead, "NBA Shoots for TV Deals by Year-End," *Multichannel News,* October 30, 2006.

101. R. Thomas Umstead, "NBA, Nets Talk Renewal; ESPN, Turner Are Eyeing Television, Digital-Content Rights," *Multichannel News,* April 23, 2007.

102. Paulsen, "ABC's NBA Season Is Lowest Rated Ever on Broadcast TV," *Sports Media Watch*, April 14, 2017.

103. John Hollinger, "How the NBA Can Raise Its Dwindling Ratings," *New York Sun*, June 20, 2007.

104. TV by the Numbers, "NBA Finals TV Ratings, 1974–2008." *Zap2it*, May 22, 2009.

105. Hollinger, "How the NBA Can Raise Its Dwindling Ratings."

106. Steven Levy, "Covering All the Online Bases," *Newsweek*, June 25, 2007.

107. John Consoli, "NBA Cuts $7.4 Bil., 8-year Rights Pact," *Mediaweek*, June 27, 2007.

108. Terry Lefton, "At Age 50, Stern Looks Ahead," *Ad Day*, October 28, 1996.

109. "Turner Broadcasting and the National Basketball Association Broaden Partnership with Digital Rights Agreement," *Business Wire*, January 17, 2008.

110. Mark Lazarus, telephone conversation with the author, April 18, 2017.

111. Hellmuth discussion.

112. Jason Dachman, "NeuLion Takes Over NBA League Pass International," *Sports Video Group*, October 26, 2010.

113. Joe Zappala (senior manager, Digital Media Operations and Technical Services, NBA), personal communication, Secaucus, New Jersey, July 26, 2017.

114. Dachman, "NBA Season Tip-Off."

115. Jason Dachman, "NBA Streamlines B2B Content Delivery with Cloud-Based NBA Content Network," *Sports Video Group*, January 20, 2017.

116. Zappala discussion.

117. Chris Halton (senior vice president, Media Distribution and Technology, NBA), personal communication, Secaucus, New Jersey, July 26, 2017.

118. Julia Alexander, "NBCUniversal Officially Enters the Streaming Wars with Peacock Launch," *The Verge*, April 14, 2020.

119. Julia Alexander, "Charter Customers Who Pay for HBO Will Get HBO Max Free When It Launches Next Month," *The Verge*, April 15, 2020.

120. Malika Andrews, "NBA Fans in China Now Have Access to View Games on NBA League Pass," *Sports Illustrated*, October 14, 2016.

121. Matthew Helvick (senior operations technician, Endeavor Streaming), personal communication, Plainview, New York, July 21, 2017.

122. Braun, "Transparent Intermediaries," 126.

123. Ramon Lobato and Julian Thomas, *The Informal Media Economy* (Cambridge, UK: Polity, 2015), 105.

124. Chuck Tryon, *On-Demand Culture: Digital Delivery and the Future of Movies* (New Brunswick, NJ: Rutgers University Press, 2013), 47–48.

125. Frank Pingue, "'World Feed Truck' Allows NBA to Be a Globetrotter," *Reuters*, February 16, 2016.

126. John Ourand, "NBC Sports Enters Video Streaming Business with Playmaker," *SportsBusiness Journal*, May 23, 2016; SVG Staff, "Turner Acquires Majority Stake in iStreamPlanet," *Sports Video Group*, August 14, 2015.

127. Connie Loizos, "Amazon Acquires Elemental Technologies for a Reported $500 million in Cash," *TechCrunch*, September 3, 2015.

128. Andrew Wallenstein, "Endeavor Buys Streaming Provider NeuLion for $250 million," *Variety*, March 26, 2018.

129. Amanda D. Lotz, *The Television Will Be Revolutionized*, 2nd ed. (New York: NYU Press, 2014), 28.

Chapter 4. The Office

1. The NBA occupies three of the floors and the fourth is occupied by the publishing company Scholastic, the only other tenant in the building for many years. In "Virginia Company Buys Secaucus Building Housing NBA Entertainment, Scholastic," *Jersey Journal*, November 24, 2013, https://www.nj.com/hudson/2013/11/virginia_company_buys_secaucus_building_housing_nba_entertainment_scholastic.html.

2. Sam Borden, "Basketball Players' Night Off Makes a Stand for Sitting Out," *New York Times*, November 30, 2012.

3. Chuck Klosterman, *X: A Highly Specific, Defiantly Incomplete History of the Early 21st Century* (New York: Penguin, 2017), 178.

4. John Nelson, "NBA Takes Its Shot in a Global Market," *Associated Press*, November 25, 1996.

5. Jeff Coplon, "Legends. Champions?" *New York Times*, April 21, 1996.

6. John Tomlinson, *Cultural Imperialism: A Critical Introduction* (London: Continuum, 1991), 175.

7. Silvio Waisbord, "McTV: Understanding the Global Popularity of Television Formats," *Television and New Media* 5, no. 4 (November 2004): 371, 380; Michele Hilmes, *Network Nations: A Transnational History of British and American Broadcasting* (London: Routledge, 2011), 310.

8. Daya Kishan Thussu, "Mapping Global Media Flow and Contra-flow," in *Media on the Move: Global Flow and Contra-Flow*, ed. Daya Kishan Thussu (London: Routledge, 2007), 23, 28.

9. Thomas Lamarre, "Regional TV: Affective Media Geographies." *Asiascape: Digital Asia* 2 (2015): 94, 109.

10. Qtd. in Walter LaFeber, *Michael Jordan and the New Global Capitalism* (New York: W. W. Norton, 1999), 48.

11. Bill Simmons, *The Book of Basketball* (New York: Ballantine), 138.

12. "Video Vision: Network Sports Executives Assess the Future," *Washington Post*, June 21, 1981.

13. Chris Cobbs, "Widespread Cocaine Use by Players Alarms NBA," *Los Angeles Times*, August 20, 1980.

14. Harvey Araton and Filip Bondy, *The Selling of the Green: The Financial Rise and Moral Decline of the Boston Celtics* (New York: HarperCollins, 1992), 83.

15. Todd Boyd, *Young, Black, Rich, and Famous: The Rise of the NBA, the Hip Hop Invasion, and the Transformation of American Culture* (Lincoln: University of Nebraska Press, 2008), 39.

16. Ibid., 167.

17. Nick Schwartz, "Julius Erving Breaks Down His Legendary Fight with Larry Bird," *USA Today*, May 3, 2018.

18. John Fortunato, *The Ultimate Assist: The Relationship and Broadcast Strategies of the NBA and Television Networks* (Cresskill, NJ: Hampton, 2001), 99.

19. Travis Vogan, *Keepers of the Flame: NFL Films and the Rise of Sports Media* (Urbana: University of Illinois Press, 2014), 2.

20. Ibid., 4.

21. Fortunato, *Ultimate Assist*, 99.

22. Todd Boyd and Kenneth L. Shropshire, "Basketball Jones: A New World Order?" in *Basketball Jones: America above the Rim*, ed. Todd Boyd and Kenneth L. Shropshire (New York: NYU Press, 2000), 3–5.

23. Fortunato, *Ultimate Assist*, 99.

24. Ibid., 99–100.

25. Terry Lyons, "30 Years of NBA Success: Started in a CBS Sports Truck in '83," *Huffington Post*, April 16, 2014.

26. Fortunato, *Ultimate Assist*, 140.

27. Joseph Turow, *Breaking Up America: Advertisers and the New Media World* (Chicago: University of Chicago Press, 1997), 3.

28. Ibid., 72–73.

29. John Thornton Caldwell, *Televisuality: Style, Crisis, and Authority in American Television* (New Brunswick, NJ: Rutgers University Press, 1995), 149, 84, 88.

30. Ibid., 100.

31. Vogan, *Keepers of the Flame*, 181.

32. Shawn Fury, "How NBA Entertainment Helped Save the League and Spread a Renaissance," *Vice*, June 15, 2016, https://www.vice.com/en_us/article/mgzgg3/how-nba-entertainment-helped-save-the-league-and-spread-a-renaissance.

33. Retro Basketball Highlights, "America's Game (NBA Action) Is Fannntastic!," 0:30, posted December 27, 2014, https://www.youtube.com/watch?v=ESePMHgyQIY.

34. Gary Kale, *United Press International*, November 15, 1983.

35. Fortunato, *Ultimate Assist*, 61.

36. David Kelly, *United Press International*, June 6, 1984.

37. *PR Newswire*, June 6, 1984.

38. Michael Oriard, *Brand NFL: Making and Selling America's Favorite Sport* (Chapel Hill: University of North Carolina Press, 2007), 16, 25.

39. Amy Saltzman, "The Supply Side of TV Sports," *Adweek*, August 1984.

40. TV by the Numbers, "NBA Finals TV Ratings, 1974–2008," *Zap2it*, May 22, 2009.

41. Anthony Cotton, "NBA: The Boredom Is Over," *Washington Post*, October 25, 1984.

42. Robert V. Bellamy, "Professional Sports Organizations: Media Strategies," in *Media, Sports, and Society*, ed. Lawrence Wenner (Newbury Park, CA: Sage, 1989), 129.

43. Ken Auletta, *Three Blind Mice: How the TV Networks Lost Their Way* (New York: Vintage, 1992), 282.

44. Ibid., 196, 282.

45. Victoria E. Johnson, "Historicizing TV Networking: Broadcasting, Cable, and the Case of ESPN," in *Media Industries: History, Theory and Method*, ed. Jennifer Holt and Alisa Perren (Malden, MA: Blackwell, 2009), 58, 61. Emphasis in original.

46. Susan Tyler Eastman and Timothy P. Meyer, "Sports Programming: Scheduling, Costs, and Competition," in *Media, Sports, and Society*, ed. Lawrence Wenner (Newbury Park, CA: Sage, 1989), 99.

47. Richard Tedesco, "NBA Playoffs Post Strong Cable, Broadcast Ratings," *Electronic Media*, June 6, 1988, 4.

48. Eastman and Meyer, "Sports Programming," 114–15.

49. Ibid.

50. Larry Eldridge, "Anatomy of a Sport's Turnaround," *Christian Science Monitor*, March 6, 1989.

51. William D. Murray, "American Sports Prove Bonanza for Foreign Television," *United Press International*, April 22, 1989.

52. Christine Brennan, "U.S. Sports Are Breaking All Boundaries," *Washington Post*, May 17, 1989.

53. Murray, "American Sports."

54. Brennan, "U.S. Sports."

55. Rachel Shuster, "Brown: Utilizing Magic Key to Lakers' Success," *USA Today*, June 8, 1989.

56. Doug Smith, "Championship Series Hooks the World's Attention," *USA Today*, June 5, 1989.

57. Shuster, "Brown."

58. Associated Press, "David Stern, a Little Man among Giants, Stands Tall," *Los Angeles Times*, February 3, 1985.

59. Sports Video Group, "SVG Summit: Keynote Conversation with Dick Ebersol and David Stern," YouTube, 41:34, posted June 1, 2015, https://www.youtube.com/watch?v=X6zAFPu74sU.

60. Joseph Durso, "A Billion-Dollar Bid by CBS Wins Rights to Baseball Games," *New York Times*, December 15, 1988.

61. John Kosner, personal communication, New York, July 20, 2017.

62. Ed Desser, telephone conversation with the author, May 9, 2017.

63. "Basketball Takes $600 million Bounce to NBC," *Broadcasting and Cable*, November 13, 1989.

64. Larry Stewart, "NBC Gets NBA for Four Years, $600 million," *Los Angeles Times*, November 10, 1989.

65. Jim Benson, "NBC to Air New Basketball Show," *Palm Beach Post*, November 22, 1989.

66. E. M. Swift, "From Corned Beef to Caviar," *Sports Illustrated*, June 3, 1991.

67. Kosner discussion.

68. Armen Keteyian, Harvey Araton, and Martin F. Dardis, *Money Players: Days and Nights Inside the New NBA* (New York: Pocket Books, 1997), 233.

69. Kosner discussion.

70. Ibid.

71. "TNT Keeps NBA for $275 million," *Broadcasting*, December 4, 1989.

72. Stewart, "NBC Gets NBA."

73. *Chicago Professional Sports Ltd. Partnership v. National Basketball Ass'n*, 874 F. Supp. 844 (N.D. Ill. 1995), 1345.

74. Fortunato, *Ultimate Assist*, 54.

75. *Communications Daily*, January 28, 1991.

76. Fortunato, *Ultimate Assist*, 59.

77. Ibid.

78. Ibid.; Richard Sandomir, "NBC and NBA Agree to $750 million Pact," *New York Times*, April 29, 1993; Barry Layne, "NBA Scores $350 Mil in 4-Year Turner Extension," *Hollywood Reporter*, September 22, 1993.

79. Layne, "NBA Scores."

80. Steve McClellan, "One-on-One with David Stern," *Broadcasting and Cable*, October 4, 1993.

81. Michael Curtin, "On Edge: Culture Industries in the Neo-network Era," in *Making and Selling Culture*, ed. Richard Ohmann (Middletown, CT: Wesleyan University Press, 1996), 197.

82. Waisbord, "McTV," 361.

83. In April 1989, the governing body of international basketball, FIBA, voted to allow professional players to compete in the Olympics and other international tournaments. This enabled NBA players to compete in the 1992 Summer Olympic Games and also allowed international athletes to join the NBA without relinquishing the ability to compete for their home countries (Associated Press, *New York Times*, April 8, 1989).

84. John Harris, "NBA Top Man Looks Ahead," *St. Petersburg Times*, February 9, 1992.

85. Luke Cyphers, "The NBA's Global Marketing Machine Is Launching a Drive to the Pacific Rim," *Wall Street Journal*, April 7, 1992.

86. Michelangelo Rucci, "NBA Is Coming to Spread the Word," *Herald Sun*, February 10, 1992.

87. Jean K. Chalaby, "The Quiet Invention of a New Medium: Twenty Years of Transnational Television in Europe," in *Transnational Television Worldwide: Towards a New Media Order*, ed. Jean Chalaby, 43–65 (New York: I. B. Tauris, 2005).

88. "The Global Appeal of NBA Television," *Variety*, February 2, 1992.

89. David Aldridge, "U.S. Basketball Team Ready to Perform a Professional Lesson," *Washington Post*, September 21, 1991.

90. Ibid.

91. Mike Downey, "Michael Jordan Plans to Retire," *Chicago Sun-Times*, October 6, 1993.

92. Michael Wilbon, "Morality, Popularity and Reality in the NBA," *Washington Post*, June 11, 1993.

93. Robert Mason Lee, "Hoop-la! NBA Franchise Means Big Money," *Vancouver Sun*, February 19, 1994.

94. Ibid.

95. An NBA office in Miami had formerly served as the Latin American headquarters (*Associated Press*, March 1, 1994).

96. McClellan, "One-on-One."

97. "NBA G League Expands to Mexico City with Landmark Partnership with Capitanes," press release, *NBA.com*, December 12, 2019, https://www.nba.com/news/nba-g-league-expands-mexico-city-official-release.

98. Terry Lyons, personal communication, New York, December 20, 2017.

99. Ibid.

100. McClellan, "One-on-One."

101. Stuart Foxman, "The NBA in Canada: Celebrating Season II," *Strategy*, January 6, 1997.

102. Ibid.

103. Ibid.

104. Albert Moran, *Understanding the Global TV Format* (Portland, OR: Intellect, 2006), 20.

105. Ibid., 65, 30.

106. Curt Schleier, "NBA Commissioner David Stern," *Investor's Business Daily*, March 11, 1999.

107. Marcel Danesi, *Brands* (New York: Routledge, 2006), 122.

108. Ibid.

109. Swish NBA, "NBA.Finals.2007.06.07.G1.Cavaliers@Spurs HD," YouTube, 1:24:14, posted October 12, 2016, https://www.youtube.com/watch?v=Z4hjcq_qAoo.

110. John Branch, "Fans' Uniform Look Is a Team Effort," *New York Times*, May 18, 2015.

111. Chris Chase, "Dear Warriors Fans: You Look Ridiculous," *USA Today*, June 5, 2015.

112. Richard Giulianotti, "Supporters, Followers, Fans, and Flaneurs: A Taxonomy of Spectator Identities in Football." *Journal of Sport and Social Issues* 26, no. 1 (2002): 37.

113. Douglas Kellner and Hui Zhang, "Sports, the Beijing Olympics, and Global Media Spectacles," in *A Companion to Sport*, ed. David L. Andrews and Ben Carrington (Malden, MA: Blackwell, 2013), 448.

114. Marwan Kraidy, *Hybridity, or the Cultural Logic of Globalization* (Philadelphia: Temple University Press, 2005), 94.

115. Ibid.

116. Rudy Martzke, "Women's Pro League to Open with NBC on Board," *USA Today*, June 28, 1996.

117. Jeff Schultz and Len Pasquarelli, "The Proposed League: NFL's a Tough League to Sack," *Atlanta Journal and Constitution*, May 29, 1998.

118. Bob Raissman, "The Check Is in the Mail," *New York Daily News*, June 21, 1998.

119. When the NBA pulled out, Turner followed, and NBC eventually found another collaborator in the World Wrestling Federation's Vince McMahon, resulting in the XFL.

120. "NBA and Brazil's LNB Announce Groundbreaking Partnership," press release, *NBA.com*, December 14, 2014; Jeff Zillgitt, "NBA, FIBA Launching 12-Team League in Africa; Barack Obama to Have Hands-on Role," *USA Today*, February 16, 2019.

121. "NBA Seeks to Block Use of Famous Name by Chinese League," *Agence France Presse*, December 13, 1996.

122. Emma Batha, "Rams Lock Horns with NBA," *South China Morning Post*, December 14, 1996.

123. Ibid.

124. Ramon Lobato and Julian Thomas, *The Informal Media Economy* (Malden, MA: Polity, 2015), 151.

125. During the Atlanta Hawks' 1988 tour of the Soviet Union, David Stern recalled fans cheering loudest for Spud Webb, whom they had watched on videotapes pirated from Turkey (Kevin Scheitrum, "Opening the Curtain," *NBA.com*, September 2013); Lobato and Thomas, *Informal Media Economy*, 43.

126. "NBA and INDES Bring First-Ever Jr. NBA Program to El Salvador," press release, NBA Communications, February 26, 2020, https://pr.nba.com/nba-indes-jr-nba-program-el-salvador/.

127. Aanu Adeoye, "Senegal Gets Africa's First NBA Training Center," *CNN*, November 18, 2018, https://www.cnn.com/2018/11/27/africa/nba-senegal-gets-africas-first-training-center-int/index.html.

128. SI Wire, "Basketball without Borders Camp to Be Held during All-Star Weekend," *Sports Illustrated*, February 5, 2015, https://www.si.com/nba/2015/02/05/basketball-without-borders-camp-all-star-weekend.

129. Troy Justice, telephone conversation with the author, September 25, 2017

130. Brian Martin, "Trio of Basketball without Borders Alumni Mark NBA Africa Game 2018 Rosters," *NBA.com*, August 3, 2018, https://www.nba.com/news/basketball-without-borders-alumni-joel-embiid-luc-mbah-moute-pascal-siakam.

131. Terhi Rantanen, *The Media and Globalization* (Thousand Oaks, CA: Sage, 2005), 99.

132. Jay Posner, "Disney-AOL In, NBC Out in New NBA TV Accord," *San Diego Union-Tribune*, January 23, 2002.

133. Jeffrey D. Zbar, "Ball's Bounce Goes ESPN, TNT's Way," *Advertising Age*, June 10, 2002, S12.

134. Paula Bernstein and Justin Oppelaar, "NBA Scores $4.6 billion in Disney, AOL TW Deals," *Variety*, January 23, 2002.

135. Russ Granik, telephone conversation with the author, March 22, 2018.

136. "The National Basketball Association Signs Historic Six-Year Television Agreements with AOL Time Warner, ABC and ESPN," *Business Wire*, January 22, 2002.

137. Mark Lazarus, telephone conversation with the author, April 18, 2017.

138. Rudy Martzke, "AOL, Turner Double-Team and Close In on NBA Deal," *USA Today*, December 12, 2001.

139. "NBA Concentrating on Cable Package," *Associated Press*, July 11, 2002.

140. "Where Did the Primetime Broadcast TV Audience Go?" *TV by the Numbers*, April 12, 2010.

141. Leonard Shapiro and Mark Maske, "'Monday Night Football' Changes the Channel," *Washington Post*, April 19, 2005.

142. Robert McChesney, "Media Made Sport: A History of Sports Coverage in the United States," in *Media, Sports, and Society*, ed. Lawrence Wenner (Newbury Park, CA: Sage, 1989), 49.

143. Amanda D. Lotz, *The Television Will Be Revolutionized*, 2nd ed. (New York: NYU Press, 2014), 25–28, 40.

Chapter 5. The Couch

1. Steve Aschburner, "NBA Changes Timeout Rules to Improve Game Flow," *NBA.com*, July 12, 2017, https://www.nba.com/news/nba-board-governors-timeout-rules-game-flow-trade-deadline.

2. Danny Meiseles (president of content, NBA), telephone conversation with the author, September 22, 2017.

3. Ibid.

4. Andrew Marchand, "Inside Amazon's Plan to Transform the Sports Broadcasting World," *New York Post*, April 15, 2021, https://nypost.com/2021/04/15/inside-amazons-plan-to-transform-the-sports-broadcasting-world/?utm_campaign=iphone_nyp&utm_source=pasteboard_app; Sam Byford, "Amazon and WNBA Strike Multi-year Streaming Deal," *The Verge*, May 12, 2021, https://www.theverge.com/2021/5/12/22433578/wnba-amazon-prime-video-streaming-deal-announced.

5. Andrew Liptak, "The MPAA Says Streaming Video Has Surpassed Cable Subscriptions Worldwide," *The Verge*, March 21, 2019, https://www.theverge.com/2019/3/21/18275670/mpaa-report-streaming-video-cable-subscription-worldwide.

6. Clay Travis, "ESPN Loses Two Million More Subscribers in Fiscal 2018," *Outkick the Coverage*, November 23, 2018.

7. Liptak, "MPAA Says."

8. Anthony Ha, "ESPN Launches Its Streaming Service ESPN+," *TechCrunch*, April 12, 2018.

9. Nicole Laporte, "This Is How Disney Is Going to Compete against Netflix," *Fast Company*, February 5, 2019.

10. Todd Spangler, "Amazon Adds NBA League Pass Live-Streaming Games to Prime Video Channels," *Variety*, December 14, 2019.

11. Steve Hellmuth, telephone conversation with the author, June 28, 2018.

12. Ibid.

13. Jennifer Holt and Kevin Sanson, "Introduction: Mapping Connections," in *Connected Viewing: Selling Streaming, and Sharing Media in the Digital Era*, ed. Jennifer Holt and Kevin Sanson (New York: Routledge, 2014), 1.

14. Ibid.

15. Tyler Hersko, "Nearly Half of U.S. Consumers Are Frustrated with a Bloated Streaming Market," *IndieWire*, June 13, 2019, https://www.indiewire.com/2019/06/too-many-streaming-services-television-decentralization-1202149596/; Julia Alexander, "The Entire World Is Streaming More Than Ever—and It's Straining the Internet," *The Verge*, March 27, 2020, https://www.theverge.com/2020/3/27/21195358/streaming-netflix-disney-hbo-now-youtube-twitch-amazon-prime-video-coronavirus-broadband-network.

16. Ibid.

17. "Pay TV Forecast Update," *Digital TV Research*, October 2020, https://www.digitaltvresearch.com/products/product?id=303.

18. "SVOD Forecasts Update," *Digital TV Research*, September 2020, https://www.digitaltvresearch.com/products/product?id=302.

19. "Desktop vs. Mobile vs. Tablet Market Share Worldwide (2011–2021)," *StatCounter*, May 2021, https://gs.statcounter.com/platform-market-share/desktop-mobile-tablet/worldwide/#yearly-2011-2021.

20. Holt and Sanson, "Introduction," 7, 9.

21. "Home Box Office Plans Multiplex Delivery of HBO and Cinemax," *PR Newswire*, May 8, 1991.

22. Ibid.

23. John Dempsey, "Multiplexing Sparks Multicriticisms," *Variety*, May 5, 1992.

24. Ed Desser, telephone conversation with the author, May 9, 2017.

25. John Kosner, personal communication, New York, July 20, 2017.

26. Ibid.

27. Prentis Rogers, "TBS, TNT Give Fans Access to All Openers," *Atlanta Journal and Constitution*, April 1994.

28. Fritz Quindt, "So Many Playoffs, So Many Dilemmas," *San Diego Union-Tribune*, April 29, 1994.

29. Scott Hettrick, "NBA Playoffs Multiplexed on TNT, TBS," *Hollywood Reporter*, April 27, 1994.

30. Jim McConville, "TNT Says It's Tops in Basic," *Broadcasting and Cable*, December 16, 1996.

31. William N. Wallace, "Pro Football Gets Four-Year TV Pact," *New York Times*, January 27, 1970.

32. HamptonRoadsTVFan, "1997 NBA on TNT/TBS Promo (NBA Playoffs: Longer Version)," YouTube, 00:35, posted September 3, 2014, https://youtu.be/PcMQvdqsSfo.

33. John Romano, "NBA Doubles Fans' Playoff Options," *St. Petersburg Times*, April 29, 1994.

34. Bernard Miège, *The Capitalization of Cultural Production* (New York: International General, 1989), 146.

35. Ibid., 123.

36. Victoria E. Johnson, *Sports TV* (New York: Routledge, 2021), 145.

37. Michael Sanson, "Football Fever," *Restaurant Hospitality* 79, no. 8 (1995): 35.

38. "For the Win: Out-of-Home Viewers of Fall Sports on Linear TV Watch in Multiple Locations and Are Engaged," *Nielsen*, January 24, 2019, https://www.nielsen.com/us/en/insights/article/2019/for-the-win-out-of-home-viewers-of-fall-sports-on-linear-tv-are-engaged/.

39. Victoria E. Johnson, "Everything New Is Old Again: Sport Television, Innovation, and Tradition for a Multi-platform Era," in *Beyond Prime Time: Television Programming in the Post-network Era*, ed. Amanda D. Lotz (New York: Routledge, 2009), 116.

40. Hellmuth discussion.

41. Phil Gulick, "Choose Your Fantasy Sports Sites Carefully," *St. Petersburg Times*, August 1, 1996.

42. Colin Brown, "Field of Dreams," *Screen International*, January 5, 1996, 12.

43. *National Basketball Association v. Motorola, Inc.*, 105 F.3d 841 (2nd Cir. 1997).

44. Associated Press, "America Online Sued by N.B.A.," *New York Times*, August 29, 1996.

45. Lawrie Mifflin, "Sports Service Battles NBA in Round Two," *New York Times*, October 21, 196.

46. Ibid.

47. Ibid.

48. "NBA Sues America Online over Usage of Game Data," *Wall Street Journal*, August 29, 1996.

49. *NBA v. Motorola*.

50. Paula McCooey, "They Click, They Score! Fantasy Sports Players Get a Big Assist from the Internet," *Ottawa Citizen*, January 8, 2001.

51. Richard Tedesco, "CNNSI Makes Its Play in the Internet Game," *Broadcasting and Cable*, July 21, 1997.

52. Richard Tedesco, "ESPN Getting into More Fantasy," *Broadcasting and Cable*, October 6, 1997.

53. "Fox Sports Online and Small World Sports Partner to Provide the Ultimate in Online Fantasy Sports," *PR Newswire*, October 31, 1997; "Small World, the Invisible Powerhouse in Online Fantasy Sports, About to Flex Its Football Muscle," *PR Newswire*, August 31, 1999.

54. Michael Hiestand, "Online Leagues of Their Own," *USA Today*, October 6, 1999.

55. Chris Jenkins, "Web Is a Dream Come True for Fantasy League Fanatics," *USA Today*, March 7, 2000.

56. Hiestand, "Online Leagues."

57. Tom Watson, "Net's a Natural for Fantasy Baseball," *New York Times*, March 26, 1998.

58. "News Corporation's News Digital Media Acquires Stats, Inc., Leading Supplier of Real-Time and Historical Sports Information," *Business Wire*, January 19, 2000.

59. "ESPN SportsZone Launches Baseball's ESPN GameCast, the Site's Most Ambitious Interactive Application," *Business Wire*, August 20, 1997.

60. *CBC Distribution v. Major League Baseball*, 443 F. Supp. 2d 1077, 1103–1104 (E.D. Mo. 2006).

61. Ibid.

62. "Industry Demographics," *Fantasy Sports and Gaming Association*, https://thefsga.org/industry-demographics. Accessed August 1, 2019.

63. John Lombardo, "NBA Signs Four-Year Deal with FanDuel That Includes Equity Stake in Fantasy Company," *Sports Business Journal*, November 12, 2014, https://www.sportsbusinessjournal.com/Daily/Issues/2014/11/12/Marketing-and-Sponsorship/NBA-FanDuel.aspx.

64. Michael McCarthy, "How Legal Sports Betting Helped Drive NFL's First Half TV Ratings," *Front Office Sports*, October 31, 2019, https://frontofficesports.com/nfl-ratings-betting-first-half-2019/.

65. Ariane de Vogue and Maegan Vazquez, "Supreme Court Lets States Legalize Sports Gambling," *CNN*, May 14, 2018, https://www.cnn.com/2018/05/14/politics/sports-betting-ncaa-supreme-court/index.html.

66. Ryan Rodenberg, "United States of Sports Betting: An Updated Map of Where Every State Stands," *ESPN.com*, April 7, 2021, https://www.espn.com/chalk/story/_/id/19740480/the-united-states-sports-betting-where-all-50-states-stand-legalization.

67. Darren Rovell and David Purdum, "FanDuel to Open Sportsbook at Meadowlands in New Jersey," *ESPN.com*, July 12, 2018, https://www.espn.com/chalk/story/_/id/24077347/fanduel-open-sportsbook-meadowlands-racetrack-new-jersey; Hilary Russ, "DraftKings Launches Mobile Sports Betting in New Jersey," *Reuters*, August 1, 2018, https://www.reuters.com/article/us-usa-betting-draftkings-new-jersey-idUSKBN1KM60H.

68. Bill King, "Broncos-FanDuel Deal Marks First NFL Team Sportsbook Sponsorship," *Sports Business Journal*, June 15, 2020, https://www.sportsbusinessdaily.com/SB-Blogs/Breaking-News/2020/06/Broncos-Fanduel.aspx; Corey Davis, "FanDuel Goes All In with Memphis Grizzlies Sponsorship," *Memphis Business Journal*, November 4, 2020, https://www.bizjournals.com/memphis/news/2020/11/04/fanduel-corporate-sponsor-grizzlies.html.

69. "DraftKings Signs Multi-year Partnerships with Three NBA Franchises," *DraftKings*, February 13, 2020, https://www.draftkings.com/about/news/2020/02/draftkings-signs-multi-year-partnerships-with-three-nba-franchises/.

70. Jason Dachman, "How Sinclair Pulled Off the Gargantuan Bally Sports Networks Rebrand amid the Pandemic," *Sports Video Group*, March 30, 2021, https://

www.sportsvideo.org/2021/03/30/how-sinclair-pulled-off-the-gargantuan-bally-sports-networks-rebrand-amid-the-pandemic/.

71. Todd Spangler, "Dish Network Adds DraftKings Sports Betting App to Set-Tops," *Variety*, March 3, 2021, https://variety.com/2021/digital/news/dish-draftkings-sports-betting-app-1234920547/.

72. Kevin Stankiewicz, "Legalized Sports Betting Has Had 'Big Influence' on Increased NFL Ratings, Giants Co-owner Says," *CNBC*, December 5, 2019, https://www.cnbc.com/2019/12/05/giants-co-owner-sports-betting-has-big-influence-on-nfl-ratings.html.

73. Johnson, "Everything New," 115.

74. Ethan Tussey, *The Procrastination Economy: The Big Business of Downtime* (New York: NYU Press), 55, 53.

75. "Zach Lowe on Tanking, Tom Thibodeau, and Trades," *The Full 48*, January 10, 2019, at minute 62:11.

76. Harvey Araton, telephone conversation with the author, August 4, 2017.

77. Michael Serazio, *The Power of Sports: Media and Spectacle in American Culture* (New York: NYU Press, 2019), 58–59.

78. Michael Freeman, *ESPN: The Uncensored History* (Lanham, MD: Taylor, 2000), 283.

79. James Andrew Miller and Kevin Belson, "N.F.L. Pressure Said to Lead ESPN to Quit Film Project," *New York Times*, August 24, 2013, https://www.nytimes.com/2013/08/24/sports/football/nfl-pressure-said-to-prompt-espn-to-quit-film-project.html.

80. John Koblin, "ESPN Gets Back into the *League of Denial* Game (Sorta)," *Deadspin*, October 2, 2013, https://deadspin.com/espn-gets-back-into-the-league-of-denial-game-sorta-1440202980.

81. Alex Reimer, "CBS Analyst Phil Simms Appears to Be a Big Fan of Greg Hardy," *Boston Magazine*, October 12, 2015, https://www.bostonmagazine.com/news/2015/10/12/phil-simms-greg-hardy/.

82. Cindy Boren, "Jerry Jones Does an About-Face on Greg Hardy," *Washington Post*, October 11, 2015, https://www.washingtonpost.com/news/early-lead/wp/2015/10/11/jerry-jones-does-an-about-face-on-greg-hardy/.

83. Travis Vogan, *ESPN: The Making of a Sports Media Empire* (Urbana: University of Illinois Press, 2015), 176.

84. Paulsen, "The NBA Probably Prevented ESPN from Hiring Stan Van Gundy," *Sports Media Watch*, October 2012, https://www.sportsmediawatch.com/2012/10/the-nba-probably-prevented-espn-from-hiring-stan-van-gundy/.

85. Jason McIntyre, "Stan Van Gundy on NBA Countdown: ESPN Is Lying," *The Big Lead*, October 10, 2012, https://www.thebiglead.com/posts/stan-van-gundy-on-nba-countdown-espn-is-lying-that-s-a-bunch-of-bs-from-espn-01dkhtcadaw4.

86. Michael Hiestand, "Jeff Van Gundy Says NBA Kept Stan Out of ESPN," *USA Today*, October 21, 2012, https://www.usatoday.com/story/sports/columnist

/hiestand-tv/2012/10/21/hiestand-tv-stan-van-gundy-espn-jeff-van-gundy-nba-60-minutes/1647505/.

87. Ben DuBose, "Today in 2019: Daryl Morey's Hong Kong Tweet Ignites Firestorm," *USA Today*, October 4, 2020, https://rocketswire.usatoday.com/2020/10/04/today-in-2019-daryl-moreys-hong-kong-tweet-ignites-firestorm/.

88. Sopan Deb, "N.B.A. Expects to Lose 'Hundreds of Millions' from China Rift, Silver Says," *New York Times*, February 15, 2020, https://www.nytimes.com/2020/02/15/sports/nba-adam-silver-china-kobe.html.

89. Staff, "China's CCTV Sports Channel to Show NBA Games from Saturday: State Media," *Reuters*, October 9, 2020, https://www.reuters.com/article/us-china-basketball-nba-cctv/chinas-cctv-sports-channel-to-show-nba-games-from-saturday-state-media-idUSKBN26U1OV.

90. Laura Wagner, "Internal Memo: ESPN Forbids Discussion of Chinese Politics When Discussing Daryl Morey's Tweet about Chinese Politics," *Deadspin*, October 8, 2019, https://deadspin.com/internal-memo-espn-forbids-discussion-of-chinese-polit-1838881032.

91. Lauren Theisen, "Stephen A. Smith Pauses between Bootlicks to Tell Daryl Morey to Grow Up," *Deadspin*, October 7, 2019, https://deadspin.com/stephen-a-smith-pauses-between-bootlicks-to-tell-daryl-1838854121.

92. Sopan Deb, "LeBron James Faces Backlash Unseen since 'the Decision,'" *New York Times*, October 15, 2019, https://www.nytimes.com/2019/10/15/sports/basketball/lebron-china-burned-jerseys.html.

93. Steve Fainaru and Mark Fainaru-Wada, "ESPN Investigation Finds Coaches at NBA China Academies Complained of Player Abuse, Lack of Schooling," *ESPN.com*, July 29, 2020, https://www.espn.com/nba/story/_/id/29553829/espn-investigation-finds-coaches-nba-china-academies-complained-player-abuse-lack-schooling.

94. Sopan Deb, "Report: N.B.A.'s Academies in China Abused Athletes," *New York Times*, July 29, 2020, https://www.nytimes.com/2020/07/29/sports/basketball/nba-china-abuse.html.

95. Ryan Glasspiegel, "Only One ESPN TV Show Discussed ESPN's Bombshell NBA China Story Thursday," *OutKick*, July 31, 2020, https://www.outkick.com/only-one-espn-tv-show-discussed-espns-bombshell-nba-china-thursday/.

96. Terry Lyons, "Experience," *Terry Lyons Sports Marketing*, https://terrylyons.com/index.php/timeline/, accessed June 23, 2021.

97. Terry Lyons, personal communication, New York, December 20, 2017.

98. Ibid.

99. Jeff Bercovici, "Turner Buys Bleach Report, Next-Gen Sports Site, for $175M-Plus," *Forbes*, August 6, 2012, https://www.forbes.com/sites/jeffbercovici/2012/08/06/turner-buys-bleacher-report-next-gen-sports-site-for-175m-plus/?sh=2a3d2d5a7843.

100. Alex Putterman, "How Bleacher Report and House of Highlights Teamed Up to Take Over Instagram," *Awful Announcing*, November 9, 2017, https://awful

announcing.com/online-outlets/bleacher-report-house-highlights-teamed-take-instagram.html.

101. Joe Lemire, "The Inside Story of How House of Highlights Scored 10 million Instagram Followers," *SportTechie*, July 30, 2018, https://www.sporttechie.com/bleacher-report-house-of-highlights-omar-raja-10-million-instagram/.

102. Andrew Marchand, "ESPN Plucks House of Highlights Founder Omar Raja from Bleacher Report," *New York Post*, October 23, 2019, https://nypost.com/2019/10/23/espn-plucks-house-of-highlights-founder-omar-raja-from-bleacher-report/; Eben Novy-Williams, "Beating ESPN on Instagram Isn't Enough for Bleacher Report's House of Highlights," *Bloomberg*, September 4, 2019, https://www.bloomberg.com/news/articles/2019-09-04/bleacher-report-s-house-of-highlights-builds-gen-z-empire.

103. Serazio, *Power of Sports*, 69.

104. Ibid., 81.

105. Ibid., 72.

106. Sara Fischer, "New Bleacher Report CEO Says Revenue Up 4–5x since Turner Acquisition," *Axios*, February 26, 2019, https://www.axios.com/bleacher-report-ceo-revenue-turner-acquisition-a455bb9d-c1ff-4601-bd91-b94b1d5679d7.html.

107. "Advertise with Us," *Bleacher Report*, https://bleacherreport.com/pages/advertise. Accessed June 20, 2021.

108. Kevin Kinkead, "The NBA's Social Media Numbers Are Staggering," *Crossing Broad*, August 9, 2018, https://www.crossingbroad.com/2018/08/the-nbas-social-media-numbers-are-staggering.html.

109. "Social Media Fact Sheet," *Pew Research Center*, April 7, 2021, https://www.pewresearch.org/internet/fact-sheet/social-media/.

110. Hellmuth discussion; Glen Dickson, "Hellmuth Promoted at NBA Entertainment," *Broadcasting and Cable*, November 18, 2007.

111. Jessica Golden, "NBA Using Artificial Intelligence for Highlight Clips This All-Star Game," *CNBC*, February 11, 2020, https://www.cnbc.com/2020/02/11/nba-using-artificial-intelligence-for-highlight-clips-this-all-star-game.html.

112. Ibid.

113. Steven Impey, "WSC Sports, the NBA and Starting the Personalised Video Evolution," March 5, 2020, *SportsPro*, https://www.sportspromedia.com/from-the-magazine/nba-g-league-amazon-premier-league-ai-highlights-wsc-sports-interview.

114. Rick Maese and Cindy Boren, "Sports Video Clips Are Now Ubiquitous on Social Media. Can the NFL Put the Genie Back in the Bottle?" *Washington Post*, October 13, 2015.

115. Hellmuth discussion.

116. Ibid.

117. Maese and Boren, "Sports Video Clips."

118. Ben Golliver, "The NBA Isn't Surprised Its Ratings Are Way Down. Radical Change Already Was Afoot," *Washington Post*, December 24, 2019, https://www

.washingtonpost.com/sports/2019/12/24/nba-ratings-decline-explanation-espn-tnt-abc-adam-silver/.

119. Gerry Smith, Christopher Palmeri, and Brandon Kochkodin, "NFL Ratings Keep Sliding, Even with Kid-Friendly Telecast," *Bloomberg*, January 12, 2021, https://www.bloomberg.com/news/articles/2021-01-12/nfl-fails-to-stem-ratings-slide-even-with-kid-friendly-telecast.

120. Alex Reimer, "Why Sports TV Ratings Will Likely Still Suffer in 2021," *Forbes*, December 16, 2020, https://www.forbes.com/sites/alexreimer/2020/12/16/why-sports-tv-ratings-will-likely-still-suffer-in-2021/?sh=334e7f002acf.

121. Dan Wolken, "Falling TV Ratings across Most Sports? Here Are Four Reasons to Explain Drop during Pandemic," *USA Today*, October 8, 2020, https://www.usatoday.com/story/sports/media/2020/10/08/pandemic-why-tv-ratings-sports-have-been-down-since-returning/5913720002/.

122. Michael Schneider and Kate Aurthur, "R.I.P. Cable TV: Why Hollywood Is Slowly Killing Its Biggest Moneymaker," *Variety*, July 21, 2020, https://variety.com/2020/tv/news/cable-tv-decline-streaming-cord-cutting-1234710007/.

123. Dade Hayes, "Cable Network NBCSN to Go Dark by Year-End, with Live Sports Telecasts Shifting to USA Network, Peacock," *Deadline*, January 21, 2021, https://deadline.com/2021/01/cable-network-nbcsn-to-go-dark-by-end-of-2021-sports-streaming-peacock-1234678611/.

124. Brandon Costa, "Bleacher Report, House of Highlights Bring Video-Filled Fan Activation to NBA All-Star," *Sports Video Group*, February 13, 2019, https://www.sportsvideo.org/2019/02/13/bleacher-report-house-of-highlights-bring-video-filled-fan-activation-to-nba-all-star/.

125. Dak Dillon, "'NBA on TNT' Expands to Tuesday Night with Social Media Focus," *Newscast Studio*, January 22, 2020, https://www.newscaststudio.com/2020/01/22/nba-on-tnt-tuesday-night/.

126. "NBA on TNT's 2020–21 Regular Season Schedule to Feature 66 Games," news release, *NBA.com*, December 4, 2020, https://www.nba.com/news/nba-on-tnts-2020-21-regular-season-schedule-to-feature-66-games.

127. Todd Spangler, "Turner Sports Unveils 'Bleacher Report Live' Pay-Streaming Service," *Variety*, March 27, 2018, https://variety.com/2018/digital/news/turner-sports-bleacher-report-streaming-service-uefa-nba-1202737168/.

128. Joe Lemire, "NBA Commissioner Adam Silver Details Plan to Sell Short Game Segments," *SportTechie*, March 28, 2018, https://www.sporttechie.com/nba-adam-silver-microtransactions-turner-sports-bleacher-report-live-ott-streaming/.

129. John Ourand, "Four OTTs. Four Strategies," *Sports Business Journal*, October 28, 2019, https://www.sportsbusinessdaily.com/Journal/Issues/2019/10/28/In-Depth/OTT-strategies.aspx.

130. "TNT to Televise Capital One's the Match: Champions for Change," media release, *WarnerMedia*, November 19, 2020, https://pressroom.warnermedia.com/us/media-release/tnt-televise-capital-ones-match-champions-change-phil-mickelson-charles-barkley-vs?language_content_entity=en.

131. Fischer, "New Bleacher Report CEO."

132. Hilary Russ, "Turner Sports Inks Deal with Caesars for Bleacher Report Betting Content," *Reuters*, February 7, 2019, https://www.reuters.com/article/us-turner-broadcast-caesars-sport/turner-sports-inks-deal-with-caesars-for-bleacher-report-betting-content-idUSKCN1PW2PF.

133. SVG Staff, "NBA Revamps Digital Products with Betting, Other Interactive Elements on League Pass," *Sports Video Group*, December 22, 2020, https://www.sportsvideo.org/2020/12/22/nba-revamps-digital-products-with-betting-other-interactive-elements-on-league-pass/.

134. Michael McCarthy, "After Successful Tests, Sports Betting-Driven NBA Telecasts Here to Stay," *Front Office Sports*, October 19, 2020, https://frontofficesports.com/nba-sports-betting-streams/.

135. 42 Analytics, "SSAC19: Who Says No? A 1-on-1 with Adam Silver and Bill Simmons," YouTube, 1:04:49, posted March 1, 2019, https://www.youtube.com/watch?v=RJ1lFirN91E.

136. Tommy Beer, "NBA Top Shot Collectibles Continues Meteoric Rise with Over $50 million in Sales in a Week," *Forbes*, February 20, 2021, https://www.forbes.com/sites/tommybeer/2021/02/20/nba-top-shot-collectibles-continues-meteoric-rise-with-over-50-million-in-sales-in-a-week/?sh=7d4491f713cd; Chris Bumbaca, "Dapper Labs, Company behind NBA Top Shot, Raises $305 million While Being Valued at $2.6 billion," *USA Today*, March 30, 2021, https://www.usatoday.com/story/sports/nba/2021/03/30/nba-top-shot-dapper-labs-valuation-funding-round/7058307002/.

Conclusion

1. "Everything to Know about the NBA's 22-Team Restart at Walt Disney World," *ESPN.com*, July 29, 2020, https://www.espn.com/nba/story/_/id/29256449/everything-know-nba-22-team-restart-walt-disney-world.

2. Andrew Greif, "ESPN's NBA Bubble Broadcasts Are an Olympian Effort," *Los Angeles Times*, August 25, 2020, https://www.latimes.com/sports/story/2020-08-25/espn-nba-bubble-broadcasts-are-an-olympian-effort.

3. Ibid.

4. "NBA Partners with Disguise to Give Fans a True 'Home Game' Experience," *Disguise*, https://www.disguise.one/en/insights/news/nba-bubble/. Accessed June 20, 2021.

5. Ibid.

6. Ibid.

7. Stephen Haynes, "How a Red Hook Company Brought the NBA 'Bubble' to Audible Life for Players, Fans," *Poughkeepsie Journal*, October 26, 2020, https://www.poughkeepsiejournal.com/story/sports/2020/10/26/nba-bubble-red-hooks-firehouse-productions-created-sounds-audio/3734477001/.

8. Ibid.

9. Ibid.

10. Ibid.

11. Ibid.

12. Greif, "ESPN's NBA Bubble Broadcasts."

13. Jason Dachman, "NEP Rolls Out Ultra-flexible EN3 with SMPTE ST 2110 IP Core for ESPN," *Sports Video Group*, May 8, 2018, https://www.sportsvideo.org/2018/05/08/nep-rolls-out-ultra-flexible-en3-with-smpte-st-2110-ip-core-for-espn/; Ken Kerschbaumer, "Super Bowl LIV: ESPN International Calls NEP EN2 Home for the Big Game," *Sports Video Group*, February 1, 2020, https://www.sportsvideo.org/2020/02/01/live-from-super-bowl-liv-espn-international-calls-nep-en2-home-for-the-big-game/.

14. Kristian Hernández, "NBA Finals: ESPN Operations Team Looks to Tie a Bow on Peculiar NBA Bubble in Orlando," *Sports Video Group*, September 30, 2020, https://www.sportsvideo.org/2020/09/30/nba-finals-espn-operations-team-looks-to-tie-a-bow-on-peculiar-nba-bubble-in-orlando/.

15. Greif, "ESPN's NBA Bubble Broadcasts."

16. Frank Pingue, "'World Feed Truck' Allows NBA to Be a Globetrotter," *Reuters*, February 16, 2016.

17. "[NBA] LeBron James Bravely Rescued the Lakers from Desperation" (Google Translate), CCTV, 0:47, posted October 10, 2020, https://cbs.sports.cctv.com/match.html?spm=C67245673465.PkkdRPUWEakd.0.0&id=4993827.

18. Ibid.

19. "2018–19 Season NBA Playoffs Raptors vs Bucks Fifth Game" (Google Translate), CCTV, May 24, 2019, http://sports.cctv.com/2019/05/24/VIDEo1f1fDZCf4fd3r45Hlfi190524.shtml.

20. "Season Restart to Feature 89 International Players from 34 Countries," press release, *NBA.com*, July 29, 2020, https://www.nba.com/news/season-restart-international-players-official-release.

21. Shlomo Sprung, "NBA TV Ratings Grow Internationally during Seeding, Playoff Games," *Forbes*, September 4, 2020, https://www.forbes.com/sites/shlomosprung/2020/09/04/nba-ratings-international-growth-spain-canada-mexico-doncic-jokic-siakam/?sh=2fadef46b605.

22. Steven Kubitza, "NBA Ramps Up Drama with Start Times for Final Day of Regular Season," *Fansided*, May 9, 2021, https://fansided.com/2021/05/09/nba-ramps-up-drama-with-start-times-for-final-day-of-regular-season/.

23. Anthony Crupi, "Record-Low NBA Finals Ratings Belie Bubble Success as Networks Salvage Cash, Players Stay Healthy," *Sportico*, October 13, 2020, https://www.sportico.com/business/media/2020/nba-finals-ratings-belie-bubble-success-1234614838/.

24. Ibid.

25. Ibid.

26. Sprung, "NBA TV Ratings."

27. John Lombardo, "NBA Preserved $1.5 billion in Revenue at Disney, but Losses Are Steep," *Sports Business Journal*, October 19, 2020, https://www.sportsbusiness

journal.com/Journal/Issues/2020/10/19/Leagues-and-Governing-Bodies/NBA-bubble.aspx.

28. Greif, "ESPN's NBA Bubble Broadcasts."

29. Paul Adam, "NBA 2020 Broadcasting Rights (Worldwide TV Channels)," *Sports Maza*, January 2, 2020, https://sportsmaza.com/nba/nba-broadcast-tv-channel/.

30. Vinnie Iyer, "NFL's New TV Rights Deals, Explained: What $100 billion Package Means for Fans in 2023 and Beyond," *Sporting News*, March 19, 2021, https://www.sportingnews.com/us/nfl/news/nfl-tv-rights-deals-explained/z4rlycwog3jz1f6pqdqoegbxf.

31. Rick Porter, "WarnerMedia Snags Remaining NHL TV Rights as NBC Bows Out," *Hollywood Reporter*, April 26, 2021, https://www.hollywoodreporter.com/tv/tv-news/warnermedia-turner-nhl-tv-rights-nbc-out-4173675/.

32. Geoff Baker, "Here's What the NHL's TV Deals with ESPN, Turner May Mean for the Kraken and the Rest of the League," *Seattle Times*, April 30, 2021, https://www.seattletimes.com/sports/kraken/heres-what-the-nhls-tv-deals-with-espn-turner-may-mean-for-the-kraken-and-the-rest-of-the-league/.

33. Chaim Gartenberg, "Topps Is Releasing Official NFT Baseball Cards on April 20th," *The Verge*, April 12, 2021, https://www.theverge.com/2021/4/12/22379645/topps-mlb-basecall-cards-nft-collectible-date.

34. Vildana Hajric, "NFT Platform Dapper Labs Tackles New Sport with NFL Partnership," *Bloomberg*, September 29, 2021, https://www.bloomberg.com/news/articles/2021-09-29/nft-platform-dapper-labs-tackles-new-sport-with-nfl-partnership.

35. 42 Analytics, "SSAC19: Who Says No? A 1-on-1 with Adam Silver and Bill Simmons," YouTube, 1:04:49, posted March 1, 2019, https://www.youtube.com/watch?v=RJ1lFirN91E.

36. Rudy Martzke, "AOL, Turner Double-Team and Close In on NBA Deal," *USA Today*, December 12, 2001.

37. Michael McCarthy, "NBC Sports Seeks New U.S. TV Deal with English Premier League," *Front Office Sports*, April 21, 2021, https://frontofficesports.com/english-premier-league-nbc-sports-tv-deal-u-s-super-league-espn-cbs-sports/.

38. Joe Reedy, "La Liga Switches U.S. Broadcast Rights to ESPN with 8-Year Agreement," *Chicago Sun-Times*, May 14, 2021, https://chicago.suntimes.com/2021/5/14/22436230/la-liga-switches-us-broadcast-rights-to-espn.

39. Travis Vogan, *Keepers of the Flame: NFL Films and the Rise of Sports Media* (Urbana: University of Illinois Press, 2014). Vogan followed his work on the NBA with *ESPN: The Making of a Sports Media Empire* (Urbana: University of Illinois Press, 2015), and *ABC Sports: The Rise and Fall of Network Sports Television* (Berkeley: University of California Press, 2018).

40. David Stern, telephone conversation with the author, February 12, 2018.

Index

4K video, 1, 55, 68, 69

ABC: contracts, 9, 36, 93, 102, 121, 134; programming, 8, 14, 39, 87, 118, 133; ratings, 8, 65, 101
ABC/ESPN, 11, 65, 101, 133–35, 139
advertising: sales, 2–4, 8, 33–38, 56–57, 95, 99, 116–19, 124, 149, 156–57; digital, 77–78, 91–92, 102, 168, 170–71
Allen, Paul, 91, 92
Amazon, 2, 11, 15, 66, 69, 108, 138–39, 158, 173–74
Amazon Prime, 139, 158, 173
Amazon Web Services, 173
American Basketball Association (ABA), 9–10, 111, 118
Americanization, 21
America Online (AOL), 133–34, 145
Antetokounmpo, Giannis, 47–49, 168
Apple iPads, 67
apps. *See* mobile applications (apps)
arena: construction, 26, 55, 59–64, 68–71, 78–81, 171; demolition, 64, 71; digitization, 15, 27–28, 55–58, 67–70, 79, 103–4, 168; lifecycle, 64, 72; public funding, 26, 65, 71, 75
Arledge, Roone, 8–9, 118
AT&T, 85, 92, 106, 138, 174
Atlanta, GA, 27, 85, 102, 105, 172
Atlanta Falcons, 56
Atlanta Hawks, 25, 30, 35, 38–39, 120, 123

Atlanta Journal and Constitution, 76, 141
audience: commodity, 42; global, 7, 12, 17–19, 31, 40, 45–51, 73–77, 86, 98, 107–10, 124, 131, 142–43, 168–70, 172; home, 22, 30, 33, 37, 52, 55, 60, 171–72, 174–75; in-person, 5, 15, 33, 37, 41, 53, 57, 70, 166

Ballmer, Steve, 66–67, 69
Bandeirantes, 37, 74
Barcelona, 27, 123, 125, 127
Barkley, Charles, 118, 125
Baseball Advanced Media (BAMTech), 84, 94, 109, 175
Basketball Africa League (BAL), 76, 131
Basketball Association of America (BAA), 8
basketball-related income (BRI), 2, 10
Basketball Without Borders, 132
BBC, 37
Berlusconi, 37
Bettman, Gary, 173
Big3, 31
Bird, Larry, 115, 118, 125, 155
bitcoin, 72
blackouts (television), 107
Bleacher Report, 2, 137, 151–52, 155, 161, 173
blockchain, 163, 174
Bodenheimer, George, 102
Bohuny, Kim, 39
Boston Celtics, 116, 119, 126, 150

branding, 67–68, 84, 92, 116, 150
Bristol, CT, 24, 172
B/R Live, 161
Broadcasting & Cable (magazine), 24, 93, 98, 99, 124
Brooklyn Nets, 50–51
Burns, Bryan, 121
business-to-business (BTB), 85, 104

cable: aesthetics, 116–17; contracts, 79, 99, 101, 117, 122–23, 134; distribution, 2, 6, 10–14, 25, 35, 87–91, 97, 109, 118–19, 133–35, 163–64, 172; ratings (NBA), 119, 142, 144, 174; revenue, 11, 38, 92, 95, 117, 120, 123, 138–41; subscriptions, 28, 138–39, 159–60; technology, 2, 24, 69, 85–86, 104
Cabral, Marco Antonio, 74
Caesars Palace, 162
camera placement, 1, 26, 61–62, 77–79, 88–89, 95, 104
Candlestick Park, 71
Cap Cities, 93–94
CBC Distribution and Marketing, 148
CBS: contracts, 8–9, 35, 60, 99, 119, 121–22, 142; production, 30, 36, 69, 87–88, 94, 113–15; ratings, 10, 114; scheduling, 135
CBS All Access, 11
CenturyLink, 84
Chant, Mike, 32, 49, 51
Charlotte Hornets, 43, 49
Chase Center, 56, 80
chatbots, 68, 72
Chicago Bulls, 2, 66, 87, 95, 123, 126, 131
Chicago Professional Sports Limited Partnership and WGN Continental Broadcasting Company v. NBA, 203
China Central Television (CCTV), 83, 104, 168–70
Chinese Basketball League (CBL), 132
Chinese National Basketball Alliance (CNBA), 132
Cinemax, 140
Cleveland Cavaliers, 1, 10, 66, 79, 101, 169
CNN, 39, 96, 116
CNN/SI, 134, 147, 174
Coca-Cola, 40
collective bargaining agreement (CBA), 2–3, 10
colocation, 24, 85, 86, 105, 108
Comcast-NBCUniversal, 106, 108

connected viewing, 139–40
copyright holders, 20, 51
court designs, 26, 48, 51
COVID-19, 14–15, 55–56, 77, 79, 96, 140, 160, 165
creative autonomy, 47, 52, 60
creative labor, 42
Crown Castle, 85
Cuban, Mark, 99
cultural hybridity, 130

Daily Fantasy Sports (DFS), 148, 174
Dallas Cowboys, 153
Dallas Mavericks, 99, 100, 170
dance cam, 44, 51, 52
dark fiber, 83, 85–86, 103, 110
data center, 1, 68–71
DAZN, 11, 138
Deadspin, 159
Denver Nuggets, 9, 62
deregulation, 4, 6, 87
Desser, Ed, 6, 35–38, 60, 87, 90–92, 97–98, 113, 116–17, 120–22, 141
Detroit Pistons, 100, 119
digital ticketing, 79
digitization, 11, 15, 79, 88, 110, 156, 172, 175
direct broadcast satellite (DBS), 83, 90–91, 95–97
direct-to-consumer (DTC), 6, 83–84, 94, 97, 100, 106, 131, 144, 151, 156–57, 162
DirecTV, 6, 83, 90, 97, 143
Dish Network, 90, 150
Disney, 71, 84, 93–94, 101–2, 124, 160
Dončić, Luka, 12, 168, 170
DraftKings, 148, 150
drug abuse, 114, 117
Dunk Street, 15, 27, 128

EA Sports, 74
Ebersol, Dick, 60–61, 95, 121, 122
Elemental Technologies, 109
Embiid, Joel, 133
Endeavor Streaming, 24, 27, 85, 106–9, 138, 175
English Premier League, 4, 17, 174
Erving, Julius, 9, 115, 118
ESPN: cable operations, 10, 23, 117, 120, 131, 133–34, 138, 147, 153; contracts, 6, 15, 74, 84, 87, 173; global operations, 101–2, 104, 166, 168, 174; news coverage, 2, 24, 66, 112, 151–52, 154–56; website, 91–92, 94, 144, 159, 164

ESPN Gamecast, 148
ESPN Internet Ventures, 98
ESPN+, 15, 28, 109, 138, 139, 160, 173
Euro step, 16, 18
event: organization, 28, 34–38, 52–53, 80; rundown, 1, 41–43, 45; script, 29, 35, 40–47, 166; script coordinator, 40–41, 45; script department, 40–42; script supervisor, 40; script writer, 40, 43

Facebook, 47–48, 157, 159, 170, 174
facilities requirements, 60–62
fandom, 69, 129, 130
FanDuel, 138, 148–50, 164, 174
fantasy sports, 144–52, 174
Fastbreak, 27, 128
FedEx, 87
fiber optics, 2, 24, 27, 71, 83–86, 89, 103–4
FIFA World Cup, 31
Firehouse Productions, 166–67
First Amendment, 145, 148
Fleisher, Larry, 10
Forbes, 24, 66, 125
Fox, 5, 15, 94, 145, 173
Fox Sports, 103, 108, 144, 147–48, 150–51
fuboTV, 138
Full 48, 151
Fuse Technical Group, 165
future proofing, 72

Garvey, Ed, 10
gate revenue, 2, 14, 171
geofencing, 107
geolocation, 106–7
geotargeting, 107
Ginobili, Manu, 100, 111
globality, 16, 86, 112
globalization, 12, 15, 19–22, 25, 30, 52, 86, 99, 110, 112, 124, 172, 175
glocalization, 29, 45, 46, 51
Golden 1 Center, 24, 55, 56, 68–72, 78–80
Golden State Warriors, 1, 26, 42, 49, 56, 66–68, 96
Goodwill Games, 31, 38, 76
Gostelradio, 38–39
Granik, Russ, 2, 96, 134,
Greece, 12, 26, 30, 39, 120, 170

halftime, 41, 45, 88, 90, 95, 122, 131
Harden, James, 151
hardware, 56, 78, 84, 103, 140
HBO, 15, 17, 84, 108, 110, 140–41

HBO Max, 106, 139, 173
HBO Now, 11, 84
Hellmuth, Steve, 60, 62, 95, 102–3, 139, 144, 158–59, 165
high-speed arena network (HSAN), 104, 105
Hindi, 20, 31, 48, 49
home video, 35, 90, 95, 122
Hong Kong, 19, 27, 101, 132, 154
House of Highlights, 137, 156–62
Houston Rockets, 1, 16, 25, 49, 79, 83, 138, 151, 153, 173
Hulu, 11, 107

Iger, Bob, 36
Iguodala, Andre, 67
Imevision, 37
IMG, 132
imperialism, 19–20, 112, 125, 129
India, 26, 44–51, 132, 138,
Indiana Pacers, 9–10, 150
infrastructure, 73–76, 79, 81, 83–88, 102–3, 106–10
Inside Stuff, 15, 90, 97, 122, 123, 172
Instagram, 156–59, 170
instant replay, 33
Intel, 70, 98
intermediaries, 83–86, 91–92, 98, 100, 103, 106–9, 175
International Basketball Federation (FIBA), 36–39, 73, 76
International Broadcast Systems (IBS), 37
internationalization, 15, 17, 22, 31, 100, 113, 133, 172
Intuit Dome, 56, 69, 79–81
Israel, 158
iStreamPlanet, 108–9
Italy, 30, 35–39, 119, 120, 169–70

James, LeBron, 100, 111, 112, 149, 165–68
jerseys: city edition, 48–51, 111; short-sleeved, 1, 16–18
Jeunesse Arena, 73
Johnson, Magic, 114, 118, 125, 155
Jordan, Michael, 1, 6, 64–66, 95–96, 111, 118, 125–26
Junior NBA, 74, 132

kiss cam, 1, 31, 44, 51–52
Klosterman, Chuck, 112
Kosner, John, 121–22, 141
Kurtinaitis, Rimas, 40, 47

Index 219

labor lockout, 96–97
La Liga, 174
Las Vegas, Nevada, 2, 80, 162
Lazarus, Mark, 6. 102, 134
League of Denial, 152–54
Levi's Stadium, 68–69
Levy, David, 102,
Liga Nacional de Basquete (LNB), 11, 73, 131
live production, 29, 40, 51
localization, 20, 27, 30–31, 44–45, 50–52, 107, 113, 128–29
London, England, 44
Los Angeles Clippers, 43, 56, 66–69, 78–81, 170
Los Angeles Lakers, 66, 114, 162, 165
lotería, 31, 49, 50
Lowe, Zach, 73, 151, 154, 164
Lunar New Year, 49
Lyons, Terry, 75, 126, 155

Madison Square Garden, 64
Major League Soccer (MLS), 100–101, 158
Manhattan, NYC, 1, 111
Manifest Destiny, 111–13, 119, 124
March Madness, 99
marketization, 4, 7, 12, 21, 172
Mastercard, 40
McDonald's, 35–40, 45–46, 51, 120, 123
MCI Communications, 144
McIntyre, Bryan, 60
media events, 30–32, 42, 52
media industry studies, 23, 26, 30, 53, 86, 163, 172
media obsolescence, 71, 73
media rights contracts, 15, 35, 39, 52
MediaSport, 5
mediatization, 4–5, 7, 21, 26, 56, 69, 71, 121, 172
Meiseles, Danny, 46–47
Melbourne, Australia, 27, 125
Memphis Grizzlies, 65, 101, 150
Mexico, 1, 27, 40, 44, 46, 76, 126, 128, 132, 169–70
MGM, 150, 163
Miami Arena, 64
Miami Heat, 64, 100, 112, 166
Microsoft, 66–67, 91–92, 144
Milwaukee Bucks, 26, 32, 36–37, 47–51, 65, 72, 80, 169, 173
mise-en-scène, 129

MLB: contracts, 108, 121, 148; COVID-19, 14, 77; fantasy sport, 148; global, 37, 44, 119; revenue, 4, 11, 14, 66; streaming, 99–100, 101, 174; television, 87, 169
MLB Extra Innings, 143
MLB.TV, 142
mobile applications (apps), 56, 58, 69, 79, 140, 149, 151, 157, 161, 164, 171
Monday Night Football, 8, 14, 118, 135, 153
Morey, Daryl, 154
Motorola, 145–46, 148, 151
MTV, 6, 15, 39, 46, 116
multi-channel transition, 135
multiculturalism, 16, 22, 45, 131
multiple-system cable operators (MSO), 141
multiplexing, 141
Murphy vs. National Collegiate Athletic Association, 150

NASCAR, 101
National Academy of Television Arts and Sciences, 112
National Basketball League (NBL), 8, 125
National Basketball Players' Association (NBPA), 10, 67
National Cable Television Association, 117
National Collegiate Athletic Association (NCAA), 99–100, 108, 150, 175
NBA 2K, 163, 166
NBA Academy, 154
NBA All-Star Game: coverage, 35, 47–48, 95; memorabilia, 111; production, 41, 87–88, 149, 160, 166; rights, 133; scheduling, 96, 122, 123; weekend, 40, 125, 132, 134, 161
NBA Asia, 132
NBA Basketball Operations, 39, 87, 137
NBA Beat, 98
NBABet, 162, 163
NBA Bubble, 28, 55, 77, 78, 165–71
NBA Canada, 127, 128
NBA China, 11, 44
NBA.com, 83, 91, 93–102, 128, 135, 142, 144, 151, 158–59
NBA.com TV, 95, 97–99, 109, 135
NBA Content Network, 104–5, 141
NBA Digital, 2, 27, 102
NBA Draft, 88, 123, 133, 134
NBA Dunk Contest, 161
NBA Entertainment (NBAE): archive, 37, 96–98, 118; commercials, 95, 102,

116; creation of, 35, 87, 115, 117, 158, 159; editing, 60, 88–89, 95–96; global, 87, 98, 102, 126; home video, 35, 116, 122; infrastructure, 39–40, 105, 109; production, 88, 90, 95, 97–98, 121–22, 175
NBA Game Distribution Center (GDC), 89, 159
NBA G-League, 76, 126
NBA Global Games, 29, 42–43, 45, 51, 73
NBA House, 73
NBA India, 11, 44
NBA International (NBAI), 6, 37, 120
NBA Latin America, 44
NBA League Pass: international, 103, 106–8; satellite service, 6, 128; streaming service, 6, 18, 24, 28, 47, 83–84, 90–94, 97, 100–2, 109, 135, 139, 142–43, 149, 159–64, 170
NBA Live Programming & Entertainment (LP&E), 40
NBA media relations, 155
NBA Most Valuable Player (MVP), 12, 100, 111
NBA on NBC, 121
NBA on TNT, 161
NBA playoffs, 1, 93, 116, 119, 134, 141–42
NBA regional offices, 27, 46, 113, 126, 129, 131
NBA Replay Center, 3, 103
NBA Technology Summit, 67
NBA Television Ventures, 90
NBA Three-Point Contest, 40, 42, 161
NBA Top Shot, 163, 173–74
NBA Traffic Ops Center, 103
NBA TV, 2, 6, 101–2, 107, 135
NBA Video Library, 88, 97
NBA vs. Motorola, 147–51
NBC: advertising, 95; contracts, 8–10, 15, 60, 64, 113, 121–24, 131–34, 144; production, 26, 60–62, 90, 135, 142; ratings, 65, 96; revenue, 13, 134; rights, 2; streaming, 139
NBC Peacock, 28, 109, 139, 160, 173–74
NBC Sports, 103, 108
NBCUniversal, 27, 106, 108–9, 114
neo-network era, 124
Netflix, 6–7, 12, 15, 17, 27, 46–47, 73–76, 107–10, 114
network era, 14, 135
NeuLion, 83, 85, 103, 106, 109, 175
Newark, NJ, 85, 105
New York Knicks, 66, 97, 107, 162

New York Times, 24, 66, 74, 112, 129, 145, 152, 154
NFL: contracts, 8, 15, 89, 90, 138, 144, 173, 174; coverage, 14, 29, 87; COVID-19, 77; global, 44; labor, 152, 153; ratings, 29, 151, 160; revenue, 4, 11, 14, 92; social media, 83, 90–92, 109, 150, 155, 157–59; stadiums, 56, 64, 68; television, 6, 8, 14, 117
NFL Films, 14, 35, 115, 116, 175
NFL GamePass, 107, 142
NFL Sunday Ticket, 90, 143
NHL: contracts, 15, 173–74; COVID-19, 14; global, 4, 119; revenue, 4, 14; social media, 103, 158, 175; sports betting, 150; television, 29, 169
Nickelodeon (Nick at Nite), 116, 160
Nike, 2, 48, 67
non-fungible tokens (NFT), 174
Nowitzki, Dirk, 100

Oakland, CA, 78
Obama, Barack, 76
O'Brien, Larry, 87–88, 117
off-track betting, 57
Olympics, 27, 31, 39, 123, 125, 128, 155
over-the-top platforms (OTT), 11, 17, 102, 110, 160

Paramount+, 109, 173–74
Pepsi Center, 62
PGA Tour, 158, 161
Philadelphia 76ers, 65, 114, 116, 150
policymakers, 56
Popovich, Gregg, 112
Portland Trail Blazers, 91
post-network era, 14, 15, 108, 109, 135, 142, 151, 172
PricewaterhouseCoopers (PWC), 11, 76, 100
public broadcasting, 38
Public Broadcasting Service (PBS), 152
public subsidies, 59, 80

Qantel, 88–89
Qualcomm, 70

Rafaga, 27, 128
Raja, Omar, 156
Ranadive, Vivek, 65, 67, 69–70, 72–73
Rashad, Ahmad, 95
RayV, 103
RealAudio, 92

Index 221

RealNetworks, 99
regional sports network (RSN), 168
revenue sharing, 2, 131
Rio de Janeiro, Brazil, 1, 46, 73–74; Rocinha, 74–75
Roy, Tommy, 61, 122

Sabol, Steve, 115
Sacramento, CA, 1, 71–72
Sacramento Kings: arena, 1, 26, 55, 71; franchise, 24, 48–49, 65; global, 26, 31, 51, 69, 99, 138, 173; technology, 67–69, 80
San Antonio Spurs, 9, 31, 49, 50, 51, 97, 100–101, 111–12, 169
San Francisco, CA, 59, 67, 71, 78, 80, 81
San Francisco 49ers, 68, 71
satellite distribution, 6, 10–12, 37–39, 83, 85–88, 90, 99, 101, 103, 106, 109–10, 141–43
satellite offices, 27, 46, 52, 107, 124–27, 133
SB Nation, 159
Secaucus, NJ, 1–3, 23–27, 85–90, 97–98, 102–6, 111, 122, 168–72
Shanghai, China, 1, 42–44, 46
Shenzhen, China, 43–44, 46, 52
Silver, Adam, 17, 76, 96–98, 113, 137, 159–62, 174
Sky Channel, 39
Slade, Mike, 91, 94
Sleep Train Arena, 71
Small World, 144, 147
smart devices, 28, 59, 137, 140, 150
smart house, 57, 59
Smith, Stephen A., 154
soccer, 4, 17, 18, 39, 74–77, 129–30, 174–75
Sofi Stadium, 81
software, 56, 72, 78, 84, 91, 106, 140, 158
Soviet television, 25, 38
Soviet Union, 25, 30, 36–40, 75–76, 120, 132, 172
Spain, 37, 39, 104, 119, 120, 169
spending leakage, 63
sponsorship, 3–4, 21, 34, 36, 40–41, 47, 53, 67, 80, 99, 129, 170, 176
sports betting, 28, 136, 144, 150–52, 162, 164, 174
Sports Illustrated, 24, 129, 134, 147, 152, 156
sports journalism, 25
sports-media symbiosis, 31, 123, 135
Sports Team Analysis and Tracking System (STATS), 145, 147
SportsTrax, 145
SporTV, 74
stadium boom, 62, 64
Stanley Cup, 160, 169, 173
Staples Center, 78, 129
Starwave, 23, 83–85, 91–94, 100, 106, 109, 144–47
Stern, David: arenas, 60, 62, 65; international distribution, 112–13, 123–26, 128–29, 131; media distribution 92, 98, 102, 112–13, 120–21, 124, 142; NBA Entertainment, 35, 87, 115; role as commissioner, 8, 10, 67, 96, 117–18, 137, 153, 175; Soviet Union, 25, 38–39
St. Louis, MO, 63
StorageTek, 104
St. Petersburg, Russia, 76
streaming: contracts, 4, 11, 77; COVID-19, 140; global, 4, 51, 83–85, 98, 107–10, 142, 172; platforms, 15, 17–18, 47–48, 67, 79, 84, 100, 106–8, 150, 162, 172, 175; revenue, 15, 84, 92, 94, 138, 174; rights, 6, 99, 173; subscriptions, 28, 135, 138–40, 160; technology, 11–12, 17, 86, 99, 101, 108–9
Sunday Night Baseball, 168
Super Bowl, 63, 168
Superchannel, 39

TBS: Atlanta Hawks, 25, 123, 124; contracts, 10, 36, 108, 117, 123, 14; ratings, 119, 160; revenue, 94, 119; subscriptions, 108, 117, 123; technology, 38
Techwood, 27, 105
Telecommunications Act of 1996, 93, 109
television formats: adaption, 18–22, 30, 45, 52, 113, 129–33; definition, 18, 20, 44, 46, 128
television ratings, 1, 8, 15, 29, 64–65, 87, 101–2, 117–19, 141–44, 159–60, 169
Tencent, 1, 4, 106, 174
Texas Rangers, 72
Thursday Night Football, 138, 173
TikTok, 161, 170
timeouts, 137
Time Warner, 94, 102, 126, 133–34, 156
TNT: contracts, 65, 123, 124, 134; ratings, 101, 160; revenue, 2
Toronto Raptors, 16, 126, 127, 169
Tracer Milan, 36, 37
transculturalism, 19, 22, 45, 130
translation, 44, 45, 52

T-shirt toss, 31, 41
Tubi, 173
Turner: contracts, 6, 11, 65, 94, 101, 122, 124, 133–34, 138, 155, 163; football, 27, 113, 131; global, 38–39, 76, 103, 104, 172; programming, 102, 133, 141–42, 161, 166; streaming, 27, 106, 109, 161, 162, 164
Turner, Ted, 25, 31, 38, 75, 117
Turner Entertainment Group, 6, 102, 134, 174
Turner Sports, 2, 77, 92, 101–2, 142, 161–62
TVE, 37, 39
Twitter, 2, 47, 137, 151, 156–57, 159, 164, 170, 174

Ueberroth, Heidi, 98
Ueberroth, Peter, 121
UFC, 109, 138, 175
Univision, 83
USA Network, 10, 87–88, 117, 120
U.S. Supreme Court, 150
Utah Jazz, 10, 79, 95

Vancouver Grizzlies, 126–27
Van Gundy, Stan, 153
Variety, 24, 91, 125, 160
venture capital, 59, 66–67
Verizon, 85
ViacomCBS, 109, 126, 174

video board, 1, 43, 104, 165, 170
videotape, 88, 158
virtual reality, 26, 67–68, 70
VOKE, 67, 70, 72

Walt Disney World, 28, 55, 77, 165
WarnerMedia, 2–3, 12, 27, 106, 114, 173–74
Washington Post, 10, 24, 99, 114, 118, 119, 160
Washington Wizards, 16, 65
WatchESPN, 84
Weibo, 49
WGN, 123, 124
Wide World of Sports, 8, 135
WNBA, 27, 113, 131, 138
WOR, 123
World Basketball Open (McDonald's Open), 35–39, 45, 51, 120, 123
WSC Sports, 158–59
Wussler, Robert, 9, 38

XFL, 31

YouTube, 24, 56–57, 151, 156–57, 159, 170

Zayo Group, 24, 27, 84–85, 103, 106
Zoom, 67, 68
Zucker, Jeff, 173

Index 223

STEVEN SECULAR is an independent scholar.

Studies in Sports Media

Six Minutes in Berlin: Broadcast Spectacle and Rowing Gold
   at the Nazi Olympics   *Michael Socolow*
Fighting Visibility: Sports Media and Female Athletes
   in the UFC   *Jennifer McClearen*
The Digital NBA: How the World's Savviest League
   Brings the Court to Our Couch   *Steven Secular*

The University of Illinois Press
is a founding member of the
Association of University Presses.

———————————————

University of Illinois Press
1325 South Oak Street
Champaign, IL 61820-6903
www.press.uillinois.edu